FRENCH CAPITALISM IN THE NINETEENTH CENTURY

GUY P. PALMADE

French Capitalism
in the
Nineteenth Century
(1961)

Translated, with an introduction, by
Graeme M. Holmes
Lecturer in Economic History
University of Wales Institute of Science and Technology

DAVID & CHARLES : NEWTON ABBOT

ISBN 0 7153 5326 8

*Set in 10/12 point Plantin
and printed in Great Britain
by W J Holman Ltd Dawlish
for David & Charles (Publishers) Limited
South Devon House Newton Abbot Devon*

Contents

TRANSLATOR'S INTRODUCTION

The Study of Entrepreneurship in Nineteenth-Century France

Until recently the economic history of France has been a neglected subject. Perhaps French historians have been somewhat more engrossed with the importance of political issues rather than economic ones while Anglo-Saxon historians have accepted the concept of a state of apparent stagnation in the French economy in the nineteenth century. Economic historians have long tended to assume rather a low growth rate in the French economy between 1800 and 1914. 'Taking the century as a whole, it is quite clear that the rate of growth of all relevant variables was substantially below that of other Western industrial nations: growth in the period 1883-96 was so slow as to justify the term "stagnation".'[1] A natural conclusion has been that one has little to learn from a study of the French economy. Besides the glittering panorama of politics, besides the barricades and the revolutionary ideas and the eternal quest for liberty, equality and fraternity, the narrow activities of businessmen and the slothful appearance of French economy and society have seemed to offer an insubstantial historical diet. Yet during the last twenty years or so there has been a change of emphasis among some writers who have studied the problem of the French economy. The complex problem of economic development and the difficulties of promoting economic growth in underdeveloped countries since 1945 have prompted the belief that France before 1914 may be a highly interesting case-study in showing where the obstacles to growth may occur. After all, in its natural resources, in its size and in the ability and intelligence of its people, France in 1800 might be thought to have considerable advantages. Why did higher growth not occur? One explanation could lie in the quality of its businessmen. Theories like those of Schumpeter which stress the central importance of the entrepreneur in the process of economic growth seem to suggest that French entrepreneurship may have been singularly deficient. Yet what are the facts? Immediately questions are posed about French entrepreneurship it becomes clear that the literature is not over-abundant. Hence arises the justification for now offering to the English reader a translation of the work by Guy Palmade which was on its appearance in 1961 a work of pioneer synthesis.

As a work of synthesis Palmade's book shows some of the heart-searching which the study of entrepreneurship has created for French historians. To the English reader such an analysis is a familiar exercise. During the 1960s there has been considerable discussion among British historians about the quality of the British entrepreneur, especially during the period between 1870 and 1914 when the growth rate of the British economy was rather lower than earlier in the century. The key question has been by what criteria does one, in fact, judge the entrepreneur. The controversial article of D. H. Aldcroft in 1964 tended to condemn the British entrepreneur on the basis of comparison with German and American rivals. Replies to Aldcroft have come from both Charles Wilson and S. B. Saul. Wilson pointed out that Aldcroft's evidence was highly selective and that the later nineteenth century saw many dynamic entrepreneurs such as Lever, Beecham, Boot, Courtauld, Rowntree and a host of others who took the boundaries of entrepreneurship far beyond the limits of iron pigs and cotton stockings. The approach of S. B. Saul in studying the problem from the viewpoint of the mechanical engineering industries was to show the influence of the market. Because of a different market situation comparisons between Britain and America were hardly fruitful. Nevertheless, these comparisons were taken up again in an article by P. L. Payne which considered the difference in size between the largest British and American firms in 1905 and concluded that sociological factors were responsible for the smaller size of British firms operating in similar areas of activity. He stressed particularly the dead hand of family influence and the haemorrhage of ability from industry into landowner-ship, politics and the professions. The controversy seemed to be laid at rest for the time being when in 1969 Aldcroft wrote the general introduction on British industry dealing with the period between 1875 and 1914. He revised his earlier global strictures and conceded that the performance of British industry was highly uneven, but at its best equalled the performance of industry anywhere in the world.[2] In the same way the treatment of French entrepreneurship in the nineteenth century is bound to depend on the viewpoint adopted. If one asks whether the poor quality of entrepreneurship was a prime cause of the low growth rate in nineteenth century France another question immediately arises—how does one judge the quality of entrepreneurship? Is it true, as Landes has stated, that 'the businessman gets the demand he deserves'? Such a typically American outlook tends to view the entrepreneur as an autonomous innovator or motivator who can manipulate conditions to suit his own purposes. It was, therefore, no accident that some of the foremost criticisms of French entrepreneurs should have come from American historians soon after World War II at a time when there seemed to be such a contrast between French complacency and narrowness of outlook and American dynamism. The condition of France, like that of Britain, was a somewhat sorry one in 1945-48 and an outside observer who had never seen France in happier times might be forgiven for receiving an impression of backwardness. The arguments of David S. Landes and John F. Sawyer were representative of such an approach.

Sawyer concentrated his attention 'on the ways in which different societies, with different interests, attitudes, systems of stratification and the like, operate to produce different kinds of entrepreneurial behavior'. France carried forward elements of the European past that have remained widely diffused to this day. Over the centuries when commercial capitalism was enlarging its place in the national life, a series of historical turnings kept aristocratic values and patterns peculiarly alive. The nobility discouraged the entrance of its sons into trade; and the French bourgeoisie never gained control of government and the fisc, a position of social prestige, or a dominance of the national capital comparable to that of the merchants of London. Among institutional complexes which had their influence on French entrepreneurship were: firstly, a strong centralised state combining policies of protection focused on national power and a bureaucratic tradition; secondly, the artificial perpetuation of the institutions of petty bourgeois capitalism and peasant agriculture creating a system built around small units, small volume and small horizons; and thirdly, the growth of Marxist and related movements and ideologies that have mobilised deep and pervasive anticapitalist sentiments against business and the businessman. The impact of the heritage may be seen in terms of recruitment, where inherited institutional patterns have operated restrictively by discouraging the flow of Schumpeter's 'strong wills and strong intellects' into business careers and by tending to close off economic positions at the top as the special preserves of selected kinship groups. Inherited patterns have affected motivation with individual entrepreneurial aspirations tending to be defined more in terms of differential class goals than of boundless economic achievement. The purely economic rewards of entrepreneurial success have been less significant, socially and culturally, in France than in the United States. The social order in France has thus undervalued the very prizes and penalties that have urged on the capitalist process. The motivation has been typically to run the business so as to assume the preservation over time of the family status and the family honour involved in it. Traditional social structure has influenced behaviour by preventing the emergence of aggressive entrepreneurship. Conspicuous rebels (of whom the Péreires are the best-known example) have found themselves destroyed by the economic community for trying to break the system. The social inheritance has operated against organising economic pressures in the direction of mass production for mass consumption. 'If France has had its great entrepreneurs they have come from groups less directly subject to the dominant social impress such as Protestants, Freemasons, Jews and métèques.' French entrepreneurship has repeatedly failed to exploit the very great scientific and technological innovations that France has produced. The place and role of the businessman has been fundamentally different in European and American society. On any relative scale the American institutional system was overwhelmingly favourable to entrepreneurship. Social structure by itself does not offer *the* explanation of the differences between European and American entrepreneurship. It constitutes a significant part of the explanation, however, and without reference to it the differing economic decisions and actions of businessmen in different societies cannot be understood.[3]

David S. Landes was equally explicit.

> The study of French enterprise and entrepreneurship is rewarding for two major reasons. In the first place, anything that will help explain the present weakness of French industry and commerce throws light in turn on one of the most important political phenomena of the last 150 years: the fall of France from hegemony under Napoleon to the position she holds today. Secondly, the history of French business and businessmen is significant precisely because of France's relatively minor place in the economic world ... In the case of France, to what extent have the character and mentality of the French financier, industrialist or merchant been responsible for the relatively retarded status of the country's economy?

Landes pointed particularly to the family character of French business and its self-imposed goal of financial self-sufficiency and the slow adoption of the corporative form. The inferior place of the businessman meant that he was continually attempting to rise into the 'superior group' either directly or through marriage. Another aspect of inferiority was that the non-business elements of the bourgeoisie generally relegated the businessman to the bottom end of the ladder. Moreover, the pressure of literary and artistic opinion was one aspect of a general atmosphere that could best be termed as anticapitalistic. Nevertheless, Landes was not quite so overwhelmingly sceptical as Sawyer in that he gave due importance to the diversity of France and was aware of regional and sectoral variations. Change occurred which was sometimes impressive. Companies like Paturle-Seydoux at Cateau-Cambrésis and Holden at Reims in the wool industry represented important concentrations of capital and labour as did the Schneider plant at Le Creusot and the de Wendel mills at Hayange and Stiring in the iron and steel industry. There were important innovators such as Boucicaut with his retail store of Bon Marché, Potin producing the first packaged foods for sale through branch outlets, Révillon revolutionising the French fur business and the whole group of Saint-Simonians with their considerable influence on the French industrial revolution. Nevertheless, the general conclusion was that 'the influence of French entrepreneurial psychology on her general economic structure has been and is extremely important' or, in other words, the French entrepreneur bore considerable responsibility for the poor performance of the French economy.[4]

Palmade at least has no temptation to use American comparisons as the ultimate yardstick for judgement of entrepreneurial performance. At the end of his volume he quotes the French trade union leader Griffuelhes who regretted in 1910 the inability of French capitalism to adapt itself to the modern world and wanted French employers to become like American employers. The comment made by Palmade is that the comparison between France and America was out of proportion and the wish to become more like America was not to the point. Support for such scepticism has come from some recent American writers who have been more sympathetic towards the difficulties of European entrepreneurs in the nineteenth century and have shown that, however great the effort might be, it was impossible for American entrepreneurs to be emulated. Notable among such contributions has been that of Peter Temin in his study of the British iron and steel industry, an industry which British historians such as D. L. Burn, W. E. Minchinton and D. H. Aldcroft have found a fruitful sphere for criticism.[5] Although Temin found some defects in the British iron and steel industry and believed that with greater dynamism entrepreneurs could have raised the annual rate of growth in the industry by about 1 per cent, the optimum growth rate for Britain was about 3.6 per cent compared with the actual growth rate of 9.6 per cent for the American industry and 9 per cent for the German. In other words, overall conditions were such that British steel entrepreneurs had much greater handicaps to overcome than their American and German counterparts. Although no such comparative single-industry study appears to exist for France it is noticeable that Rondo Cameron in his magnum opus appearing in 1961 was much less inclined to criticise French economic performance than in his earlier writings. For example, he could point out that 'in two crucial sectors of the international economy, banking and railways, French enterprise played a role out of all proportion to France's share in total economic activity'. Or again, he made the point that French engineering, like French industry generally, was handicapped by the high price of raw materials —coal and iron in particular—but it surmounted the handicap by superior technical efficiency.

> Even proud Albion, the original fount of modern industrialism, called on the French for assistance and advice; a French firm sank the foundations for the great Forth river bridge; another used dredges of a special design to help dig the Manchester ship canal; and—most humiliating of all, no doubt—British steel mills had to call on French metallurgists for advice on the manufacture of fine alloy steels.[6]

Similarly, David Landes is somewhat less critical of French entrepreneurship than he once was. In dealing with the period before 1850 he can still find fault with the business firm in France, Germany and the Low Countries as being far more likely to be exclusively familial and to be so closely identified with the family as to be almost indistinguishable from it, whereas the British entrepreneur had come a long way towards seeing a given industrial venture as a means to an end, as a device to be rationally utilised for making money. Nevertheless, he can describe the period from 1850 to 1873 as Continental industry's coming-of-age, when there was unprecedentedly rapid growth. Among the positive forces for expansion in the 1850s and 1860s was a creative entrepreneurial response to a combination of long-run opportunity and short-run facility. He is now aware that what sociologists call the analysis of ideal types, such as two contrasting types of entrepreneurs (say British and German), is inevitably a dangerous technique of historical comparison because it rests on the averaging of the unmeasurable and does violence to the complexity and variety of human behaviour. He is also aware of the argument that the human factor of entrepreneurial and technological creativity may be nothing more than a reflection of economic determinants, and quotes Svennilson and Habakkuk as exponents of the 'feedback approach' which sees the growth of an economy or even an industry in any period as a function of its growth in the preceding period. Nevertheless, he still disagrees with the feed-back approach because it offers

> an explanation for one side of economic behaviour, that of the stimulus to economic activity which comes from the side of demand. But it slights the supply side and thereby truncates historical reality. Nothing succeeds like success ... but why do some succeed and others fail? Why do some front runners fade and laggards pick up?

He appreciates the fundamental point that neither empirical evidence nor theoretical reasoning is likely to settle the dispute. The precise imputation of weights to each of the many determinants of economic development is impossible and likely to remain so. Scholars tend to choose those interpretations which they find not only plausible but congenial. Because of the profound implications of the drama of economic development for the status of the participants, the explanations offered for success or failure are themselves crucial to the self-esteem of these societies and their members. 'Under the circumstances the identification of the scholar with the problem he studies has often been as important a determinant of his approach as the objective data.'[7]

For such reasons the debate over the quality of French entrepreneurship, like that of British entrepreneurship, is by no means closed. Whether in Palmade's book or in the writings of later scholars it is not difficult to discern an uneasy element of uncertainty in establishing satisfactory criteria of judgement. Few French writers would probably be in complete agreement with Roger Priouret in his recent book *La France et le management* in which he castigates the historical traditions of French entrepreneurship with its aura of absolute and hereditary monarchy with the entrepreneur-king disdaining technical advice or market considerations.[8] No doubt such a work is a popular *pièce d'occasion* which itself reflects the changing business atmosphere in France in the 1960s and which marks a realisation that contemporary France has something to learn from American experience. Equally Priouret's criticism may reflect the perennial political tendency in France for a writer of somewhat left-wing political persuasion to assail the quality of the French entrepreneur. Yet the picture is surely over-drawn when Priouret holds up for admiration those two dazzling American examples of businessmen who rose to success by their exploitation of the market: Richard Warren Sears and William C. Durant. The obvious caution to urge from such examples is that even in America entrepreneurs who thought of market expansion as an immutable and inevitable tendency fell into difficulties. Sears and Durant were both deficient because they had too narrow a view of the entrepreneurial function and needed a multi-dimensional definition of entrepreneurship such as that provided by Arthur H. Cole.[9] If neither man's firm ceased activity the reason was that in the one instance at Sears Roebuck the deficiencies of Sears were remedied by Rosenwald and Doering, and in the other instance at General Motors, Sloan and Donaldson Brown had a clearer insight than Durant into the firm's problems. It is one of these cherished and indestructible historical myths that American entrepreneurs must always have experienced success; but any general student of economic history knows that downturns in the American economy such as those of 1893 and 1907, let alone the cataclysm between 1929 and 1933, brought wholesale bankruptcies to entrepreneurs who had made miscalculations about the state of the market. *Pace* Landes the entrepreneur does not exist independently of the market which he supplies, and the potential ability of the entrepreneur to change market conditions at any particular time and place is always a difficult matter to estimate.

The market itself is a sociological phenomenon. When buyers change their habits the reasons for change are complex, but there is a sense in which the entrepreneur responds to the needs of his customers; his role is to make their needs explicit, to make a fruitful reality for them out of previous vague and perhaps subconsciously held aspirations. If demand changes more rapidly in one society than another the reasons are complex, but clearly a society that experiences higher economic growth is likely to have more rapidly changing demand patterns and hence to experience more dynamic entrepreneurship. Hence one comes back to the essential problem of whether entrepreneurship is cause or effect (or partly both) of the social and economic environment with which it is associated. In the example of France, therefore, it is necessary to be sure that the main assumptions about the slow rate of growth in France are correct. Recent work done by Jean Marczewski and Tihomir Markovitch confirms that the overall rate of growth between 1780 and 1913 was 1.8 per cent, which was lower than that of other advanced industrial countries. Nevertheless, not all previously accepted generalisations are necessarily valid. In the early part of the nineteenth century, for example, Markovitch questions whether France was a retarded industrial nation. On the contrary, he is able to state categorically on the basis of now known statistics that France at the beginning of the nineteenth century was the first industrial power in the world. The only industrial sectors in which Britain was ahead of France were coal and cotton. In wool the quantity of production was much the same, but in a great many products French industrial production was superior to that of Britain, such products being silk, linen, leather goods, metal products both ferrous and non-ferrous, fatty substances, glassware, paper, tobacco and sugar. In a country whose population was two and a half times that of Britain it was hardly surprising that the same point was true of milling, bakery and pastry-making. At a time when even British historians are beginning to view the industrial revolution as a far more complex process than change occurring merely in cotton, coal and iron, and are emphasising changes, for example, in the brewing industry or in papermaking, the point made by Markovitch is timely. Moreover, Markovitch concludes that during the first half of the nineteenth century the growth rate of French industry was relatively high at an average of nearly 3 per cent per annum but that a slackening occurred in the second half. French performance until 1845 was not so very much inferior to that of Britain, but at times between 1845 and 1895 it was demonstrably sluggish. Between 1895 and 1914, however, there was some revival and during those twenty years French performance was better than that of Britain. Equally important is the distinction drawn by Markovitch between three kinds of industry which he terms declining, progressive and dynamic. Clearly French industry, like British industry, had the problem of uneven performance.[10]

Not unnaturally French historians, like their American counterparts, have tended to write about the success stories of the dynamic firms rather than about the laggards or the failures. In his bibliography Palmade notes that existing French business histories, such as those by Sédillot on Peugeot and de Wendel, have tended to be uncritical and laudatory and lacking in value as serious economic studies. In spite of the generalisations about family influence and its harmful effects, no French writer seems to have produced studies equivalent to those of Addis and Rimmer dealing with the Crawshay dynasty and Marshall of Leeds respectively—both of them studies showing how the attitudes of the founding father in a family business could create a harmful tradition leading to the ultimate demise of the firm. The strictures of Paul M. Hohenberg in dealing with the European chemical industry on a comparative basis have drawn attention to the way in which French chemical entrepreneurs failed to make the best use of their technically trained personnel compared with German entrepreneurs, a feature explained by the reluctance of French entrepreneurs to yield up family control. Nevertheless, the strictures of Hohenberg seem to be remarkably undocumented and further research may well modify his generalisations. It is clear that family influence need not be detrimental to effective entrepreneurship if only because families differ so much among themselves in competence and ability.[11] Kindleberger points out that in French textiles there were substantial differences in the temperament, character and behaviour of entrepreneurs from one area to another. Perhaps the most striking defence of family influence in industry is provided by T. C. Barker's study of the British firm of

B

Pilkington Brothers in the glass industry, where it is shown that continuing family influence and control need not exclude the granting of considerable influence to outsiders possessing technical expertise. Pilkingtons possessed the happy knack of appreciating their own deficiencies and of being able to supplement those deficiencies by drawing on the abilities of capable outsiders. Was there, then, a complete failure on the part of French chemical firms to utilise technical men? As Palmade notes, the firm of Kuhlmann owed its origins and rise to technically trained men such as Kuhlmann himself and Kolb. The firm of Péchiney, much criticised for its conservative outlook when controlled by Alfred Rangod, who assumed the name of Péchiney and imposed that name on the firm from 1877, again owed its origins to two technocrats, Henry Merle and J. B. Guimet. Although there are few doubts that on balance the German chemical industry was the most dynamic and thrusting of all European chemical industries after 1850, there is still a problem of how far that dynamism was due to particularly favourable circumstances and how far to the efforts of particular men. As with so many industries, the chemical industry was not a homogeneous sphere of activity. In the two main branches of organic and inorganic chemistry, the Germans were particularly progressive in the latter, with their achievements in the distillation of coal and tar. One need hardly emphasise the French shortage of coal which has been the subject of frequent comment. The problem has been facetiously described as 'coal versus role'. Yet if the role of certain men was important one can only say that we know too little about the employment of personnel, whether in the chemical industry in particular or in French industry in general. As Roger Priouret notes in his *Origines du Patronat Français*, no sociologist or social historian has made a study of recruitment or career patterns in French entrepreneurship. France still awaits its Mabel Newcomer or its Charlotte Erickson to show whether the traditional strictures about family influence and the exclusion of newcomers to industry are fully justified or not.[12]

Nevertheless, some weighty studies have shown that a great deal of change occurred in France and that any picture of total stagnation would be far from the truth. After all, France even in 1914 was considered one of the great powers of Europe and merited that status on the basis of her economic activity even if her relative industrial importance had become less than that of America, Britain or Germany. Perhaps not unnaturally, serious economic study has tended to be concentrated on the period when change seems to have occurred in relatively spectacular fashion. The obvious features of change are the relative overall dynamism which the French economy possessed between 1815 and 1845 and the structural change in French industry and economic institutions which occurred between 1848 and 1882. That structural change has so impressed Palmade that he can describe it in his third chapter as 'The Great Upsurge'. At first sight the statistical work of Marczewski and Markovitch appears to show that, except for the middle years of the Second Empire between 1855 and 1864 when there was some recovery, the growth rate of the French economy between 1850 and 1870 was rather low. Hence his use of the term 'upsurge' could be called into question. Yet Palmade would probably defend his title at least for the period between 1850 and 1870 on three grounds: firstly, that the statistical sources of recent quantitative history are not always firmly based; secondly, that some especially bad years in the late forties or in the fifties bring down the average figures; and thirdly, that the expansion of the French economy during the fifties in a number of spheres is a matter of commonsense observation by any real student of the period. Nevertheless, it may well be true that until recently the study of economic change, whether in terms of performance or of politics, has been inspired, even if subconsciously, by considerations of politics. Historical studies of France, and for that matter of Britain, have tended to be written from the viewpoint of governmental and political change. For example, the influence of banking and railways on the social and political life of France was considerable, especially since the two activities were closely interlinked, with bankers providing a good deal of railway finance. Equally, the effect of the bankers on society has been taken as a token of the triumph of the bourgeoisie with bankers exhibiting the merits and demerits of bourgeoisie as a class. Perhaps it is on some such lines that one explains the relatively important literature which has appeared on banking with weighty contributions by Jean Bouvier, Bertrand Gille and Maurice Lévy-Leboyer, whereas such an industry as the sugar industry which Markovitch is able to demonstrate as a fast-growing consumer industry in the nineteenth century has apparently still to await its historian. No doubt archives and their accessibility constitute part of the explanation.

The important work of Lévy-Leboyer, published in 1963, presents a favourable view of French bankers before 1850. Their role was to guide national or foreign savings into sectors in course of expansion. The doubts expressed by some observers on the usefulness and efficiency of banking institutions have little foundation. One has to recognise that serious deficiencies existed in the economy from the point of view of credit, since credit grew only in certain towns such as Paris, Lyon and Mulhouse and for special reasons. Yet considered against the background of the legacy of the Napoleonic Wars and of France's geographical and technical handicaps it was not surprising that bankers concentrated their efforts in particular sectors such as quality textiles and fashion ware, or in transport with its link with coal and with engineering. The Napoleonic Wars had temporarily destroyed the French capital market and it was necessary to invest where opportunities were promising. In spite of the strictures of the Church or of the critical tone of writers such as Stendhal, Balzac, Dumas, Zola and Daudet, who denounced the misdeeds of men showing insatiable cupidity and immoderate thirst for wealth, the activity of banks on an overall scale was beneficial. The truth was that there were two kinds of banker. One type was a legacy from the eighteenth century who worked in the service of the state and whose practices drew deserved criticism. The criticism of such activity was that it weakened the economy and created fictitious capital. The other type, who was the subject of Lévy-Leboyer's volume, worked in the service of the economy by receiving capital and distributing it according to his best judgement in the most useful sectors of industrial expansion. Lévy-Leboyer thus distinguishes between the 'financier' and the 'banker' and regrets that in spite of their different functions the two types became mixed up in the eyes of public opinion, with 'financiers' eclipsing 'bankers'.

> The banker was not responsible for the weaknesses which emerged in several sectors of the economy; he intervened only to further their progress and it is really an affront to commonsense to daub him with that spirit of monopoly which characterised the measures of the state. The financier may wish to make industry servile to him but the banker's objective is to free it from hindrances.

Lévy-Leboyer shows, then, the complexity of the situation as it affected banks and the feeling of anticapitalism among a vocal section of the French intelligentsia, an outlook on which Landes has previously commented. In his own scholarly way Lévy-Leboyer shows that there were forward-looking bankers but that limits existed to the fruitful employment of capital. If the chronological limitations of his study had allowed him to take it beyond 1850 it would have been interesting to have his comments on the careers of Émile and Isaac Péreire, especially during their dazzling years after 1855, for no episode in French business history of the nineteenth century can illuminate more clearly the subjective prejudices of the historian. If Sawyer can depict them as conspicuous rebels who were destroyed for trying to break the system, the reply to Sawyer might be that in their reckless speculation they were little better than the Chase Manhattan Bank or some other American banks whose operations during 1928 and 1929 brought so much harm and dislocation to the American economy. In the history of comparative banking American historians have to beware of criticising the bankers of other nations overmuch. Palmade's succinct but balanced account of the Péreires and their activities, which is based on the work of Girard, Bouvier and Schnerb, is probably as fair a conclusion as one is likely to find. Altogether, the history of French banking as far as the great national institutions are concerned has been well studied. With the work of Lévy-Leboyer on the earlier part of the century supplementing Bertrand Gille's study of the Rothschilds and Jean Bouvier's study of the Crédit Lyonnais, besides other important contributions, the historian has a fair body of evidence. The existence of such literature explains why Palmade spends a good deal of space on banking and rather less on other activities which one hopes will be illuminated by further studies.[13]

It may be that the preoccupation of some historians with banking has led them to study some economic activities rather than others. Bankers, as Lévy-Leboyer points out, tended to invest in textiles and railways. If some important studies have been made of aspects of the textile industry by Claude Fohlen and by Jean Lambert-Dansette, the study of railway entrepreneurship in France, as in Britain, still awaits an equivalent treatment of the classic American work of T. C. Cochran, *Railroad Leaders: 1845-90*. Nevertheless, a recent thesis by François Caron deals with the history of the important railway network in the north of France from the viewpoint of problems of management and control.[14] It is noteworthy that Caron, like Cochran, comments on the social and community influences bearing on railways which tended to diminish their zeal for profit maximisation. Both textiles and railways had their links with banking but the investment problem for the iron and steel industry was somewhat different. The definitive study of the iron and steel industry between 1814 and 1864 by Jean Vial shows that with changing structure and technique the capital needs of the industry were great. Recourse to banks could hardly be avoided, yet one preoccupation of the ferrous metal entrepreneurs was to avoid falling too much into the hands of the banks with resulting loss of control. Hence Vial's work contains important sections dealing with entrepreneurship and it is hardly an exaggeration to say that it has more of the appearance of a work by Cochran than anything hitherto produced in French economic history. At the opening of the work Vial poses the problem of how the French iron and steel industry managed to free itself from the old forms of production based on forests and charcoal with an associated routine mentality in organisation and technique. The period with which he deals was essentially a period of great change even if old techniques persisted among a certain number of producers. Technical change had to be accompanied by a changing outlook among entrepreneurs and managers. The essential feature of the period was a move away from the dominant importance of landholding for entrepreneurs (because of the necessity of ensuring supplies of wood or of coal or of raw materials) towards a period in which the complexity of operations created considerable need for capital. If there was some recourse to banks there was a relative diminution of banking influence in the 1860s. Nevertheless, the financial considerations involved when large sums were at stake in an uncertain economic climate meant that administration of firms became more complex. Although change might be difficult for firms with a long tradition it was not impossible. Vial is well aware of the criticism which can be made of many entrepreneurs, yet he is insistent that a new kind of entrepreneur was born. Those two shining examples of success so often mentioned in many books—de Wendel and Schneider—are considered by Vial to show the importance of men possessing technical knowledge. He confirms a previously held opinion of Rondo Cameron that the high quality of the French system of technical education was a distinct advantage for the supply of the necessary skilled manpower. As the industry moved into the fifties and sixties, however, technical knowledge was not enough. Commercial foresight was necessary. Only those whose outlook was alert and resourceful and knowledgeable could meet the conditions for success in a new age. Among those who met such requirements were Dufaud, de Wendel, Schneider, L. Talabot, Petin and Gaudet. Technical rationalisation and commercial centralisation favoured firms capable of satisfying both a varied group of regional customers which constituted its original basic market and a specialised national market. In such a complex situation the entrepreneur had to be sure that he took care of investment, of supplies of raw materials, of changing technology and of markets. Although he might allocate greater priority to one activity than to the rest he neglected any of them at his peril. In short, a new type of entrepreneur was born who was more an economist than a technologist.[15]

What is so noticeable to the English reader of Vial's work is that his treatment not only reveals the complexity of the situation, with the best entrepreneurs being credited with a considerable measure of achievement, but that it points to the importance of market and institutional factors. From this point of view Vial justifies rather than condemns the creation in 1864 of the employers' association known as the Comité des Forges, since he shows that it was the creation of some of the ablest of the entrepreneurs. In other words, his approach is one to commend itself to Professor Saul. No doubt future work in French business history will be upon similar lines and will show the extent to which change was possible in a country which experienced considerable obstacles to the attainment of rapid economic growth especially in the second half of the nineteenth century, and in which social change remained extraordinarily slow by American, British or German standards. The overwhelming impression is that the market did not change as rapidly in France as in the other major industrial countries. No doubt part of the explanation lies in the well-known feature of low French population growth, but part of the explanation must lie equally in the relatively low pace at which transfer of labour and of resources took place from the agricultural sector to the commercial and industrial sector.

Overall, France did not experience the relatively rapid increase in urban population which was so marked a feature of the German and British scene in the seventies and eighties. Hence one may enquire how far it was possible for new methods and organisation to be applied to French retailing. As Palmade notes, the firm of Bon Marché organised by Boucicaut was among the most advanced to be found anywhere. Its success was based on new commercial methods such as a deliberate restriction of profit margins, a conscious effort at public relations and propaganda and a policy of freedom for each department or section of the store. Yet it is still a question how far in the circumstances of late-nineteenth-century France it would have been possible for a Sears or a Lipton to have created a retailing revolution of the kind which was achieved in America or Britain. It is noticeable, for example, that Palmade's short account of French retailing is based entirely on Paris and on the four departmental stores of Bon Marché, Printemps, Galeries Lafayette and Samaritaine which were to be found in certain areas of Paris. It was a different ethos from that in which Lipton and others brought cheap food to the British working-class household in Liverpool, Glasgow, Manchester, Birmingham and London. Undoubtedly we need to know a good deal more about the market in France and urban studies on the lines of the recent study of Bordeaux by Louis Desgraves and Georges Dupeux will partly remedy the deficiency. Change certainly did occur in Paris, Lyon, Marseille and Bordeaux but they hardly had the same proportional rapidity of urban growth as Bremen, Hamburg, Manchester and Birmingham. Such market factors are presumably some part of the explanation for the plight of the French winegrowing industry described by C. K. Warner in *The Winegrowers of France and the Government since 1875*, even though the difficulties stressed by Warner emerge more from the supply side, with the havoc and uncertainty resulting from the phylloxera epidemic and the overproduction that followed attempts to remedy the situation. The winegrowing industry seems to epitomise both the general factors of retardation in the French economy and to confirm the traditionalism and narrow outlook of the French producer. Equally, the volume on the history of Bordeaux in the nineteenth century shows that although change did occur in the town the general ethos was one of conservatism and cautious readjustment.[16]

Palmade, at least, can hardly be accused of being unaware of factors of retardation but it may well be that he overstates some of them. In particular, the problem of the export of French capital and the question of the performance of the French economy after 1895 are matters for further discussion. For the English reader the strictures on the high proportion of French capital sent abroad bear a familiar sound, yet whether one is studying the scene in France or in England the crucial question is whether capital exported could have found a more fruitful use at home. Can one show that entrepreneurs were seriously deprived of capital for potentially promising schemes of development? If bankers tended to become less involved with internal industrial development the reasons, well illustrated by Jean Bouvier in his study of the Crédit Lyonnais and of its leader Henri Germain, were twofold. Firstly, the speculative nature of many industrial ventures and the money lost in them made bankers understandably cautious. France was not lacking in speculative ventures that failed; these in their own way were equivalent to some of the chancy colliery or tinplate enterprises described by Morris and Williams or Minchinton in their studies of South Wales in Britain.[17] It is idle to condemn bankers who had had their fingers burnt and equally idle to condemn entrepreneurs for not resorting to the banks if they knew that the bankers were cautious about them. Yet one may still ask why more small regional banks possessing links with local industry did not arise in France. The bank of Charpenay at Grenoble, mentioned by Palmade, was a good example of the kind of organisation which might have injected more dynamism into local capitalists if it had had widespread imitators in other regions. Nevertheless, the existence of speculative ventures, of which Panama and Suez were among the most notable, showed that the spirit of business enterprise so much lauded in America was not totally lacking in France. The ventures of Panama and Suez, however, owed nothing to the enterprise of bankers since there was government support, especially for Suez, and bankers merely provided loan funds under conditions of guaranteed repayment. Furthermore, French capital might also have been directed abroad partly because successful French firms were obsessed with the perils of falling too far into the hands of the banks. Hence it might be argued that external investment opportunities were easier for bankers. Vial shows how steelmasters were concerned not to allow banks to obtain overmuch control, Schneider being a particularly good example of an advocate of internal ploughback of profits. In this connection it would be interesting to have a comparative treatment of the 'general entrepreneur' in France, Britain and America: this is the term used by Cochran in his study of railroad leaders to designate the man who came to exercise managerial control over a firm because of the extent of his investment in it. It might well be found that the 'general entrepreneur' was more common in nineteenth century America than in Britain and France.

Ploughback of profits and retention of control in a few hands did not necessarily mean that French industry was stagnant. A good deal of writing has tended to suggest that before the First World War backwardness was the order of the day, especially between 1900 and 1914. Palmade writes in his final section of chapter four of an *essoufflement*, of a snuffing out of French capitalism. '*La machine commence à s'essouffler.*' Yet such an interpretation seems to be at variance with some of the production figures which have been established. Marczewski and Markovitch have been able to demonstrate that the growth rate of the French economy took a new upturn after 1895. François Crouzet has shown the same tendency of an upsurge in the French economy after 1895 in his recent article on trends in French industrial production.[18] Markovitch is able to point to the growth of productivity in a number of industrial sectors such as cotton, wool, metal production and metal processing and chemicals. Markovitch is extremely critical of Anglo-Saxon writers—shades of J. H. Clapham!—who have tended to write of British industrial production as if it necessarily grew faster than French industrial production. On an overall view the point might be true since British population grew much faster than French population, but if the growth of industrial production were measured by each head of population or by each person actively employed then French industrial production grew more rapidly than that of Britain in a number of periods.

Between 1895 and 1914 it is not difficult to point to some sectors of French industry which could rival anything in Europe. The reasons for French superiority in European motor vehicle manufacture, for example, need further illumination, since on the basis of engineering tradition Britain might be thought to have the greater initial advantages for success. Current research is likely to show that there was considerable vigour in French industry in the years before 1914. It is probable, for example, that the researches of Patrick Fridenson will show the technical efficiency and foresight of Renault, who were unsurpassed in Europe before 1910 and well aware of opportunities in markets outside France, especially in Russia. Nevertheless, a doubt about Renault still arises because of the firm's hesitation to adopt moving assembly-line production which would have involved considerable increase in capital and therefore some loss of control, since capital would have had to be brought in from outside. In fairness to Renault, however, it should also be pointed out that the labour force did not always take kindly to innovations in management, and a strike in 1912 against the introduction of methods deriving from 'Taylorism' urged caution on the firm's directorate. Elsewhere, the researches of Miss Carol Kent on Camille Cavalier (1854-1926) will no doubt show that Cavalier was an outstanding entrepreneur by any standards. He spent considerable efforts in ensuring that the quality of pipes at Pont-à-Mousson were the best in the world at a reasonable price. He was not content with operating merely in the French market and achieved substantial success in exporting to North America. Finally, the work of Henri Morsel on the electrical industry in the French Alps shows the vitality of that industry before 1914.[9] If any further evidence is needed about the vitality of the French economy around the turn of the twentieth century Jean Bouvier is able to show in a collective volume dealing with the movement of profit during the nineteenth century that the profits of the Crédit Lyonnais between 1891 and 1913 more than quadrupled, from 17.7 million francs to 79.3 millions. Even if the growth of those profits owed a good deal to share and stock issues, a goodly proportion of which were issues connected with Russia and other foreign countries, the very existence of such profits (since they derived from savings at home) hardly provided evidence of a stagnating economy. [20]

In other words, in spite of the known and accepted sluggishness of the French economy during certain phases of the nineteenth century the overall condemnation of French entrepreneurs has still to be established. Kindleberger, himself an American, has concluded that

> it is difficult to see that the Landes-Pitt thesis has been established . . . the greatest weakness in attaching first importance to the nature of entrepreneurship in shaping France's and Britain's economic development is that the model is incomplete. What needs to be established is not why business behaved as it did, but taking this for granted, why other firms did not come along and challenge existing enterprise.

Such a conclusion clearly points to the importance of the economic environment, even if Kindleberger himself attempts to avoid judgement between Landes on the one hand and Habakkuk on the other.[21] Palmade's own conclusion equally points to the environment: 'No doubt it was necessary—if there is necessity in history—that French capitalism of the nineteenth century was what it was'. Presumably in time the prolific and valuable work of Bertrand Gille, the literature indicated in this introduction and the work now being done in French universities will be brought together in a new synthesis which will, one may forecast, throw more favourable light on French entrepreneurship than some writing in the past.[22] Already the American criticisms of fifteen and twenty years ago are beginning to look somewhat shoddy and superficial. Yet at least they have had the effect of provoking the French themselves to study the question of entrepreneurship and to begin the process of bringing the great traditions of French scholarship to bear on hitherto largely neglected territory. Yet until such scholarship provides a new synthesis, Guy Palmade's succinct and, on the whole, sympathetic treatment remains the best account that we have.

NOTES

1. Rondo E. Cameron, 'Economic Growth and Stagnation in France: 1815-1914', *Journal of Modern History* March 1958, reprinted in *The Experience of Economic Growth*, ed B. E. Supple (Random House, New York 1963), 329. It is only fair to add that Cameron has somwhat changed his emphasis since that article and now tends to point to dynamic features in the French economy. Vide *Annales* January 1971

2. D. H. Aldcroft, 'The Entrepreneur and the British Economy: 1870-1914', *Economic History Review* XVII 1, August 1964
Charles Wilson, 'Economy and Society in Late Victorian Britain', *Economic History Review* XVIII 1, August 1965
S. B. Saul, 'The Market and the Development of the Mechanical Engineering Industries in Great Britain: 1860-1914', *Economic History Review* XX 1, April 1967
P. L. Payne, 'The Emergence of the Large-Scale Company in Great Britain: 1870-1914', *Economic History Review* XX 3, December 1967
D. H. Aldcroft (ed), *The Development of British Industry and Foreign Competition: 1875-1914* (Allen & Unwin 1968)

3. John F. Sawyer, 'The Entrepreneur and the Social Order: France and the United States' in *Men in Business*, ed William Miller (paperback, Harper & Row 1962), 7-22

4. David S. Landes, 'French Entrepreneurship and Industrial Growth in the Nineteenth Century', *Journal of Economic History* May 1949, reprinted in B. E. Supple, op cit, 340-53

5. D. L. Burn, *Economic History of Steelmaking: 1867-1939* (Cambridge University Press 1940)
W. E. Minchinton, *The British Tinplate Industry, a History* (Oxford 1957)
Peter Temin, 'The Relative Decline of the British Steel Industry: 1880-1913', in *Industrialization in Two Systems*, ed H. Rosovsky (John Wiley, New York 1966)

6. Rondo E. Cameron, *France and the Economic Development of Europe: 1800-1914* (Princeton University Press 1961) 89, 100-101

7. David S. Landes, *The Unbound Prometheus* (Cambridge University Press 1969) 131, 193, 201, 353-58

8. Roger Priouret, *La France et le management* (DeNoel 1968)

9. A. H. Cole, 'An Approach to the Study of Entrepreneurship' in *Explora-*

tions in Enterprise, ed H. G. J. Aitken (Harvard University Press 1967), 35

10. J. Marczewski and T. Markowitch, *Histoire Quantitative de l'Economie Française* (Cahiers de l'ISEA, 7 vols, Institut de Science Economique Appliquée). See especially volume 7, T. J. Markovitch, *l'Industrie Française de 1789 à 1964. Conclusions Générales*

11. Paul M. Hohenberg, *Chemicals in Western Europe: 1850-1914* (Amsterdam, North Holland Publishing Co 1967)

12. C. P. Kindleberger, *Economic Growth in France and Britain: 1851-1950* (Harvard University Press), 122

    T. C. Barker, *Pilkington Brothers and the Glass Industry* (Allen & Unwin 1960)

    Roger Priouret, *Origines du patronat français* (Grasset 1963), 189, 191

    Mabel Newcomer, *Big Business Executive* (Columbia University Press 1955)

    Charlotte Erickson, *British Industrialists: Steel and Hosiery; 1850-1950* Cambridge University Press 1959)

13. Maurice Lévy-Leboyer, *Les banques Européenes et l'industrialisation internationale dans la première moitié du XIXᵉ siècle* (Presses Universitaires de France 1964)

14. T. C. Cochran, *Railroad Leaders: 1845-90* (Harvard University Press 1953)

    François Caron, 'L'Histoire de l'exploitation d'un grand réseau français. La Compagnie du Chemin de Fᵕ. du Nord' (Thèse: Doctorat d'Etat, Université de Nanterre 1969)

15. Jean Vial, *L'Industrialisation de la sidérurgie Française: 1814-64* (Mouton 1967)

16. Louis Desgraves and Georges Dupeux 'Bordeaux au XIXᵉ siècle', *Histoire de Bordeaux 6* (Fédération Historique du Sud-Ouest, Bordeaux 1969)

    Charles K. Warner, *The Winegrowers of France and the Government since 1875* (Columbia University Press 1960)

17. J. H. Morris and L. J. Williams, *South Wales Coal Industry: 1841-75* (University of Wales Press 1958)

    W. E. Minchinton, *The British Tinplate Industry, a History* (Oxford 1957)

18. François Crouzet, 'Essai de construction d'un indice annuel de la production annuelle française au XIXᵉ siècle', *Annales* No 1, 25 année, Janvier-Février 1970

19. Patrick Fridenson, University of Nanterre, is undertaking research on the history of Renault. Useful references are:

    J. M. Laux, 'Some notes on entrepreneurship in the early French automobile industry', *French Historical Studies* 1963, 129 et seq

    J. M. Laux, 'Rochet-Schneider and the French motor industry to 1914', *Business History* July 1966, 77-85

    Anthony Rhodes, *Louis Renault, a biography* (Cassell 1969)

    Miss Carol Kent of St Antony's College, Oxford, is investigating the career of Camille Cavalier

    Henri Morsel, 'Les industries électrotechniques dans les Alpes françaises du Nord de 1869 à 1921'. (paper presented at Colloque International du C.N.R.S.: 'L'Industrialisation en Europe au XIXᵉ siècle', Lyon October 1970)

20. Jean Bouvier, François Furet, Marcel Gillet, *Le Mouvement du profit en France au XIXᵉ siècle* (Mouton 1965)

21. C. P. Kindleberger, *Economic Growth,* op cit 123, 124
22. Bertrand Gille has written a great number of contributions on different aspects of French enterprise, many of them as articles. Three of his works are:
   Recherches sur la formation de la grande entreprise capitaliste (S.E.V.P.E.N. 1959)
   Histoire de la Maison Rothschild, 2 vols, two further volumes to appear (Droz, Geneva)
   La Sidérurgie Française au XIXe siècle (Droz, Geneva 1968). This is a selection of articles reprinted.

INTRODUCTION

Capital, Capitalist, Capitalism

Voltaire once told the story of a man with forty sovereigns who met a friend, the nephew of a merchant who had made his fortune at Cadiz and Surat; the fortune was already entirely in liquid wealth. 'I don't possess a scrap of land,' said this pioneer capitalist, 'all my wealth is in contracts and in bills of exchange.'[1] This was in 1768 and Voltaire was following his usual practice of inventing an example in order to support his argument. In this case he was particularly aiming to show the absurdity of the tax on real property advocated by the physiocrats. One might ask whether his 'capitalist' was not a mere fiction, an argument to prove his point. Yet at the time he was writing the word was coming into use and such usage was already a sign of the existence of the capitalist. In Lucien Febvre's opinion,

> tracing the evolution of a word is never a waste of effort. Whether the journey is short or long, monotonous or varied, it is always an instructive one. In the language of any great civilisation there are only about ten words—sometimes rather fewer but never more—whose history is not the province of the language expert. They are the province of the historian in the full sense of the word historian.

It is a pertinent question whether to put among these key-words of historical vocabulary at least one of those which concern us in this book—'capitalist', 'capitalism', or simply 'capital'.[2]

The original meaning of capital, first used as an adjective and then as a substantive, was perfectly clear and its etymology was obvious. In the seventeenth century the 'capital' of a business still connoted its essential feature of activity; according to the first Dictionary of the Academy in 1694 it meant the 'principal aspect'. However, as early as 1567 there was a specialisation of the word which applied also to 'principal', the word 'capital' being used more specifically to denote the actual amount of a debt or of a bond as opposed to the additional interest accruing on it. A second meaning was soon added to the first which had been specifically an economic or financial one. In 1606 Jean Nicot in his 'Treasury of French Language' spoke of 'the capital of a merchant'. Furetière accepted this meaning of the word in 1690 as applying to 'the sums of money invested in an enterprise, the funds a merchant puts in his business or brings into a firm'. The theorists among the physiocrats, followed by those of the liberal school, adopted the word and broadened its meaning in their turn, giving it a general and abstract twist. J. B. Say, who in his works on political economy written during the Consulate established the principles and language of classical doctrine, considered 'capital' as a key term of the production cycle. It existed as the result of previous activity but its function was to allow new productive work to be done. 'All capital is an instrument of production.' As soon as some form of liquid wealth or income is put to reproductive use' its nature alters, it becomes capital and perpetuates itself through reproduction. 'The meaning of the word was widened to such an extent that after Lavoisier referred in 1791 to 'the situation in the kingdom with its abundance in men, in production, in industries and in accumulated capital' Say could talk of 'the capital of a nation which was made up of all individual capital'. Yet no matter how widely used the noun 'capital' had become it could not be applied to any kind of wealth. Indeed, it was common ground in economic and social studies of the nineteenth century (in the writings of the Liberals as well as those of the Reformers, in Saint-Simon as well as in Bastiat, in Fourier or in Louis Blanc as well as in Joseph Garnier or in Wolowski) to distinguish besides capital other factors of production among which were human attributes such as labour and 'ability' as well as natural factors of which land was the most important. Land represented wealth but it was not 'capital'. Why not? It was precisely because land was a gift of nature and not the result of an act of production. Littré confirmed the meaning of 'capital' and gave the following explanation: 'Wealth is the totality of things which contribute to satisfy our needs and which result from previous efforts. Capital and landed wealth are often contrasted with each other'. In 1829 Guizot gave an illustration:

> As soon as a man owns some land and makes use of it ... he brings into play forces which he does not derive from the soil but from himself. By his workmanship and by the buildings which he puts on it he adds a certain value to the land and, to use the present language of economists, he adds to it a certain amount of capital.

This distinction might seem purely theoretical but it concealed a more weighty contrast of meaning with important implications for the economist. Materially considered, what was this 'capital' which contributed together with labour and 'natural factors' to 'the satisfaction of our needs'? At that point another meaning of the word appeared which was perhaps most common in everyday conversation. Capital was liquid wealth such as money or any liquid currency. In their dictionary, which was shorter than Littré's, Hatzfeld and Darmesteter had no hesitation in combining in a single definition the two main aspects of the word. For them capital was 'money considered as an instrument of production'. Certainly, the capital of a debt or of an annuity could already be considered as money. For a long time lending or the drawing up of an annuity represented about the only way of using a fortune in money without depriving it of its liquidity. However, in the combination capital-interest or capital-income, capital was the durable element meant for long-term savings. In general terms and regardless of its use, the capital of an individual was the 'total wealth owned by that individual in accumulated products'. Following that definition, which put more stress on the wealth itself and its ideal stability than on the way in which wealth could be put to effective use, Littré commented, probably not without some misgiving, that it was in such a sense that one talked about 'a tax on capital'. The idea of stable wealth remained but a far more dynamic meaning came to be added. Logically the new meaning seemed almost to be in contradiction with the previous one and yet in fact was perfectly compatible with it. The new meaning was even complementary, for in it lay the secret of progressive accumulation. Capital was no longer something to be retained but something to be transferred and changed in form, to be shifted and to be reproduced. If held on short term it was circulating capital; it was—still following Littré's definition—'that which is transformed in the production process, which changes from one form to another as with raw materials or foodstuffs' or, again, something which served to 'pay the costs of development'. If on longer term it was 'fixed or immobilised capital; it was capital which served under a permanent or fixed form for durable objects and whose use endured in numerous acts of production, such as buildings, machinery and land improvements'. There was no fundamental contrast between these two forms of use of capital. In both cases it was useful and showed its economic effectiveness. In both cases it could be converted into cash and was capable of being expressed in monetary terms. 'Money is fixed capital

c

in relation to society and is circulating capital in relation to the individual.' From an historical standpoint the essential features of the evolution of the word and of its changes in emphasis can be summarised as follows: Capital is not a form of wealth which man has received from nature but which he has created by his own effort. It is a type of wealth which is essentially movable. It is the symbol of the coming of a new form of economic society in which landed wealth is neither the only form of wealth nor even the most important one. This is a society in which money, currency or paper money are no longer only means for patient hoarding, meant in their turn (when the stocking is full) to be used to purchase new land or (for as long as the old régime lasts) to provide for the purchase of an office which together with landed property is the surest way to acquire social prestige. On the contrary, it is a society in which money is circulating more and more readily, giving to the whole economic machine an ever increasing impetus and efficiency. Ernest Labrousse has emphasised the contrast between the two structures in striking terms. On the one hand there was the fixed unchanging society of the landed nobility based on a rigid rural economy, and on the other there was a commercial and industrial environment, a fast changing society in which wealth, ideas and élites were in rapid flux. It was the new importance of capital which constituted the fundamental difference between the two.

The man who typified this new society, our 'capitalist', made his distinctive appearance rather late, apparently in the second half of the eighteenth century. 'I am neither a great lord nor a capitalist, I am poor and happy,' a correspondent wrote to Rousseau in 1759. When he made his entry into the world the capitalist already cut a fine figure, being placed as he was on the same level as the aristocrat, the typical great man of the last years of the old régime. On the evidence it seems that he did not enjoy any higher a reputation. For the Marquis de Mirabeau in 1780 'stock-holders are naturally antisocial. The capitalist aims for the highest possible interest, a state of affairs which is bound up with public misery.' Lemontey, a lawyer from Lyon, protested against the opening of a canal which would destroy a whole system of irrigation and declared indignantly: 'It is callous to let a whole province dry up in order to enrich some capitalist'. With the Revolution this lack of sympathy towards the capitalist turned into a feeling of open hostility. In 1789 the publicist Linguet declared: 'The capitalists are inspired by love of money rather than by love of country'. The next year the National and Anecdotal Dictionary went even further:

'This word denotes a money monster, a man with heart of stone, who is fond of nothing but cash'. During the 'Second Revolution' in November 1792 social tension was increasing and the capitalist was sometimes regarded as a class enemy of the poor. Goujon, a member of the Convention, declared:

> Freedom of the corn trade is not in accordance with the existence of our Republic. What does our Republic consist of? A small number of capitalists and a great number of poor people. Who deals in the corn trade? That small number of capitalists. Why do they deal? In order to become rich. How do they become rich? By raising the price of corn... Yet that class of capitalists and landowners which enjoys complete freedom in determining the price of corn is also the class that determines the length of the working day. Indeed, every time a workman is needed ten apply for the job and the rich man has plenty of choice... He goes for the man who demands least. He lays down the wage and the workman abides by his ruling because of the need for bread, a need which cannot be postponed.

However, the National Dictionary also gave some more information of a positive nature concerning the usage and exact meaning of the detested word.

> This word is known only in Paris and in a few French towns... In the days of the old régime the capitalist used to keep his precious wealth in his portfolio. Since the Revolution he has turned it into liquid assets, an operation which has caused the disappearance of liquid currency which is now sought on all sides.

A *cahier de doléances* mentioned 'capitalists and people with a portfolio'. Thus the word kept the relatively narrow meaning which Turgot, Morellet and Necker had previously understood by it; it was never used to refer to a large landowner. The capitalist was not a wealthy man, considered apart from his specialised kind of wealth; he was the possessor of liquid currency or of transferable capital—'capitalists or holders of money' as Turgot explained in 1777. More often than not the capitalist was someone who invested his wealth by lending it to the state or by financing an industrial or commercial enterprise. He was a stock-holder or a sleeping partner. In May 1792 the Monthly Chronicle referred to 'the capitalists and those citizens possessing abundant movable wealth'. Cambon had the same idea in mind when, on 15 August 1793, he urged the Convention to include in the same register of the National Debt the loans contracted under the old régime and those contracted under the Revolution. He then declared: 'The capitalist is in favour of the king as long as the king remains his debtor because he is afraid of losing his debt if the debtor is not reinstated. You will see that he will be in favour of the Republic once it becomes his debtor for he will be afraid of losing his capital if the Republic disappears'.

At first, therefore, it was the nature of his wealth and the way in which he used it that marked the capitalist. In 1835 the Academy still followed the definition which it had accepted in 1798: 'A man who has a considerable amount of money and who invests it in commercial enterprises'. Jean-Baptiste Say did not go much beyond that meaning but he undoubtedly suggested an extension of it. 'In the best circles only men who derive their income or at least their main income from interest on capital are considered capitalists. Yet people in general describe all those who possess capital in large or small amounts or who possess a share in a capital holding as capitalists.' That 'share' was not precisely defined and, in fact, Say still saw the moneylender or sleeping partner behind the capitalist. For example, he asked: 'Will the manager be entitled to deny the capitalist any share in an increase in production when that increase is so largely due to his capital?' Even more specifically, he mentioned the capitalist who had made loans to a manufacturing concern in order to obtain interest from it. In 1829 the Saint-Simonians in their 'Outline of Doctrine' depicted 'the present state of affairs where distribution of instruments of production was done by capitalists and landowners'. They retained the traditional meaning of the word, a meaning which could still be used by Thiers in 1845. According to him, the tax-collectors under the Empire discounted their own debts either with public funds or with money which they obtained from capitalists at a high rate of interest. For Thiers capitalists remained 'owners of capital'. With that meaning the capitalist could sometimes be distinguished from the speculator. On 1 January 1846 the *Revue des Deux Mondes* acknowledged that the shares of the Lyon railway had not opened very buoyantly but declared optimistically that 'this bad start gives speculators the chance of a probable rise in price and provides capitalists, along with other cautious people, with an investment safeguarded against the falls which follow an inflated market price'. All the time our capitalist seemed to be characterised primarily by his economic function of investing in firms or in public funds. Indeed, a specialist review appearing between 1836 and 1840 had for its title: 'The Journal of the Industrialist and Capitalist'. Of course, the capitalist could also possess landed property, buildings and mortgages. As we shall see, that was generally the case. However, the money invested in property and so on had been acquired through investments of a different kind. As early as 1792 a deputation protested in the Convention against a 'coalition of rich capitalists' who 'would

gain possession of all the great estates' and thus set up a new 'aristocracy'. In the Chamber of Peers in 1826 Count Siméon pointed to the
'power of capital concentrated on building' and Baron de Barante
declared that 'large estates are nothing more than one aspect of large-
scale capital investment. Therefore, estates must grow at the same time
as capital and wherever there are great capitalists there will be great
landowners as well'. During the July Monarchy a local paper, *L'Opinion, journal du Gers*, published 'advertisements for the sale of all sorts
of property, undoubtedly very useful advertisements for solicitors,
notaries, surveyors, capitalists and so on'.

Nevertheless, this functional sense of the word capitalist, used as a
noun and then as an adjective (definitely being used as an adjective in
1832) came gradually to be superseded by a broader meaning. The
fact that Lamartine could write indignantly in 1843 that 'instead of
labour and industry having their freedom, France is sold to the capitalists' was a sign that the shift in meaning had already begun. Soon after,
as J. B. Say had foreseen, when one wanted to define the capitalist, the
social type that he represented was more important than the role he
played in the economy. In 1848 Scribe made one of his characters in
Le Puff say: 'My sister, whom I could not afford to keep with me, has
found an ideal position with that respectable old capitalist'. In *Les
Paysans*, written by Balzac between 1844 and 1847, old Fourchon,
anxious to exchange the two crowns he had just been given for bottles
of old wine, exclaimed: 'To your good health! I am becoming a
capitalist'. However far-fetched this example might be, it was revealing
all the same. The capitalist was now a rich man; the source of his
wealth and the way that he used it were only secondary considerations.
He might be the owner of a firm or a manager or an investor as distinct
from a workman. This was what Proudhon was referring to in his
theory of surplus value when he pointed out that the capitalist gained
his independence and his security for the future by wealth produced by
the workmen. In the same way Audiganne in 1841 in the *Revue des
Deux Mondes* stressed, before Marx, the contrast between the workmen who supplied their labour and the capitalists who only supplied
their capital. Additionally it could be said that landed wealth and
landed income were not usually included in the new and wider meaning. Yet the lack of distinction in everyday speech between wealth in
general and 'transferable wealth' was extremely significant. The typical
rich man was now the owner of railway shares or of government bonds.
Contemporaries were vaguely becoming aware of the process by which

the predominant and motivating part played by agriculture in the economic structure of the country was being taken over by industrial, commercial and financial activities, even if the change was not complete. Thus, in the always valuable evidence of change in language the evolution of the two words, 'capitalist' and 'capital', shows the same shift in meaning.

The coming of a new economic order as well as of a profoundly changed social structure roughly coincided with the emergence of the abstract noun 'capital' which served as a label for the whole system. It was the end of an evolution which has been admirably summed up by Marc Bloch:

> Capital was a word used originally by usurers and accountants but it acquired a much wider meaning when used by economists. The word 'capitalist' came from old jargon used by speculators in the early days of European stock exchanges. Yet capitalism, which enjoys a much more important place today in our major economic classics, is quite recent: its inflexion shows its derivation from *Kapitalismus*.

It was only in 1867 that 'capitalism', ignored by learned dictionaries such as Littré and Hatzfeld, was noted by Larousse which was concerned more for the richness than for the purity of the language. For Larousse the word was a 'neologism' denoting the 'power of capital and of capitalists' and used with that meaning by Proudhon. The year 1867 came at the crucial point in time during the Second Empire when old France, even if not yet entirely overthrown, was at last experiencing the thoroughgoing effects of the economic revolution of the nineteenth century. The 'New France' was the title of a book written in 1868 by Prévost-Paradol—who, incidentally, meant something entirely different by it—but for that New France the word 'capitalism' arrived just in time to serve as a symbol.

1
The Prelude to Capitalism

In the words of François Perroux, 'Capitalism stands for a slogan of warfare. Karl Marx and his followers brought the word into the arena of class struggles. They made it a word of dynamite and it has never entirely lost its explosive meaning'.[1]

An opponent of a system is bound to be lucid when he becomes a fervent apologist of that system. Although he prophesied the inevitable collapse of the capitalist order, Marx exalted its historical importance in unforgettable words. Its role in history was vital since it was 'essentially revolutionary'

> The bourgeoisie has been the first to show what man's activity can bring about. It has accomplished wonders for surpassing Egyptian pyramids, Roman aqueducts, and Gothic cathedrals; it has conducted expeditions that put in the shade all former exoduses of nations and crusades. The bourgeoisie cannot exist without constantly revolutionising the instruments of production and thereby the relations of production and with them the whole relations of society. Conservation of the old modes of production in unaltered form was, on the contrary the first condition of existence for all earlier industrial classes.[2]

Thus unending change motivated capitalist society and an untiring dynamism urged on the bourgeoisie which was its ruling class. It was an alteration in tempo and a striking acceleration of historical change by comparison with the stability of previous centuries.

From a subsistence economy to one of profit

In *Das Kapital* Marx analysed the economic structure of bourgeois society in a more technical way and explained the forces that drove it. In doing so, he helped us to understand how capitalism came into being inside the old system of production and exchange. 'The origin of capital', he wrote, 'lies in the circulation of goods.' In the first stage 'simple circulation—or buying and selling—is merely a way of obtaining goods outside one's immediate sphere of operations; this goal consists of the acquisition of wealth in use, of articles meant to satisfy particular needs'. It can be expressed by the formula M-A-M: the sale of an article for a sum of money which can then be used for the purchase of another article. However, 'if we isolate the exchange of wealth in use, that is the material aspect of the circulation of goods, simply to consider the economic operations which it brings about, in the end we find money'. The formula then becomes A-M-A or rather A-M-A', A' representing A + A, or A plus 'added value'. This time money is used to buy goods which can be resold at a higher price.[3] 'This final end-product of circulation is the first sign of the appearance of capital.' The economic structure in which it appears is completely different from the system of 'simple circulation' from which it originated. 'The circulation of money as capital contains its goal within itself; for it is only through constantly renewed circulation that wealth continues to increase. Therefore there is no limit to the movement of capital.'

These were the terms in which Karl Marx defined[4] the features common to capitalism in its various aspects, aspects such as the economic activities on which it was based, the social structures in which it was moulded and in which it expressed itself, and the state of mind which it created and which inspired it in turn. These economic activities were no longer undertaken to satisfy the elementary needs of individuals or of human groups living at subsistence level. Their essential driving force was the search for profit through free enterprise, with acceptance of strife, competition, risk and even adventure. It might be true, as Georges Lefebvre thought, that capitalism considered in this way was 'the inheritance by the bourgeoisie of the instincts of the warrior'.

Obviously capitalism defined in such a way had a long history. According to Marx, 'the modern history of capital began with the creation of commerce and trade between the two worlds in the sixteenth century'. There were already capitalists in the economic system of the middle ages, let alone in the economy of the ancient world. Yet such capitalists, even the most progressive of them, did not have the

same impact as those of the early modern age. Pierre Vilar has re-
minded us that 'the true merchant, the bourgeois-type of the middle
ages', may nave been in a sense the opposite of our latter-day bourgeois. For 'he made his money through adventure, monopoly and
usury. Now, capitalism flourished only after destroying—through a
widening of the market—these previous means of making money,
which were limited in any case'.[5] Therefore, the fact that there were
enterprises, sectors or regions which were inspired by a capitalist outlook does not enable us to conclude that the whole economy and the
entire social setting were of a capitalist nature. They consisted only
of 'islets' which had no close links with economy and society as a
whole and exerted no positive influence on them.[6]

It was the part played by the capitalists and their relative importance
in the whole economy which mattered most. If, by the beginning of
the nineteenth century, France had been accustomed for a long time
to certain forms of capitalism, she still offered considerable resistance
to its progress and diffusion.

The difficulties of early accumulation

In 1815, just as in 1789, the French economy was still the economy of
the old régime, essentially agricultural. At least three Frenchmen out
of four lived in the countryside. The value of agricultural production
was two or three times greater than that of industrial production.
Estate duties of the time showed the importance of landownership,
since landed wealth represented the greatest proportion of inherited
property.

The methods of that predominant agriculture were archaic. The
practice of leaving land fallow was widespread and collective burdens
such as common pasture had only partly disappeared. Modernisation
was taking place only in certain limited regions and the tempo of the
'agricultural revolution' was not in the least revolutionary. Output was
low and the surplus available for the market, once the producer had
put aside the amount required for sowing and for family consumption, was small. The proportion of marketable surplus was undoubtedly
increased by the abolition of manorial rights and of the tithe. At least
the more fortunate of the French peasants, who owned and farmed
land and produced enough to sell a substantial part of their crops,
certainly enjoyed several years of prosperity under Napoleon and were
able to save. Yet soon after 1815 there was a change. There began a

long fall in prices which weighed heavily on agricultural income and seriously reduced the profit of the farmer and the income of the landowner. Hence there was nothing in the rural way of life or in the circumstances of the period of elective monarchy to encourage the accumulation of capital, at least in general. Yet there were rural groups both before and after the Revolution who made a fortune and founded bourgeois families. According to Albert Soboul, the large-scale farmers in regions of extensive cultivation were 'true capitalists of agricultural exploitation'. The Thomassin family of Puiseux-Pontoise, who were the subject of one of his studies, rented 224 hectares of farmland under Louis XVI and owned only 3. During the sale of the 'national lands' they bought 74 hectares and subsequently were full owners of 150 hectares in 1822 and of 216 in 1914. Elswhere 'the ploughman' or 'the village cock of the walk' represented other sections of 'wealthy peasantry who were already producing to a greater or lesser extent for the market'.[7] The same was true of the rural merchants—who under the old régime fixed the rate of the tithe and of the manorial rights—and of innkeepers and postmasters. All of them were usually ready to lend their accumulated savings at high rates of interest. Overall, however, the French 'stocking under the bed' was still far from bulging with the hidden fortune which it would contain by the time of the Second Empire. Even then, as we shall see later, it was going to be difficult to put that fortune to productive use.

Industry was secondary in importance and had hardly been touched by technical progress. Technology was a sphere in which change was long drawn out, not only in time but also as far as various regions and different branches of production were concerned. The special reason for high production costs lay in the deficiency of readily available energy supplies at a low price. The steam engine made its appearance at the end of the eighteenth century but during the Revolution and the Empire France was preoccupied with her own destiny or with that of the continent. Since she was more or less cut off from English influence the widespread adoption of the steam engine was slow. Even in 1820 only 65 firms in France were using steam power. The restriction and separation of market outlets constituted another handicap and the 'revolution in transport' had not yet taken place. There were not enough rivers or roads, and even fewer canals, to overcome the fragmentation of the national market into zones or provinces which were virtually isolated from each other. The political and legal Revolution certainly secured freedom of production and trade in that corporate forms of organisation and internal customs duties were abolished, but it did not remove the real obstacles which hindered development and which set rather narrow limits to capital formation. In this sphere France would not be able to emulate England for a long time.

The most flourishing sector of the French economy before 1789 was maritime and colonial trade. The French ports—Nantes, Bordeaux, and especially Marseille—built their prosperity on trade with Europe, with ports in the Middle East such as Beyrouth, Tripoli and Alexandria, with the Barbary coast and particularly with the colonies known as 'the Islands', a term which meant the West Indies, Réunion and Mauritius, and the settlements in Senegal and in India. These French ports exported wine and wheat, linen and cotton cloth. Following the classical pattern of 'triangular commerce' they imported and redistributed tropical products such as sugar, coffee, cocoa, tobacco, indigo and cotton, after first supplying the plantations of the West Indies with the manufactured products required and with Negro slaves bought on the coasts of the Gulf of Guinea in exchange for shoddy goods, guns and different kinds of spirits. In addition there were foreign transactions taking place in the interior of France with the textile industry of Lyon (which was the first market in the world for silk and silkware) and the luxury trade of Paris. French foreign trade, which in 1789 was four times what it was in 1715 and exceeded 1,000 million francs, did not perform badly even when compared with British trade which was already in first place. The profits accruing from it seemed enormous alongside the meagre profits yielded from cultivation of land, and they were sometimes as high as 300 and 400 per cent. Certain ship-owners from Nantes, such as Chaurand or Delaville-Deguer, had a net profit of 60 to 80 per cent.[8] Thus, with the very excess characteristic of their heroic age, 'the last adventures of merchant capital laid the basis for the early accumulation of modern capital'.[9] Besides, it was under the influence of that capital that industry developed in seaports, with sugar refining, soapmaking and so on. Under the same influence industry developed inland, sometimes quite far afield. For example, the flour mills, the draperies and the silk manufactories of Montauban relied on shipments from Bordeaux.[10] 'The important trade of Grenoble consisting of drapery, linen manufacturing, grocery and haberdashery, could exist and prosper only through St Domingo where some of its members had invested enormous amounts of money.' The Dolle and Raby families were typical examples. 'They were owners of plantations and slaves, exporting products made in Dauphiné via Beaucaire or Bordeaux and importing sugar and rum. They were local patrons of arts and letters and owners of one of the finest estates in the town.'[11] Yet this close dependence on overseas links constituted the weakness of such an economy, since it was semi-peripheral activity and was tied to the French coasts in order to ensure trade relations with distant countries. In a way it was like Alexandria under the Ptolemies, 'on the edge of Egypt' but not in Egypt and surviving only as long as its links with Egypt lasted. Marseille likewise was completely turned towards seaborne trade; its links with the hinterland were of secondary importance and the free port which it enjoyed was maintained with jealous concern. However, the events of the Revolution and of the Empire, with their endless wars, blockades and revolts in the colonies, dealt Marseille along with other ports a severe if not fatal blow. St Domingo and Ile de France were never to be under French rule again. Other French possessions either never recovered their former prosperity or they continued to follow the various directions taken by their trade between 1789 and 1815; those directions did not always obey the rules of the old mercantilist system of exclusivity which meant the monopoly of the mother country. In the nineteenth century French trade was reorganised on new lines and it was not until the reign of Louis Philippe that it clearly recovered from stagnation.

Hence the mechanisms of production and exchange did not operate to secure the release of available capital in sufficient quantity to give a new impetus to the whole economy. The more serious drawback, however, was that a goodly part of the capital was turned away from productive investment. The way in which capital was used was no more satisfactory than the way in which its formation and accumulation were achieved. In that respect Colbert's complaints lost none of their relevance at least until the Revolution. The luxury expenditure of the ruling classes was still of some economic importance even though it was not always undertaken in the best national interest. The royal borrowings were enormous sums and the National Debt went up from 1,700 millions to 4,500 millions between 1721 and 1789; some share of this came back into the economic system thanks to the orders of the army, the navy and the various public services, but it was only a fraction. The offices which were sold in ever increasing number by a needy monarchy to the newly-rich anxious to attain higher social status—even the rank of nobility—were much in favour. Hence funds were put to this use which could have been used more efficiently.

Since the sum required to pay for an office was often borrowed, capitalists were induced to keep in reserve a plentiful amount of liquid money which was not then available for circulation. This practice tended to hold interest rates too high. It was true that the sale of offices in general disappeared with the old régime, even if the sale of ministerial offices in particular continued—or was at least restored by the law of 1816. However, the purchase of an office in the magistracy or in the treasury was not the only temptation which induced the merchant or manufacturer to leave his business and to remove the capital invested in it once he had made his fortune. The craving for land was even stronger and lasted for a longer period of time.

The craving for land was widespread. The desire to augment his place in the sun also led the wealthy peasant to use his savings to acquire new property or strips of land. The peasant even borrowed to gratify his land-hunger and encumbered his estate with heavy mortgages. The investments in landed property, which were completely unfruitful as far as industrial and commercial development were concerned, were often far from promoting the improved conditions of agricultural organisation which might have been expected. Yet they certainly did sometimes lead to an 'agrarian capitalism' which was progressive in its methods and its yield; it altered the old landed arrangements so as to achieve better production and productivity and hence left its mark on the soil. This was what happened in the Pays de Caux where a great part of the money earned by the tradesmen of Le Havre and Rouen went towards the purchase of land. Yet if this 'agrarian individualism', on which Marc Bloch has written one of his most quoted articles,[12] was quite common in the eighteenth century, the rural tradition of France did not produce farmers with a determined eye for profit in the same way as in England. There the search for profit helped to support the enclosure movement and other associated features of agricultural progress for generations. Lavoisier, who had tried to improve his land in the Blésois by using chemicals on the soil, and who knew how much the experiments cost, deplored the situation. In France, he said, country estates were quite different from estates on the other side of the Channel. 'The number of buildings which make up a farm unit is such that the amount obtained for letting them is hardly equal to the interest on the loans contracted in order to have the buildings erected.'[13] Hence the purchase of an estate and its amortisation swallowed up capital which was then not available to finance agricultural improvement. For that reason the Marquis de Mirabeau and the physiocrats wanted a close association between 'landed property' and 'movable property' which alone could provide the capital necessary for development. Their contention was that 'the extinction of movable property brings about the deterioration of landed property which then finds itself unproductive'.[14] Their policy was followed only in a few prosperous country seats where large-scale farmers could provide the funds to bring about such an association. Usually capital hoarded up over the years by peasants aspiring to higher social status emerged from its long period of sterile accumulation only to be used for the hasty purchase of land which became overvalued as a result of the ensuing competition. Only a minority of farmers were advocates of improved methods of cultivation and farming: they were the great landlords who favoured English practices or the bourgeois who had also become landed capitalists in respect of part of their wealth. The French countryside was far from having ample funds available for development; although men competed to possess land there was a serious and chronic shortage of money and credit.

The early period of capitalism

A relative scarcity of capital due to insufficient accumulation and economic errors in its use explained the weakness of capitalist organisation in France at the end of the eighteenth century. This scarcity, in turn, aggravated the weaknesses from which it sprang. It was a kind of pre-capitalism, or capitalism in its infancy. More precisely, in a well-known historical formulation, there was a predominance of commercial capitalism which preceded and foreshadowed industrial and financial capitalism.

This commercial capitalism was not devoid of outdated features even in its own sphere of the distribution of goods, and was far from having an impact on the whole of French life right down to the remotest province. The villages which were at the very heart of subsistence economy had practically no experience of a fixed and permanent distribution network and their main commercial source of supply was still the pedlar. In the towns the increasing rigidity of the social framework caused by the systematic creation of privileges led, during the old régime, to the setting up of autonomous corporations of specialised merchants: examples of these were the *Six Corps* in Paris and the activities organised in the provinces around consular jurisdictions created by royalty.[15] The tradesmen who 'treated mechanical devices with contempt"[16] were regarded all the more highly when their own personal business activity included little or no time spent in working on the bench. Typical among them were the Paris haberdashers who, according to Savary, produced nothing and did no work except to decorate articles already made and manufactured. The Parisian smallware dealer was, for the Encyclopedia, 'a dealer in everything and a maker of nothing': he dealt almost exclusively in a particular trade, whether it was luxury fabrics or skins, stationery or precious metals, hardware or coppersmith's goods, toys and knick-knacks or glassware, jewellery and ornaments. Each trade had its own district or street: the cabinetmaker who left the St Antoine area to become a dealer in luxury furniture joined his new colleagues either in the rue St Honoré or nearby.[17] Even after the corporate system disappeared many features of the commercial system of the old régime remained. At lower levels there were a host of merchant artisans and shopkeepers of all kinds who differed from proper artisans only by the wage-earners they employed and by the relative importance of their business funds. Hence they were more clearly capitalists in their own right. They were specially involved in the sale of consumer goods and food associated with the trades of baker, butcher, publican and innkeeper.

It was unusual for travelling merchants to link retail trade with wholesale trade and production. In writing in 1833 about the exploits of the famous Gaudissart under the Restoration and under Louis Philippe, Balzac described him as 'one of the strangest characters produced by the practices of the present time and the herald of an all-pervasive but levelling influence towards standardised products for a mass market, an influence motivated by a one-track cast of mind which is a recent trend in society'. Before Gaudissart the function of middleman belonged to the wandering merchant who was to some extent a wholesaler. The fairs which had been the great centres of the commercial world in former times of difficult communications still remained, especially in the south. Yet they became more concentrated: at Beaucaire they became more important at the expense of less well-known ones in the area, and their continuance at Pézenas emphasised the decline of secondary fairs.

The prosperous merchant society of the ports, mentioned in a previous section, was just becoming a capitalist society, yet it retained many features of the past. The large fortunes accumulated—the wealth of the Roux or Borély families at Marseille and of the Gradis or

Bonnafé families at Bordeaux—were usually the result of diverse activities, specialisation of function being unknown. They were at one and the same time wholesale merchants, carriers, ship-owners, commission agents, insurers, bankers and industrialists. In Rouen, for example, they sold everything from handkerchiefs to cannon. In the Pays de Caux they sold sugar and coffee, cotton for the local textile industry, wool for Elbeuf and shoddy goods of all kinds for the Islands. The richest of these import-export merchants also indulged in lending 'for high adventure', loans being repayable only if cargoes arrived safely. Some of them became involved in shipbuilding, in marine insurance and even in horse-racing. The Férays at Le Havre and the Hoüels at Caen had interests in the coffee and slave trades, in luxury crafts, in mines, in shipyards and armaments, in cotton weaving and printing, and in the making of silk lace known as 'blondes'. They lent whatever remained of their capital. Isnard, a Girondist in the National Convention, inherited from his father—a rich merchant at Grasse— an oil business, soap manufacture, corn importing, silk throwing and a wine and provision business. These constituted the basis of a fortune which was supplemented by ship-owning as well as ownership of lands and buildings.[18] At Cette [Sète], the seaport for Montpellier, the rich bourgeoisie of the capital of Languedoc financed simultaneously exports of wheat to the poorer sectors of the Mediterranean world, supplies of wholesale wine to St Valéry and to fairs at Amiens as well as small consignments of wine to Sedan or Lunéville. There was even some distant trade with America and Russia.[19]

These businessmen, the most daring entrepreneurs of the time, were provided with a system of commercial law which was only rough and ill-defined. They could only form so-called 'personal partnerships' and more often than not these were for a specific objective.[20] Besides, like most bourgeois they put their money in landed property in order to make sure of a safe income and to gain prestige for their family. The bourgeoisie at Bordeaux, in the same way as its counterpart at Rouen or Le Havre, monopolised the finest estates of the hinterland. At Nantes between 1783 and 1792—the years when the slave trade reached its high point there (in contrast to the decline already taking place at Bordeaux and Le Havre)—rich ship-owners were still prospering. Two examples at Nantes were the Michels, who had been in business for eight generations, and the Espivents de Villeboisnet, members of the noblesse d'épée in the thirteenth century who had come into business in the seventeenth century in association with

Chateaubriand's father. Nevertheless, many influential families retired from business following the example of the Bouteillers whose fortune, including their 'dwellings' in the Islands, was more than 8 million francs in 1789. The Chamber of Commerce expressed concern: 'The merchant whose transactions have been crowned with success is anxious to give up his business . . . his children soon forget their father's activity and his grandchildren despise the obscure but useful source of the titles to fame which they enjoy'. They in their turn became property holders.[21]

The prominent merchants of Marseille appeared to be rather less interested in converting their liquid wealth into land but most of them still owned rural estates which by their size as well as by their yield contradicted the legend that those estates were country retreats for leisure use only.[22] Besides, in the circumstances of the age, although landowning was a policy which was harmful to general economic advance it seemed to benefit the interests of those who pursued it. Certainly in the Beauvais area, where the problem was different from that confronting the overseas merchant, Pierre Goubert has shown that the Motte family, who disappeared from the commercial world in the eighteenth century, were nearly always opposed to the possession of country estates and to the role of rural landowners. In consequence they paid the penalty for the fortune which they had acquired too quickly, for their social recklessness, their ostentation as newly-rich and their arrogant pretensions. The Danse family, another group studied by Goubert, were 'wiser'. They firmly established themselves in the Beauvais area and because they were great landowners as well as important merchants and administrators, they endured much longer. Ploughmen in the sixteenth century, they became launderers in the seventeenth and important merchants in the eighteenth century with virtually worldwide connections. In addition to their royal privileges and their capital invested in large shipping expeditions they were well-informed magistrates of noble rank under Louis XVI, departmental administrators before and after Robespierre as well as active buyers of 'national land' and then magistrates again and deputies under the elective monarchy. The Danse family presented a typical picture of the slow but steady rise of the bourgeoisie with deep roots in the soil.[23]

The history of the Danse dynasty also confirmed that industrial capitalism as distinct from artisan organisation or from merchant or landowning capitalism did not yet exist at the end of the eighteenth century. The majority of enterprises were small in scale and old-

D

fashioned. They consisted of traditional town workshops, small pockets which were industrial and commercial at the same time since the master, who was himself a worker either on his own account or with several workmates and apprentices, had a shop where he sold the product of his labour directly to the customer. This practice was common in the building trade, in clothing and shoe manufacture, and in the wood and metal industries (in the locksmiths' trade, for example).[24] Mines, ironworks and glassworks were not so much greater in size. Near the forests which supplied them with fuel, or near the rivers which provided them with power, they gathered together a few skilled workmen and assistants who were half workmen and half peasants. Small scale metalmaking in Champagne and the 'Catalan forges' in the Pyrenees were of this kind. These works often belonged to noblemen or, before 1789, to the religious orders, because they were dependent on forest resources and on water power in which landowners usually had exclusive rights. The valuable study by Pierre Léon,[25] which enables us to follow the industrial development of Dauphiné with exceptional accuracy and continuity, describes the enterprises of the Count de Marcieu and of the Chartreux de Durbon and Barral families. The Barrals were simultaneously barristers, councillors or presidents in the *parlement* at Grenoble, great landowners as lords of Allevard where they possessed forests, iron mines, blast furnaces and tilt hammers. The magistrates of Dijon and many others provided further examples of similar enterprise.[26]

Nevertheless, landed income which had provided, and still did provide, a great part of the capital required for industrial development was, around 1800, beginning to prove insufficient to meet industry's regular financial needs. The majority of works relying on landed income found it difficult to continue. They had to appeal for 'liquid capital' which was by no means always essentially different from landed capital. Léon shows how in many instances this liquid capital came from landed income as well, being derived from patient accumulation of profits gained from cultivation of the soil. Because of prevailing eighteenth-century prosperity and of the rise in agricultural prices this capital was freed from its former use in mortgage loans to farmers in financial difficulty and was now directed to other kinds of loan, including advances to needy ironmasters. Yet the new capitalists who now helped with their available funds, and who in the long run would oust the old landowners from mining and metallurgy, also came from merchant and trading circles. In the case of the Périers, who are mentioned again later, it was through banking and commerce in Grenoble that they took over from Paulin de Barral at Allevard. In 1805 they gave Barral a yearly grant, subject to severe conditions, and then in 1816 forced him to sell to a joint-stock company which they controlled through their own men and their own capital.

Usually capitalism penetrated French industry by more old-fashioned methods. It operated through the domestic system by which workmen and peasants,[27] even if they were 'masters' in a legal sense as employers and hirers of journeymen, were still dependent on the 'putter-out' who distributed raw material to them, paid them an appropriate amount and collected the finished products for ultimate sale. In this way commercial capitalism dominated urban or rural domestic industry, and examples occurred in linen cloth manufacture in Maine, pinmaking in the Ouche region and spinning and weaving in Normandy where over two-thirds of the textiles sold in the market hall at Rouen came from 'manufacture' in the Caux district. Similarly in Paris the small-ware dealers whom we have already mentioned—the Duvaux, Hébert, Poirier and Daguerre families—put out customers' orders to cabinetmakers. They employed the best makers, who were consequently under their close control, including even the great Bernard Van Risen Burgh (B.V.R.B.).[28]

This classical structure was retained by the silk industry at Lyon for generations. On the eve of the Revolution there were about 400 master merchants or wholesalers or merchant manufacturers in the Lyon area, about 6,000 master workmen or foremen, about 20-22,000 journeymen and nearly 10,000 women warpers, reelers and throwsters. Jacques Imbert-Colomès became the leader of the counter-revolutionary movement in Lyon and was a man of culture as much as a businessman; he 'lived like a lord' and through his marriage alliance to noblemen in the magistracy could be counted as a typical representative of the upper middle class controlling the Lyon silk industry. That upper middle class did not have to contend with the old nobility, since noblemen were not numerous around Lyon, nor with any parliamentary group because no *parlement* existed in the town: hence it felt secure and confident in its power. Yet in this city, which was 'entirely devoted to commerce', it is doubtful whether the economic ambitions and modernity of the upper middle class were as great as its social dominance. Evidence on this has come from Grimod de la Reynière, an inquisitive and experienced observer as well as a great traveller and epicurean who had sold groceries on occasion at fairs in southern

France. He praised the upper middle class of Lyon for being satisfied with moderate wealth and for having less imperious needs than some, since they preferred to increase capital gradually by speedy turnover rather than by attempting to double it through involvement in long-term speculation. In any case it was a capitalist bourgeoisie whose members were more concerned with trade than with manufacturing, but they were fully aware of the fact that their prosperity was closely concerned with the low standard of living of the wage-earners employed, a situation due to the *loi d'airain* drawn up by Turgot. The manufacturer Mayet wrote in 1786:

> Everyone knows that the price of food determines the cost of labour. It is mainly due to the low cost of our labour that our fabrics are marketable in the rest of Europe... It is essential to stop the workman from ever becoming rich. He must earn just what he needs in order to be well fed and decently dressed.

He alleged, moreover—and this theme was to be widely repeated in the coming century—that 'among some categories of people too much affluence stifles hard work and engenders idleness and all the vices that go with it'.[29] It was hardly surprising, however, that Ford's doctrine of high wages as a factor contributing to higher output and greater consumption had not yet been advanced, especially by manufacturers of luxury fabrics.

The archaic economic methods and lack of social understanding prevailing in silk at Lyon towards the end of the eighteenth century were typical of employers' attitudes in the whole textile industry. Well-known names were Crespel and Barrois of Lille in the north, Cohin de la Ferté-Bernard in the west, Latune of Crest in Dauphiné—and there were many others who did not specialise in any particular branch of the industry. In 1780 Crespel founded a dynasty remarkable among the Lille bourgeoisie for its length of survival. After he added the trade of merchant grocer to his business of linen stretching the family affair went on to last for seven generations, until 1947.[30]

Nevertheless, this first form of industrial concentration tending to bring commercial capitalism to maturity went a stage beyond 'merchant manufacturing'. Large-scale merchants, who for marketing purposes continued to centralise the home-made products of artisans working to order, also set up their own workshops for the finishing, dressing or even the making of fabrics. This tendency was seen particularly in sectors already affected by mechanisation but not yet using steam engines, as in the *pacus* which were workshops in the Armentières district for the spinning of linen or cotton. A similar development took place in the silk-throwing workshops of the south-east. Hence it was a period of transition from a technical as well as from an economic point of view. These capitalists who employed both traditional labourers and real workmen in the modern sense of the word were at a stage of 'nebulous concentration', in Léon's suggestive phrase.

The expansion of trade and of manufacture was slowed down, however, by the absence of an organised network for the distribution of capital. No feature of this early type of financial capitalism was more significant than the legal and religious prohibitions which still hindered the lending of money for interest. Lending for interest was still condemned by the Church, and Benedict XIV gave a reminder of traditional doctrine in the Bull *Vix pervenit* of 1745. If the lender took some share of the risk it was only right that he should have a share in the profit, but if he declined all responsibility once he had lent the money, and if he did not care about the use to which it was put, then the resulting profit became unlawful. Common law had long followed this doctrine and under Louis XVI the *parlement* condemned 'every kind of usury forbidden by canon law'. Nevertheless, the theologians themselves tended to become less strict, and in 1765 Emery followed Salesian traditions in trying to find a middle way between the austerity of the Jansenists and the laxity of the Jesuits. He acknowledged the 'invincible ignorance' of the moneylenders, so making honest men of them. Of course, actual practice was well ahead of the slowly yielding attitudes of ecclesiastical and lay authorities.

Yet the prohibition which was so rigidly adhered to had important results. It explains why the settlement of an annuity was under the old régime the normal way of borrowing money, not only for an individual but also for a business firm, rather than straightforward lending for interest. In return for a sum which represented the actual amount of the loan, the borrower of capital sold to the lender the right to collect a yearly income on his principal, the income representing interest. In this way the bond-holder did not draw usurious profit from the capital which he was not supposed to own any more, but obtained instead a legitimate revenue from the landed property or buildings on which he had a claim during his lifetime. The purchase of an agreed bond could be considered as the purchase of a life income from capital which was never repayable. Hence it was a normal and legitimate operation in which the maximum amount was fixed by the king. Perhaps following the letter of the law in this way satisfied the scruples of those 'widows' and 'maids' from Beauvais who strangely combined the most illicit and disreputable activities with the strictest and most extreme piety, for they showed the most astonishing bravado in their zealous collection of annuities, mortgages and real estate. They were not exceptional; a great part of bourgeois wealth came from profit on loans to the nobility, to the peasants and to the merchants and artisans. In Marseille under the Empire these loans still represented a great part of the money inherited by rich and important men, even those among them who had no links with the business world.[31]

For the same reasons of religious and social psychology the lotteries of the Hôtel de Ville and the lotteries of religious communities, as well as the royal lottery which replaced them in 1776 and the *emprunts à lot* which were popular under Calonne, all played the part of our modern bonds. Such bonds were not possible then because of the prohibition on moneylending, and capitalists had few alternatives to the lottery as a means of investing their wealth. Furthermore, Raymond de Roover seems to have proved that in Catholic countries prohibition delayed the general acceptance of discounting. Until the creation in 1776 of a special office called *La Caisse*, which was like an early version of the Bank of France, it was impossible to discount a bill of exchange, since discount was regarded as interest.[32] Undoubtedly it was a special kind of interest, 'an interest which was deducted in advance from the nominal value of a bill instead of being collected at maturity or at the end of a time appointed by the contracting parties'. Nevertheless, it was interest reckoned as a certain percentage of the capital and hence illegitimate. By contrast, the buying and selling of bills of exchange, a practice of bankers of the time, was regarded as something entirely different. It consisted of 'speculations on the rate of exchange with other places' which yielded a profit; the 'exchange' itself represented the profit made on the fluctuations in price of the various metal currencies. It involved a certain amount of risk and could even result in a real loss, at least in theory. This was why the banker was officially entitled to his profit.[33]

The situation was that commercial paper had existed for a long time, had been dealt in, had circulated and had played an important part in the economy which could not rely entirely on the stock of metal currency, considerable as it was.[34] 'Between the age of [John] Law and that of the *assignats* there had been an intermediate age of "paper". Metal currency, swallowed up by state taxes and loans as well as by land investments, did not seem to return easily to commercial circulation.' Somehow the deficiency had to be made good. Yet there was hardly a 'domination by paper money'.[35] In fact, the question at issue was a long standing one—credit, which was closely linked with current commercial transactions. The four annual payments at Lyon—on Twelfth Day, at Easter, in August and on All Souls' Day—originated in the big fairs though the payments survived after the fairs had ceased to be prosperous. The payments were based on differences in value. In the same way at Marseille commercial agents opened current accounts for merchants and from 1766 to 1774 they even went as far as to issue money orders 'payable in compensation'. These functioned as banknotes and they enabled people, according to a contemporary report, to run a business of nearly 200 million livres with 7 or 800,000 in hard cash, thanks to transfers between contracting parties.[36] Even the merchants themselves occasionally became bankers and we know that they did so in the great ports; among the silk merchants of Lyon there was the remarkable example of the Guérins and at Grenoble there were the Périers. The development of banking operations such as compensation, currency exchange, speculation on bills of exchange,[37] and opening of credit accounts for industrial buyers and for suppliers of raw materials, was taking place on the fringe of commercial capitalism and yet under its aegis.

The 'merchant bankers' were not the only ones to put their capital 'to work'. Banking during the period was the province of capitalists of all kinds, and for many of them it was a way of increasing money obtained by what could only be called a real exploitation of the state by its finance officers. Farmers-general or collectors-general handled considerable amounts of money representing public revenues and knew how to use them in their own interest. There were also suppliers, purveyors, and service agents of all kinds who were expert at drawing a profit from their commercial operations. The notaries seemed to play an even more important role. Since contracts concerning sales, leases or drawing up of bonds had to be made in their presence, people were naturally inclined to leave in their care the task of investing the capital being transferred as part of those contracts. In Paris more than anywhere else they had enormous amounts of money at their disposal and had influence over a great many commercial and industrial investments. In 1782 Sebastien Mercier said they were 'financiers far more than lawyers, real Proteans, money-handlers, speculators, and unofficial brokers in financial transactions. They had become valuable to the Ministry since they persuaded private investors to lend money to the king. They obtained a profit on each loan and their wealth increased rapidly. At thirty-five years of age they could sell their office which was then worth three times what it had been ten years before.' The municipal pawnshop also handled money; established in Paris in 1777, it granted loans to tradespeople on pawned articles such as metals and precious objects; these were an anticipation of the loans on securities contracted during the nineteenth century.

Thus if 'money-handlers' were numerous they belonged to very diverse categories and banking was far from being their main occupation, let alone the exclusive one. They rendered incomplete, local and occasional service and in no way formed a coherent, unified and well-organised network. Hence their usefulness remained limited. Credit was hard to obtain and expensive almost everywhere. In Dauphiné, industry obtained it only for 10, 12, 15 and even 24 per cent. Firms, as well as individuals, tried most of the time to manage with their own resources. One could say that self-financing was the rule, and the only possible alternative was what the age itself called 'recourse to usury'. Such a primitive system of distribution of capital aggravated the difficulties inherent in the very structure of the economy. The bad management of public finances and the burden of unavoidable expenditure, set against an absurd and unfair assessment of taxes made even worse by mediocre techniques of collection, forced the state to grant outrageous advantages to the people who subscribed to its loans, advantages which tended to keep the average rate of interest too high. One more example of the archaic methods of payment and credit may be mentioned. Although the use of short-term commercial paper was already frequent, monetary circulation remained in very large measure one of metallic currency. Mercier described how

> on the 10th, 20th and 30th of the month between ten o'clock in the morning and noon one came across carriers bending under the weight of their bulging money-bags. They ran as if an enemy was about to take the town by surprise. Such a practice showed our inability to establish an acceptable and reputable token to replace metal coins. Metal ought to serve as a symbol which is usually stationary rather than in transit from one cashier's office to another.

The end of the eighteenth century and its auguries

Nevertheless, the equivalents for cash in bulk desired by Mercier began to appear, along with other requirements of a capitalist system, during the feverish years of the reign of Louis XVI when business circles were discovering the methods that were to make their fortune. Towards the end of the eighteenth century there were positive achievements and projects in hand which because of their nature and their import could be considered as real pointers to the future; they occurred especially in sectors where the timely renewal of bourgeois groups prevented the conservatism that in other sectors affected the merchants of the old patriciate.

A new financial circle began to flourish in Paris around 1780, launching into activity unequalled since the failure of the 'System' associated with John Law.[38] The circle included men like Lecouteulx de Canteleu, who came from merchant activity in Rouen, Laborde the court banker, Fulchiron from Lyon, who also owned mines in the coalfield of St Étienne, and Ducloz-Dufresnoy, a wealthy notary. There were a number of foreigners like the Englishman Boyd and the Vandenyvers, who arrived from Holland in 1752 with connections in all the big markets of Europe. The Vandenyvers owned numerous buildings in Paris and had interests in St Domingo. The so-called 'Genevese' were specially important,[39] although many of them were in fact descendants of French Huguenots who had taken refuge in Switzerland from as early as the sixteenth century. Among these early settlers were the Thelussons who had come originally from Lyon, but more usually these 'Genevese' families had fled after the Revocation of the Edict of Nantes as did the Clavières from Dauphiné, the Mallets from Nîmes and the Panchauds.[40] They formed a tightly organised group with very intricate family connections, like those binding together the great industrial families of Mulhouse who were similarly of protestant stock, and their international business connections foreshadowed those of the Rothschilds at a later date. All this explained the powerful influence of the group and the vital part it played in a country which was far from being integrated in the great European network of circulation of capital. Government affairs were conducted by a Treasury which was sometimes not too scrupulous because it was always in financial difficulty. The government could obtain loans only on exceptionally disadvantageous terms because so many risks for the lender—such as seizures, reviews, repayments and cancellations—were involved. French lenders themselves could hardly endure against such risks, and even the fortune of Samuel Bernard, the great banker of Louis XIV, did not last long after his death. The specially vital connections with London and Amsterdam, the great financial centres of the time, 'had to be made almost necessarily through Huguenot intermediaries from Geneva or from other Swiss centres—bound to be shady characters—who were represented in Paris by banks that had some tenuous connections with Geneva'. Necker was clearly the most famous of them all. He was the son of a lecturer in law who had come to Geneva from Pomerania, and was not really a self-made man but rather a successful go-between. He became (just as Laffitte was later to become) the partner of his employer Thellusson, then his successor and finally a millionaire in the true sense of the word, possessing 7 or 8 million livres in 1768 when he was practically the sole owner of his banking concern. He deserves to be remembered more as a representative figure than as an isolated case. The man himself and his doctrine and achievements were extremely disappointing. Yet his accession to power in 1777 was the first example of the rise of a commoner. He had no title, no family connections, no office, and no post as royal official. He did not belong to the nobility, the judiciary, the administrative bureaucracy or even to the organisation of the royal offices of finance. Moreover, he was a foreigner and a heretic and he did not even attempt, as Law had done, to renounce his faith and to be naturalised. Yet he managed to become very influential, thanks to an organised group of followers who knew how to sway people's opinions, and thanks also to his ability to sell to an international set of capitalists the loans of an overburdened royal treasury which taxes and traditional finance could no longer supply. In Lüthy's judgement this was something really new. Yet we may point out, without exaggerating the idea of repetition in history, that this appeal by the French monarchy for help from the best-known figures in international banking had happened many times before. It went back to the age of 'Biche' and 'Mouche' the Italian financiers who worked for Philip the Fair.

Nevertheless, Parisian business under Louis XVI certainly assumed a new dimension and a new vitality. Based to a large extent on the needs of the royal finances, its speculation mainly involved public funds. Imitating English practice, Necker left to his principal representatives the task of investing bonds with foreigners or French capitalists. The latter were mostly Parisians themselves and constituted a group which felt acutely the fluctuations of the public debt and politics, the two being clearly linked together. This was one of the groups responsible for the turmoil that preceded the Revolution. Thanks to cunningly organised competition and to manoeuvres which by well-controlled cornering of the market led to immediate success of financial issues, these bankers made substantial gains. Calonne heightened this kind of speculation by increasing the number of loans. Yet speculation occurred also in the shares of companies created by the bankers themselves. Indeed, there was a mushrooming of new enterprises. Some, like the *Compagnie des Indes* which was revived in 1785, still followed the tradition of mercantilism and met with hostility in liberal business circles, although Swiss financiers supported them. Others, however, were more dynamic. The *Compagnie des Eaux de Paris* undertook to supply houses with water from the Seine by using 'fire pumps'—in other words, steam engines—constructed at Chaillot by J. C. Périer, the company's live-wire.[41] Its rival was the *Compagnie des Eaux de l'Yvette*. The first insurance companies were making their appearance: Delessert for life assurance, for example, and Clavière for fire. Bankers and stockbrokers launched them with great publicity, employing notary clerks as canvassers and trying to raise the price of shares. Lecouteulx himself arranged a placing on the French market of shares of the *Banque de St Charles* which had been founded at Madrid by Cabarrus, the father of Madam Tallien. More important, Parisian speculators created their own bank, the *Caisse d'Escompte*, a joint-stock company founded in 1776 and soon to come under the control of Swiss bankers.[42] At last the idea, inspired by the English system and often contemplated since Law, of an issuing and discounting bank—this time practising true discount—was being put into effect. Additionally, the *Caisse d'Escompte* engaged in trade in precious metals, looked after deposits in current accounts without charging a fee, collected bills that were due, settled outstanding debts, collected interest on bonds, and overall carried on most banking activities. Yet what was new and most important was the fact that issue and discount (or rather, re-discount) were combined, a practice which tended to turn the *Caisse* into a concern dealing with credit in the second degree—that is, into a banker's bank—and so into a forerunner of the Bank of France for which it was to provide a framework. It accustomed the Parisian public to the use of the bank-note, which remained little known in the provinces. Classified together with bills of exchange, the bank-note was marked down at $\frac{1}{2}$ to 1 per cent loss in value.

In this way Paris experienced a business fever which swept away traditional restrictions. Discount weathered the veto on usury; the Stock Exchange, established in 1724, dealt in long-term transactions in spite of prohibitions[43] and brought over to the side of the capitalists names well known in literature and in high society. Beaumarchais, himself a dealer, supplier of munitions and speculator, was successful enough to be able to spend 1,700,000 livres on the building of his mansion and defended the *Compagnie des Eaux* (in which he was a partner with Périer) against the pamphleteering attacks of Mirabeau. Talleyrand, who played the Stock Exchange in expert fashion, took part in 1783 in the reconstitution of the statutes of the *Caisse d'Escompte*. He said quite openly: 'I have always been rich; wealth is a necessity'. Speculation, coming out into the open like this for the first time since the 'System', naturally created strong controversy. The leading part played by men from Geneva provoked criticism which by its xenophobic tone foreshadowed the partisan propaganda of the nineteenth century. The physiocrats, who were trying to protect national and landed wealth against 'cosmopolitan' capitalism, set the tone for the debate. The Abbé Baudeau for example, attacked in 1776 what Necker himself was unwise enough to call 'the faculty of enjoyment provided by money'. Baudeau denounced the greed driving 'those men who have a great deal of money at their disposal which they can use wherever they like' and the sterility which, he felt, affected their speculations: 'accumulated capital cannot be regarded as public wealth as long as it is not used to subsidise useful new undertakings'.[44]

In this criticism was there a call for investment? In that case his reproach was not entirely justified for the call was beginning to meet a response. Coinciding with the importation of new techniques from England which marked the beginning of the 'industrial revolution', the capitalist upsurge played its part in setting in motion a new tendency in French industry. Of course, it was in no way a general or mass movement, but besides expansion in quantity of production there were signs or hints of progress. Even in a 'static sector, one of traditional activity', the patient statistical research of Léon shows a 'slow growth' of 61 per cent on average during the eighteenth century in the cloth industry, growth which was also experienced in the traditional hemp and linen industries and in the leather trade. Growth was obviously more rapid in 'new sectors' where 'refined techniques were being applied and where the capital of an aristocracy powerful both by birth and by wealth was being used'. The production of coal, which certainly started from a very low base, seems to have increased in the same period by 700 to 800 per cent, and the production of cast iron by 72 per cent. The 'take-off' of the new cotton industry and the expansion of silk which was an 'old industry but a very active one' seemed equally important.[45] Moreover, in those branches of 'dynamic' activity firms of a new scale and dimension were appearing. Labrousse has described them as 'heavyweights' of industry.

From the middle of the century, the small coalowners began to be replaced by great capitalist mining companies among which Anzin in 1757 was the prototype; and cotton, a new textile industry, was based from its commencement on an organisation which operated on a large scale. There were 'Indian' cottons and painted and printed cloths at Mulhouse from 1746. The Dollfus and Keochlin families were already famous. Mulhouse was to witness the rising fortunes of one of the most remarkable upper-middle-class business groups which modern France has ever known. 'Mechanical devices' for spinning and weaving appeared in industry, being introduced notably by John Holker; steam engines which were either imported or made at Chaillot were used in the Anzin coalmines, in the Creusot ironworks, and in spinning mills at Orléans. The first industrial smelting for making cast iron by using coke occurred at Le Creusot in 1785 but the technique was used only occasionally at first. In 1789 there were a number of great captains of industry in the kingdom who either used new methods or concentrated a greater degree of production in their own hands. According to Arthur Young, Decretot at Louviers controlled the finest cloth factory in the world; Oberkampf at Jouy acquired letter patent of nobility in 1787 thanks to his printed fabrics; in Paris, Réveillon had a wallpaper factory and Hanriot owned saltpetre works; and Chaptal at Montpellier was a manufacturer of chemical products, and was to become a minister during the Consulate. At Lyon François Perret, a local spinning-mill owner, founded a large-scale 'cotton firm' equipped with 'English machines', the finance being provided by the king, by royal paymasters and by members of the *parlement*; a group from Geneva also created a works at Lyon for the making of cotton which employed 'under factory conditions', as we should now say, nearly 1,000 men and women workers.[46] Traditional finance was involved in this development. One might ask, in the words of Jaurès, whether there was not a kind of 'hybrid social force at the cross-roads of the old régime and of new capitalism'. The son of farmer-general Dupin de Francueil, for example, opened new factories at Châteauroux.[47] Elsewhere, this industrial capitalism, although still in its formative stages, was already altering the basis of its connections with commercial capitalism; the owners of cotton mills became the largest investors in an arms factory at Marseille.[48]

The nobility became interested in this development and we shall shortly have to describe the precise part it played. For the moment the example of the de Wendel family can be quoted. Originating from Flanders they settled in Lorraine in the seventeenth century and married into the local aristocracy, becoming noblemen themselves in the duke's service. One of their members, Jean Martin, the 'founder' of the dynasty of ironmasters, was an army officer and afterwards a leaseholder working the Ottange ironworks for an agreed period. In 1704 he bought the works at Hayange which were to become the cradle of his dynasty, needing some 30,000 livres to acquire it and to commence production. He had to borrow part of the money from capitalists in Metz and Thionville. When he died in 1737 he left a fortune of 700,000 livres. His eldest son Charles expanded the works, thanks partly to a rich marriage which connected him with a collector of taxes in Lorraine and which brought a marriage dowry of 60,000 livres. The grandson, François Ignace, an artillery expert and a stubborn but inventive technician carried out technical enquiries for the government of France, Germany and Austria, and as a result of the information obtained he was able to experiment at Hayange as early as 1769 with the smelting of iron by coke. Then he was asked to put the royal ironworks at Indret into working order, in collaboration with the Englishman Wilkinson. In order to supply the works at Indret he set up the 'royal plant' at Le Creusot in 1782. The capital was jointly supplied by the state by Périer (from Chaillot) and by farmers-general and paymasters-general. We know that the first industrial casting obtained by using coke occurred in 1785. Two years later Le Creusot was merged into a powerful company, the *Manufacture des Fonderies Royales d'Indret et de Montcenis et des Cristalleries de la Reine,* with a capital of 10 million francs divided into 4,000 shares and with Ignace de Wendel as one of its three permanent administrators. It was a fine example of initiative in industry: traditional metalmaking was given new vitality by the enterprise of a pioneer inspired by the ethos of the day, who was helped by a supply of public and private capital from landed property, from speculation in the old style and from transferable securities in the new style.[49]

Small-scale enterprise organised by an individual or a family, functioning with its own capital and if need be with a loan pledged by mortgage, undoubtedly remained the rule.[50] Furthermore, as we have just seen, there was no doubt that the state, by the orders placed by it and by the varied support it provided, was to some extent responsible for advances made. Industrial capitalism was not yet very widespread nor very self-confident. Nevertheless, these first examples of 'mammoth industry 'bore witness to the birth of a new ethos which seemed to augur an imminent industrial upsurge. There were unfavourable circumstances, of course, in the closing period of Louis XVI's reign when economic difficulties which had remained dormant for ten years cruelly erupted in 1788-89. Yet the slow underlying evolution which was taking place in spite of the downturn and of the crisis seemed really to prepare the way for a new chapter in the history of capitalism. As a final indication of this one may mention that Calonne reduced the weight of the gold louis in 1785,[51] and naturally this revaluation of gold 'by bringing the legal parity nearer to commercial parity and above all nearer to foreign parities resulted in an influx of yellow metal'. However, according to Dermigny's ingenious interpretation:

> If one considers the general ethos which prevailed at the end of the monarchy this combination of heady speculation and of growing free trade in the time of Calonne, together with the replacement of money which was the traditional currency of an outdated mercantilism by gold with a more genuinely international value ... might be taken to symbolise in reality the integration of France into a whole system headed by London and Geneva—in short, the integration of France into the most advanced capitalism of the day.[52]

Capitalism and the society of the old regime

This capitalism which was beginning to break its way through the old crust of the French economy ought logically in theory to have brought higher social status to its most brilliant representatives, especially to the great merchants. It seemed to be a favourable century for them. The Abbé Coyer set the tone with his book *Noblesse Commerçante,* published in 1756. He asked whether trade had not become 'the central focus of political interests and of balances in the game of power, the basis for the greatness of kings and for the happiness of the people'. In 1785 Sedaine in *Le Philosophe sans le Savoir* wrote in the same vein:

> What a state of affairs ... for a man with a mere stroke of his pen to be obeyed from one end of the world to the other! His name and his seal need not be guaranteed by the value of metal like the stamped coins of monarchs. The man is everything; he has signed and that is enough ... He is not serving a particular people or just one nation; he serves them all and is served by all of them. He is a universal man.

Just as lyrical but more accurate was the anonymous author of 'Patriotic Merchants, a useful manual for dealers, ship-owners, manufacturers and farmers, by a merchant who has travelled', published in Amsterdam in 1784. He particularly singled out for praise 'that outstanding class of merchants, who by their foresight, their way of life, their travels, their wisdom, their experience and their large-scale capital are called to trade with foreign countries'. He describes them as 'transcendental geniuses' and benefactors, because the merchant, wishing to employ as many men as he can find and surrounded by all manner of needy persons, brings them relief by work and industry'. These geniuses are motivated entirely by 'creative fire' and are 'bringing back a golden age'. It is the merchant 'who provides food for the poor', who supports manufacture and keeps it going, and even agriculture too. 'This latterday Atlas bears the burden of factories, of firms, of maritime activities and of land clearing. He says continually to those who work hard: keep working energetically and you will have money![53]

This élite of large-scale commerce was to be more plainly the élite of the coming age. It was a change to be achieved by the Revolution, when the notion of an élite underwent considerable alteration, such a group then being sharply distinguished from the nobility.[54] The monarchy seemed to sense a new climate of opinion as on several occasions consideration was given to the ennoblement of wholesale merchants, yet in practice titles were given to merchants only sparingly and with obvious hesitation. Undoubtedly there were rather more merchants who entered the nobility by purchasing an office, since offices like that of 'secretary-counsellor to the king' were a pure fiction and easily bought. Some were given a noble title as a result of performing municipal duties. Overall there was rather a long list of such 'noble merchants' with recently acquired titles less than a century old. There were about a thousand of them among the five or six thousand noble titles held in 1789 by those living in the seven most important French ports. They even included foreigners and protestants who were merchant ship-owners or manufacturers. There was Massieu from Caen, Oberkampf, Féray and a whole group from Bordeaux. Noblemen included members of the reformed church (Castaing, Desclaux de Latané and Laffon de Ladébat), Dutchmen (Vanduffer and Van der Brande), Germans (Bethmann), Catholic Irishmen (MacCarthy) and even Jews (Gradis and Pereyra). Yet these noble merchants often 'went over to the other side' by retiring from business life and becoming—like the Irish family of Walsh living at Nantes—noble landlords.[55] On the other hand, the efforts made by the royal government to attract true-born

noblemen to overseas commerce or to overseas trade that was considered by them as being beyond the pale met with disgust and inertia on
the part of the noblemen involved and with opposition on the part of
corporations and of the consular corps. The result was that nothing
happened. Reinhard's conclusion is that 'the commercial nobility was
still-born'.

That inactivity did not justify the curt treatment of the subject—
fashionable enough for the moment—by Siéyès on the eve of the
Revolution in his famous pamphlet 'What is the Third Estate?' In his
view, noblemen absorbing 'the best part of production without having
contributed in any way to the making of goods are surely outcasts to
the nation by virtue of being parasites'. But in fact there were 'gentle-
men' ironmasters and glassmakers, and an edict of 1744 had granted a
royal concession for the working of coalmines, which concession the
noblesse d'épée obtained very easily, occupying a key place in this
pioneering sector of the economy. The Duke of Croy and the Marquess
of Cernay owned half the shares in the Anzin Company, the Castries
controlled the Grand'Combe and the Solages controlled Carmaux.
The dukes of Humières, of Aumont and of Charost were also involved
in industrial concerns. Princes of royal blood participated in the creation of new factories: the Count of Artois in acidmaking at Javel, the
Duke of Orléans in glassmaking at Villers-Cotteret and in cotton spinning at Orléans. Some noble families—among them Lameth, Gouy
d'Arsy, Castellane and Gallifet—had extensive plantations in the
Islands. Courtiers obtained shares in the Ferme Générale; these were
rather similar to our subscriber's shares—no money was invested but
an illustrious name was linked with the enterprise. The firms of contractors to the monarchy had similar prestige shares. We know that
Talleyrand was a born speculator. Other speculations were those of the
Duke of Orléans on the allotments of the Palais Royal and of the
Cardinal de Rohan on the lands and properties of the Quinze-Vingt.
Yet the argument of Siéyès with its foreshadowing of the attitudes of
Saint-Simon could not be refuted simply by having shares in a business
or even by making speculative deals which showed genuine capitalist
activity. The fact was that the nobility. and often the highest ranking
nobility, simply because it was wealthy and up-to-date in outlook, did
not brush capitalism aside. The *Manufacture des Glaces de France,* a
powerful concern resulting from Colbert's influence and as early as
1695 calling itself by what was to be its permanent trade name of
Saint-Gobain, had on its board a number of great lords—the Duke of

E

Montmorency as chairman, a member of the Ségur family and a La Vieuville—as well as bankers from Paris and Geneva. Of the 288 deniers that constituted the capital (each one being worth 40,000 livres) 54 were later to be confiscated as property of *émigrés*.[56] Among this particular group family alliances had developed over a long time. Crozat, the financier, married his sons to a Choiseul-Gouffier and a Montmorency-Laval and his daughters to the Marquis of Gontant and to the famous Choiseul. The banker Laborde's daughters became Duchesse des Cars and Duchesse de Mouchy respectively.

The old nobility was no stranger to the business world. On the other hand, there was a certain kind of conservative bourgeoisie, with its wealth already acquired rather than in the process of being created, whose outlook in the eighteenth century was characterised by solidity rather than by dynamism, by tradition rather than by innovation. The lady president Thiroux d'Arcouville regarded the bourgeoisie in 1761 as 'solid as a rock in the middle of universal upheaval, its outlook being the same today as it was a thousand years ago'. She praised the 'good way of life' which caused the bourgeoisie to stick to their old habits and led the average merchant to forbid his daughter to follow the latest fashion 'because grandfather would object'. One must leave such unbecoming conduct 'to the common people who have no education and to the wordly wise who have no morals'. In her eyes the bourgeois 'live in a narrow circle and rarely have any ambition'.[57] In her touching description one could hardly recognise the bourgeoisie of 1789, those 'social outcasts'—for the expression used long after by Labrousse had already found favour. As outcasts they were a revolutionary force. History had moved fast since 1761 and, more important, the word 'bourgeoisie' came to be applied to a great variety of all sorts and conditions of men. The capitalist sections of that very complex social class which had been affected by the long years of the century's prosperity were in full upsurge and vigour. Even though the nobility played a part, the new capitalist vitality and wealth was essentially a bourgeois creation. The stubborn reaction of the nobility, the lack of cohesion and authority in the monarchical state and the whole set of circumstances associated with the economic downturn darkening the reign of Louis XVI were expressed in the crisis of 1788-9 which precipitated the Revolution and marked its opening phase. Those circumstances contributed to make the difficulties seem more unbearable and to quicken people's tempers. Thus the Revolution was brought about by the new distribution of wealth which as Barnave had already foreseen was bound to produce 'a new distribution of power', and in the phrase of Jaurès it became 'a historical necessity'. This revolution, as defined by *l'Histoire Socialiste*, was 'a revolution of industrial and transferable property, that is to say of bourgeois property'. Hence it was a capitalist revolution notwithstanding both the popular support for it and the inherent contradictions in its development. Thus the first achievements of capitalism prepared the ground for the Revolution, which was itself a judicial and social extension of the economic power and ideological outpouring which already characterised the bourgeoisie in 1789. The Napoleonic period, under a different political form, was to stabilise, organise and codify this pre-eminence of the bourgeoisie.

The legacy of the Revolution and Empire

In some respects, however, the years from 1789 to 1815 seemed to mark a halting point in the development of capitalism.[58] The war, the blockade and the loss of the colonies ruined an entire economic sector which was by no means the least important one. That sector comprised overseas trade but it might be argued that its collapse was offset by the fact that France became all-powerful on the continent. To some extent the argument is justified, for while the ports lay idle Lyon, Strasbourg and Paris experienced a growth in trade. For a time at least there was a noticeable shift in the main centres of French capitalism, a shift which was marked by some advance in the provision of roads. Commercial arrangements improved and a few manufacturers like Dollfus-Mieg at Mulhouse created new branches of their business or employed commercial travellers instead of relying on fairs and traditional commission agents. Overall, however, commercial capitalism saw little change.

Industrial progress was perhaps rather more in evidence. Migration, especially in the west of France, led to the disappearance of a number of ironmasters and caused the metal industry to undergo some concentration which was stimulated in any case by military needs and by the geographical widening of the market. The blockade also benefited the chemical industry,[59] and brought about the use of sugar beet. The textile industry (especially cotton, the leading textile sector of the industrial revolution) gained from a generally favourable set of circumstances linked with the relatively high level of purchasing power in France, and agricultural products—a significant general indicator—fetched a good price at least until the crisis of 1810. The average size of firms was becoming slightly larger, and 'giants of industry' such as Richard-Lenoir with its 39 establishments and its 15,000 workmen emerged at the top of the list. The change from trade to manufacturing was proceeding apace. The Morin family of Dieulefit combined their cloth trade with spinning and weaving, in which activities they were later to specialise entirely. There were even examples of 'vertical concentration' to be found, one of them occurring at Wesserling where the printed-calico factory owned by Gros, Davillier and Roman combined spinning, weaving, bleaching and printing. Production had certainly increased in general and in the newest sectors of industry it was spectacular. Cast iron production seems almost to have doubled between 1789 and 1796, and almost quadrupled between 1796 and 1811. Production of spun cotton nearly quintupled between 1806 and 1812.[60] Promising connections between banking and industry were in the course of creation; the Merian family of Bâle financed industrialists at Mulhouse, especially Dollfus-Mieg; André and Coffier supported Latune at Crest and the ironworks at Nevers; and Veuve Thézard et Fils financed textile industry at Rouen.[61] Yet it was still only occasional assistance, support given in time of crisis rather than regular financing, and it was to be a long time before financing for industry on a general basis was to be the regular practice. Hence firms founded in the exceptional circumstances of the period from 1789 to 1815 often had a precarious financial existence. The fortune of Boyer-Fonfrède the cotton industrialist at Toulouse did not, for example, endure beyond the Restoration. The progress achieved by industry showed no signs of a true, mature and self-confident industrial capitalism. The break with England slowed down the introduction of new techniques,[62] and techniques that were already known, like the use of steam, spread only gradually. Le Creusot, the cradle of modern French ironmaking, went through difficult years; the de Wendels migrated and then repurchased Hayange, but the works there was restarted only with difficulty and on a small scale, without the use of coke or of steam power. Their difficulties occurred in spite of the help of the banker Seillière who granted money to help them buy Moyeuvre.[63] The industrial concentration that was slowly taking place itself remained in the existing tradition of commercial capitalism. Even a large-scale employer like Ternaux, who was for wool what Richard-Lenoir was for cotton, used simultaneously the factory system in concentrated workshops and traditional work by the domestic system, and he practised both banking and merchant activities.

Perhaps more than any other town, Lyon revealed the characteristic ambiguities of the period. In some respects Lyon benefited from the new temporary geographical balance of French economic power. The interruption of barge transport from Provence to Italy by the presence of English cruisers, together with the opening of a road through the Mont Cenis pass, made the fortune of haulage contractors like the Bonafous, who imported raw silk from Piedmont. The number of working looms more or less reached its highest level in Lyon at the beginning of 1810 when there were more than 13,000 of them. The palatial buildings of Bellecour were in course of erection. Yet this, the Emperor's favourite town, though relatively benefiting from the Continental System, did not willingly support the blockade. Moreover, in its resentment towards the government it echoed the recriminations heard in Bordeaux and it held stubbornly to the old organisation of its economy. Still attached to the 'four payments a year', the merchants of Lyon mistrusted bank-notes and the activities of the *Comptoir d'Escompte* founded in 1808:

> By their attitude and outlook the silk-throwers of the Terreaux district differed greatly from the cotton manufacturers of Normandy or of Alsace; the bankers among them had more in common with their ancestors of the sixteenth century than with their colleagues in Paris who were barons of the Empire and guiding spirits of the new Bank of France.

This criticism applied to one of the most important firms in the town, the firm of Guérin whose history has been comprehensively studied.[64] The family were at first silk-throwers at Annonay, then silk merchants at Saint-Chamond; they settled in Lyon in 1792 where their business prospered until the great economic crisis of 1931. They claimed that the silk trade remained 'the main branch of our business'. In time of need, especially when a stagnant period in the silk trade gave them some leisure, they became importers of rice, of oil, of cotton and of colonial goods. If they also undertook banking it was because they were obliged to do so: They had consignments of raw or manufactured silks in their warehouses which they were entrusted to sell on behalf of producers in contact with them by correspondence; it was a situation which brought them naturally to grant credit to the producers; they would then deduct this from the sale of the consigned goods. Certainly, they supported manufacturers by grants of long-term credit and by doing so set in motion the extraordinarily complex machinery which constituted the silk industry. The vital link in the system was the silk merchant and not the manufacturer; banking for its own sake held no interest for the Guérin family who were men of traditional practices.

The principal contribution made during this period to the history of French capitalism lay elsewhere. It lay in the fundamental achievement of the Revolution in organising a new social order in harmony with the ideas as well as with the interests of the victorious bourgeoisie. The time had come, as Marx was to say later, when 'the feudal conditions controlling property were no longer in harmony with already well advanced productive forces. Feudal conditions hindered production instead of furthering its cause. They were turning into so many fetters. They had to be broken and they were broken.'[65] In fact, the authors of this great achievement were lawyers rather than capitalists. In the States-General the Third Estate numbered only 13 per cent business men as against 25 per cent barristers and notaries and 43 per cent office-holders. In the Convention the respective proportions were 9, 27 and 25 per cent. The majority of the successive leaders of the Revolution were 'men of learning' and not merchants. Yet despite some dissension and protests there was a deep sense of solidarity among the bourgeoisie. The 'special deputies for industry and commerce' were often able to gain a hearing in the Constituent Assembly.[66] In any event, the results were favourable to capitalism because they fitted in with the bourgeois notion of property and therefore of society.

In fact, the right of property which was at the centre of the capitalist machine triumphed over the restrictions and complications which had impaired its effectiveness under the feudal and manorial system. The implications of individual property ownership were now made clear. Property conferred political and social power in a France where only 'distinction' and the right to vote mattered. 'Landowners are the holders of power' declared Dupont de Nemours in Year III of the Revolution. Individual ownership implied the transferability of landed wealth, even when land was inherited or when possession resulted from the suppression of leases in perpetuity. It also implied 'free landowner-ship',[67] freedom of cultivation and hence the safeguarding of the position of the rural bourgeoisie. Even so, since the old collective rights were partially retained rural capitalism and large-scale exploitation were not completely dominant. In addition, the abolition of the old corporations and regulations resulted in the emergence of unregulated commercial and industrial enterprises; these enterprises had the right to produce freely without restriction, could look for unlimited market outlets and could indulge in ruthess exploitation of the labour force since a combination being forbidden by law,[68] labour had no means of defence. association or combination. It was a situation implying that a man was entitled to gain a profit from his available capital and that lending for interest was legitimate, the law merely fixing the maximum rate.[69] A further implication was that more flexible rules for the organisation of financial companies were required.[70]

Nevertheless, while the revolutionary bourgeoisie was establishing conditions of economic freedom it did not and could not appreciate the full import of its activity. Even after the producers of the day had been freed from the legal fetters that bound them, they did not seem capable of overturning existing arrangements. The object was not to overthrow artisan workshops and small retail shops for the benefit of more concentrated large-scale enterprise but rather to allow anyone who wanted to do so to become an owner of a business on his own account as an artisan or shopkeeper. Following the thinking of Rousseau, the Constituent Assembly undoubtedly espoused the ideal of a society of small producers and independent traders. Labrousse has seen in its individualism and its liberal outlook a kind of 'democratic option', a promise of universal ownership which was the ideal even of Montagnards like Robespierre. In fact, economic development followed another path and competition brought very different results. Even before technical innovation necessitated a certain degree of concentration, changes occurring within the ranks of the bourgeoisie from the commencement of the Revolution strengthened the newest and most dynamic groups, groups least encumbered by the traditional outlook and most likely to put profit before security. Moreover, they were the best fitted to make the fullest use of the new economic conditions.

There were certainly some categories of the bourgeoisie who were worse off; they were the bourgeoisie who had lived, like the nobility, on manorial privileges now abolished, or on income from mortgages now willingly paid by debtors who gave them valueless *assignats,* or on securities hit by the liquidation of two-thirds of the Public Debt under the Directory. There were bourgeois who had held offices and who were compensated in *assignats* when their offices were suppressed; and some belonged to the world of traditional finance linked with the state: farmers-general, suppliers, and shareholders of privileged companies. A number of them failed to survive. Hence it was wealth made under the old régime which was hit by structural reforms and by inflation. On the other hand, for the bourgeois whose type of income (however modest at its commencement) was directed to achieving capital accumulation and for active capitalists of whatever kind there were clear gains.[71] Whether they were merely wealthy peasants or important businessmen, the greater part of the national lands went to them and therefore they either increased their estates and their property considerably or they made profitable speculations.[72] They were the ones to benefit from profits derived from war industry and from army supplies, or from commercial and financial services given to a government which was often in difficulties. Under the Directory there was once more a golden age for supply men who were very often new entrants to the business. One of these was Colombier-Batteur, who opened a warehouse to supply ready-made clothes to the army in Holland before he settled in Lille as a dealer in linen and overalls. He retired from business in 1817 and explained how he made his fortune in the following terms: 'I merely sold 1,000,000 overalls with one franc profit on each. That was how I became a millionaire'. Seillière was another 'war profiteer': by profits earned from making and selling sheets he was able to establish a bank in 1807. Yet in spite of measures taken against the capitalists, particularly under the Convention during the summer of 1793 when the Stock Exchange was closed and joint-stock companies were suppressed, financial adventurers did not stop their activities. Perrégaux worked simultaneously for the *émigrés* and for English agents as well as for the Committee of Public Safety—which undoubtedly knew about his collusion with the enemy but thought it could not do without him to solve the problem of importing arms and of obtaining foreign commercial paper.

It was Thermidor which saw the general return of financiers and speculators to Paris. Their reappearance in the forefront of the scene resulted in the founding of an institution which was a landmark in the development of French capitalism. Since the *Caisse d'Escompte* had ceased to function along with other concerns in 1793, bankers in Paris were looking for a means of rediscounting which would enable them to increase the volume of their operations. Thus they founded the *Caisse des Comptes Courants* headed by Récamier, the *Caisse d'Escompte du Commerce* in 1797 and the *Société Générale du Commerce* headed by Lecouteulx at Rouen in 1798. They were the promoters of the capitalist revival led by Perrégaux and Lecouteulx and in 1800 they achieved the creation of the Bank of France. Lecouteulx sat as chairman on its first Board of Regents; other members were Perrégaux, Récamier, and Mallet and Périer from Grenoble. Already the general meeting of shareholders was limited to the 200 largest shareholders who were the ancestors of the '200 families'. Yet the first years of its existence were difficult and its place in the financial system badly defined. The state required it to perform important duties, particularly the discounting of Treasury bills. The Bank was also granted privileges—holding the capital of the sinking fund,[73] organising the lottery and in 1803 obtaining the monopoly of bank-note issue in Paris.[74] Yet the Bank remained an independent organisation whose essential activity was discounting.[75] Discount was controlled by the principal bankers and merchants of Paris who were predominant in its affairs. The dangers of the system became apparent in 1805-06, at the time of the affair of the *Négociants Réunis*. This was a gigantic speculation devised by Ouvrard, the boldest financial adventurer of the period.[76] He offered the Treasury Minister, Barbé-Marbois, enormous advances of money as well as the amount of the subsidy promised by Spain. In addition, he promised to supply the 'Grand Army' and the French and Spanish fleets, to deliver corn to Madrid, and also undertook to guarantee the Spanish government's credit. In return, he reckoned on transferring Mexican piastres to Europe, thanks to his links with the Hope Labouchère bank in Amsterdam and with the Baring bank in London. Meanwhile, it was the Bank of France which discounted the bonds of the promises of tax-collection which Barbé-Marbois had negotiated as security through one of its governors, Desprez, a partner of Ouvrard; it discounted also the Spanish bills and the false securities which the *Négociants Réunis* were drawing on each other. This inflation nearly ruined the Bank. As soon as he returned from Austerlitz, Napoleon put at its head a governor nominated by himself, though he preserved the Bank's nominal character as a private concern. Henceforth it was under state influence and yet it was still hardly anything more than the Bank of Paris; the branches which were opened at Lyon, at Rouen in 1808 and at Lille in 1810 did not last and the provinces resisted the use of the bank-note. Nevertheless, in the Bank of France the money market had obtained an institution which was absolutely essential. Almost at the same time the famous law of 17 Germinal Year IX (7 April 1803) created a new denomination of money: the franc, defined as a 5 gramme silver coin with nine-tenths pure metal, ended the confusion between money in accounts and real cash. As the franc was linked to gold with a ratio of 1 to $15\frac{1}{2}$ it created a true bimetallism with a free stamping of both metals, their rate of exchange not being fixed by law. Above all, since the franc was almost exactly equivalent to the livre as established in 1726 it brought France back to an age of monetary stability which, with the exception of the episode of the *assignats*, lasted for some two centuries between 1726 and 1926-28 (or 1914).

The foundation of the Bank of France and the adoption of the franc of Germinal were significant events. So, too, in another sphere was the arrival in Paris in 1810-11 of three sons of Meyer Amschel Rothschild: the youngest of them, James, settled there and created the French branch of the firm. Hence the Revolution and the Empire outlined the framework in which capitalism could flourish when general factors such as markets, the state of technology and the availability of capital allowed it to do so. A new way of thinking which characterised the situation fairly clearly was already widespread. It was in the closing years of the Empire that the publicist Jouy wrote: 'The love of gold has seized all social classes in the nation and wealth has become for us the yardstick of the esteem given to those who possess it'. Perhaps he was yielding to commonplace utterances of moralising humbug.[77] Yet we can also believe that he was noting the advent of contemporary society in which wealth has counted more than former titles to distinction and has brought to the forefront those who hold it, who manipulate it and put it to productive use. Those producers and manipulators are the subject of our book—the capitalists.

2
Progress and Delay: 1815-48

When in 1840 Count Rossi referred in the Chamber of Peers to the scheme allowing the Bank of France to renew its privileges, he regarded the achievement of the Bank with moderate optimism: 'Its progress is not fast,' he said, 'but it is steady. It is not dazzling but it is reassuring'. His remark can be extended to the development of French capitalism as a whole in the first half of the nineteenth century. The era of fast and feverish expansion was not to arrive before the Second Empire. In spite of a last attempt by the old nobility to make a comeback, France under the Restoration or during the reign of Louis Philippe was essentially that 'bourgeois France' described by Morazé. In this context 'bourgeois' was not exactly synonymous with 'capitalist'. It was the France where Benjamin Franklin's books—*Science of Robin Goodfellow* and *The Way to Wealth*—had enormous success. Franklin defined a moral code based on individual success and social usefulness, but in his view neither should bring more than a reasonable degree of affluence. He condemned all recourse to borrowing.[1]

1 THE OBSTACLES

Traditional obstacles still operated to slow down the growth of the French economy and to restrict its potentiality. They were of two closely related kinds: barriers to the circulation of men or goods and to the circulation of capital. These obstacles were soon to be overthrown by forces acting in unison but for the time being they caused some difficulty.

Archaic communications

Means of communication had undoubtedly become easier. New roads had been opened by the Department of Roads and Bridges and the existing road network was maintained; a law of 1836 had allowed an increase in the number of country lanes. Travel and transport had improved thanks to the mergers supported by powerful Paris bankers like Laffitte, and this concentration had brought about the creation of haulage firms and of great transport companies such as *Messageries Générales* in 1826, *Messageries Nationales* in 1831 and *Messageries Françaises* in 1836. These companies either eliminated many existing local firms or they absorbed them and formed amalgamations which were thoroughly illegal but completely unpunished by authority.[2] Yet transport by road remained very expensive and could be used only for light and expensive goods. Between 1815 and 1830 and then again between 1830 and 1848 the length of the canals doubled, and these new waterways altered the economic geography of the kingdom. In Paris, for instance, they enabled coal from the north and from Belgium to take precedence over coal from central France, and steam navigation made the Seine a more important route than the Loire. Yet the transport system remained defective, badly co-ordinated and still too costly. There was no 'revolution' in transport and the 'railway age' had scarcely begun. The first railways, from 1828 onwards, provided access to coalfields around St Étienne and Épinac, but the great lines of the future network took shape only in the forties and in 1848 scarcely 2,000 kilometres of line were in service. France at that period with its slow, difficult and costly communications was the France of Balzac; so many provinces were similar to the province of Limousin before the coming of the railways—the setting for his novel 'The Village Priest'. 'Without communication, there is no possibility of trade, of industry, of exchange of ideas or wealth of any kind'. Another of his novels, 'The Human Comedy', shows us the provinces from one aspect only—that of the countryside and of small, sleepy towns. If, apart from passing references, Marseille, Lyon, Mulhouse and Lille—the cradles of the incipient economic revolution together with Paris—were all ignored by Balzac, it was not because he was unaware of the importance of such towns or of their future destiny.[3] It was just that he emphasized what seemed to him in all honesty the most characteristic features of the period, and in this respect literary simplification conveyed the truth.

Dear money and its scarcity

Circulation was slow and involved small quantities, a situation which was true both of money and goods. The first half of the century was a time of scarce money because world production of precious metals experienced a setback until about 1840 and the growth of the stock of money was decelerating. Although France held large amounts, the circulation of metallic currency appeared not to rise very much over the level of 1789.[4] Hence there were signs of an archaic situation which were also indications of poverty; these were the importance given to small pieces of copper and of base coinage and the strange speculation they induced 'at the expense of the very poorest members of the community who had no reserves in gold or silver'.[5] In an economic sense the use of the stock of precious metal remained ineffective. Hoarding was still general, with all the consequences involved. Balzac, so often a source of evidence, pointed out in 'The Village Priest' that 'the burying of capital by the small bourgeoisie and the peasant meant delaying the building of railways in France'. The state itself collected considerable amounts of money which were used for non-economic purposes: the various indemnities required by the victorious enemies in 1815;[6] the milliard francs for the émigrés, which did not, incidentally, lead to a massive restoration of great aristocratic estates; money for the expeditions to Spain, to Morea and to Algeria, and for the armaments and fortifications under Louis Philippe. They absorbed a substantial part of income and increased the National Debt, hence becoming a burden on the capital market and tending to make budgets tighter because of the payment of yearly dividends and the redemption of debts. On the other hand, the volume of public finance was strictly limited by fiscal conservatism which spared the rich; public funds contributed very little to the country's social overhead capital, at least before 1842.

Private credit was insufficient to compensate for the deficiency of public investment. The more modern function of private credit was not yet accepted without reservation since the echoes of the old controversy concerning the legality of taking interest had still not died away. Rome had become more flexible without officially renouncing its doctrine. The Holy Office and the Penitentiary merely declared in 1831 that 'people who lend money at the legal rate of interest must be left alone and they should not be asked to hand back money which they have collected. It is enough to ask them to accept the instructions which the Holy See will give subsequently on the matter'. The priests from St Sulpice, loyal to the teachings of Émery, kept to a middle road. Monseigneur de Bonald, a future cardinal-archbishop at Lyon, was also in favour of Rome's compromise and in that respect differed from his father Viscount de Bonald who, under Napoleon, had been known to attack usury which was then recognised by law. The Viscount demanded that the prohibitions inspired by the wisdom of Christianity should be restored, since those prohibitions 'have made society what it is and keep it that way'. Yet Monseigneur de Bonald's clergy did not always support him and the Archbishop of Toulouse, Monseigneur d'Astros, was personally shocked by the opportunism to which the Curia was giving way.[7]

Of course, this was only a minor conflict. Yet the extension of the use of credit was marked by caution and occasional diffidence which bore witness to a stubborn outlook in favour of traditional practices. Principal banking, which represented the lynch-pin of the system, resumed its eighteenth-century traditions, during which time state loans had been unknown. It now devoted itself mainly to privileged state connections. During the years of distress at the beginning of the Restoration it had to submit to a reorganisation by large foreign banking houses; the foreigners alone were capable of guaranteeing to the government of Louis XVIII the enormous sums of money needed, and French banking had to infiltrate in their wake, as best it could, in the undertakings which were proposed or insisted upon.[8] Very soon, however, principal banking was assured of an advantage which quickly turned into monopoly. On the whole it gained exceptional profits from its massive issues; the loans of 1816-19 were subscribed at rates of 57.25; 52.52; 55.50; 61.50; 64.50 and 67. Five per cent stock was acquired by banks tendering at these astonishingly advantageous rates and resold by them at high profit since it soon went above a quotation of 120 and after 1824 did not fall below par. For principal banking it was a permanent source of substantial profit yet it was also a constant temptation to direct capital towards public funds to the detriment of productive investment, and thus to make the majority of capitalists government stock-holders rather than investors in industry.[9] Apart from discounting and short-term credit the only specifically economic activity of principal banking was its influence in the financing of raw materials.[10] Rothschild financed wool, silk, cereals and tea; Delessert and Hottinguer cottons, and Seillière wool.

However, this commercial credit was very inadequately distributed. In the last resort everything depended on the Bank of France. Yet the latter performed its main function of rediscounting only with a great deal of caution—an approach that some might describe as wisdom or circumspection. In any case, the Bank exercised strict selection among the bills offered to it. Its attitude was partly justified since it had to make a success of the delicate task of issuing, but it certainly went too far and was too open in its choice of discrimination. Thiers expounded its doctrine in the debate of 1840 and the bank struck a beautiful gold medal for him as a token of appreciation. The doctrine was stated in the following terms. The bank must accept only safe bills coming from trustworthy concerns guaranteed by the signature of a previous discounter. Bills must be less than three months old for 'industry must be forced to undertake only short term commitments. By being compelled to renew its commitments more often industry becomes accustomed not to rely too much on the future, and there are more frequent payments and hence more circulation of capital'. Above all, no attempt must be made to lower the rate of discount systematically[11] since that will enable 'all manner of incompetent people to set up in business, people who have neither ability nor money. They will spin cotton or weave linen in haphazard fashion without measuring it, and by unloading a mass of products on the market will compete with well-established merchants. These newcomers will ruin men who have been in business for forty or fifty years.' This text revealed surprisingly clearly that the Bank was in favour of a Malthusian conservatism based on the high price of capital. This approach was deeply characteristic of the French bourgeoisie and it was all the more significant to find a Malthusian attitude among one of its most renowned representatives at a time when the bourgeoisie was on its way up and full of ambition.

Therefore, the Bank of France merely discounted bank bills on the large bills of exchange. It assisted large provincial firms only through the intermediacy of firms in Paris and remained itself essentially the Bank of Paris. Even in 1840, according to Rossi, 'the bank-note is not yet known in most *départements*'.[12] In the provinces they thought of it as a convenient way of carrying large amounts of money and as a kind of bill drawn on Paris. As it was payable to the bearer it was the more liable to be stolen; hence notes were torn in half so that they could be sent in two separate pieces. Only important transactions were made by bank-note since the smallest denomination was for 500 francs; the note with a face value of 200 francs was not issued until 1847. Thus for many years regents of the Bank neglected possibilities in the provinces. After Napoleon's downfall their eagerness to close down the three branches which he had ordered them to open allowed the opening of other new banks (in the *départements*), with which the regents would have nothing to do.[13] Only in 1836 under the influence of the banker Vernes, who was one of its sub-governors, did the Bank appreciate that it was encouraging dangerous competition and commence the setting up of a network of branches under its own direct control.[14] The departmental banks and branches of the Bank of France were gradually to familiarise the public with the use of paper money; they were to regulate the credit system and encourage the development of regional banking. Yet for the moment their activity remained very limited. Economic theorists themselves saw the Bank of France as a means of obtaining facilities for the Treasury rather than as an economic regulator; in their eyes it was a handmaid of the state rather than an engine of the general economy.[15]

The distribution of credit, therefore, remained in a fair state of uncertainty. The financing of firms and the relationships between banking and industry were influenced by the relative scarcity of funds. In order to understand the period and the life of the business world as well as that of private individuals one has to conjure up a whole atmosphere of monetary shortage, an ethos once again described by Balzac. Its major recurring themes were obsession with repayment dates, the threat of bankruptcy and the success of the moneylender.[16]

> To ask for credit is quite a simple commercial operation. Every day in transacting a business deal a man has to find capital. Yet to ask for credit to be renewed is, in commercial law, as bad as a legal case being transferred from a magistrates' court to an assize court. It is a first step towards ruin in the same way that a breach of the peace leads to crime.

In time of need the small perfumery shop-owner César Birotteau, obsessed with foolish speculations, had no hope of assistance from principal bankers like Keller or Nucingen. He was forced to approach the moneylenders who appear on every page in 'The Human Comedy'.[17] One moneylender was Gigonnet 'who died with a fortune of 1,800,000 on the third floor of that house in the rue Grenéta where buildings look terrible'; and there was Gobseck 'that human guillotine of finance who is a banker to the same extent as the executioner at Paris is a doctor. His immediate reaction is 50 per cent. He belongs to the Harpagon circle and can find for you, on request, birds from the Canary Islands, stuffed boas, furs in summer and nankeen in winter'. There was also Vauvinet who was alleged by the caricaturist Bixiou to discount bills signed by his caretaker: 'they were bills no doubt without much value, but for once the borrower had the better of the money-lender by the borrower's promise to obtain railway shares at par underwritten by du Tillet and Nucingen'. Of course, these are only so many characters in a novel, but numerous sources confirmed Balzac's insight. Without going as far as Gobseck in their requirements the discount brokers in Paris added fees of all kinds to the 5 or 6 per cent legal rate of interest charged to people who had fallen into their hands; these were people who did not operate on a large enough scale or did not offer enough security for the principal banking houses to open their doors to them. There were commission fees, mortgage fees, postage, cash receipts and withdrawals which made the total climb to 11 per cent or more. The provinces were not backward—far from it! Rates of $8\frac{1}{2}$ in the Isère and from 7 to 12 per cent in the Indre could be regarded as moderate. In the Eure-et-Loir interest reached 18 per cent at times; in the Nièvre 8 or 9 per cent was usual and 10 to 20 per cent was required for renewals. The Mayor of Grenoble declared in 1839 that 'the interest borne on capital is at a rate which is quite usurious. The unfortunate rural manufacturer who is forced to resort to this perilous expedient soon meets with complete ruin'. According to the Council of Nièvre in 1845 small landowners, unlike the rich, were not able to borrow on a bill payable to order or to open bank accounts or to obtain credit. They had no other source of supply than the money-lender who granted loans only on mortgages. The question put by Count de Gasparin in the *Revue des Deux Mondes* in 1843 was: 'How can one take the ploughman out of the hands of speculators?' The same impression prevailed wherever one looked: too little money was circulating in the kingdom and, if some made their fortune because of that very scarcity, the economy in general made poor use of the money which was in circulation.

2 THE SUCCESS OF CAPITALISM

The shortage of money was only one aspect—and a possible cause—of the general stagnation which weighed on the French economy. Around 1815 the economy entered a phase of depression commencing with the crises of 1810-12 and 1817-18, and that phase ended only after 1851 with the advent of imperial prosperity. The depression, synonymous with a fall in prices, was long and severe. It was acute in the agricultural sector and disastrous for industry. Yet this very con-

F

traction, to the extent that it put firms in jeopardy and threatened their profits, contributed to progress and even imposed it. Some attempted solutions were futile, like the classical and ineffective remedy of protectionism and the exploitation of labour carried to the limit, so that around the middle of the century the condition of the working classes reached the lowest point at which survival was possible. The real remedy which suggested itself for the overcoming of such conditions was the method of mechanisation and concentration, or, in other words, of industrial capitalism.

Industrialisation

It was then and only then that the industrial revolution began in France. England had provided the pioneering example in the previous century and now contributed, whether willingly or not, to the French economic revolution. French technicians were sent across the Channel and British engineers and workers were asked to come to work in French firms. Machinery and new processes were imported, at first in secret and then openly.[18] This is not the place to tell that story. Besides, it was rather similar to the development of capitalism in general in its slow momentum and its uneven impact. Obsolete water power, even if in an improved technical form, remained in much wider use than steam but, by contrast, the textile industry modernised itself more rapidly than the metal manufacture, and cotton spinning especially experienced almost total re-equipment.

From the end of the Empire to the eve of the 1848 Revolution, the 'added value' put on raw materials by industrial processes increased by half for wool and more than doubled for cotton. In 1847 there was nearly six times more coal mined than in 1815. The production of cast iron increased at least five times by weight and three times by value. The annual percentages of growth remained moderate but positive: 4.9 per cent for coal and 2.4 per cent for cast iron from 1820 to 1850; the figure for the cotton industry between 1831 and 1850 was 3.7 per cent.[19] Thus the long depression of the years 1817-51 by no means signified stagnation. The period was marked by the development of business in general and this could in fact be seen in the volume of discount business done by the Bank of France. We know that discount was conservatively measured, yet it experienced a three-fold increase.

Urbanisation

There were, however, more solid and visible signs of economic advance. For example, urbanisation and the growth of building construction and of property speculation was no mean sector of capitalism. Here again the foremost achievements were to come only with the Second Empire. Industrialisation did not yet lead to massive migration. The Rhône *département* was still the only industrial region with a really rapid demographic rise. Paradoxically, the Haut-Rhin remained a region of emigrants. The point was that this first stage of industrialisation, especially in the textile industry, was not at all incompatible with rural life. 'Weaving is done in the countryside but rails can no longer be made there': so it was said, but not many rails were being made yet.[20] However, less spectacular indicators foreshadowed the urban movement in the years from 1850 to 1870. Especially during cyclical periods of growth the facilities provided by the sale of the national lands played a great part in migration; this was so at the beginning of the century and in other growth periods from 1820 to 1827, from 1834 to 1839 and 1842 to 1846.[21] In his 'Memories of a Tourist' published in 1838 Stendhal sought 'restrained phraseology' in which to describe the growing prosperity that France was enjoying under Louis Philippe. He wrote: 'I am afraid to be taken for a writer by the state. At every step I see bricklayers at work. They are building a multitude of houses in the cities, in the small market towns and in the villages. New streets spring up all over the place.' Especially in Paris the great works inspired by the prefect Rambuteau foreshadowed the coming 'Haussmannisation', though on a smaller scale. When in 1845-47 Hugo wrote *Les Misères* (a first version of *Les Misérables*) he felt that 'the tumbledown old city was disappearing beneath the splendour of a more wealthy and showy Paris'. The change in Paris was also a recurrent theme in Balzac who, with his usual care for detail, gave information about financial speculation which tended to alter drastically the appearance of several districts. He saw very clearly the resulting social effect:

> the trowel has a much more civilising influence in Paris than one might think! When speculators build beautiful, stylish houses with caretakers in attendance and put pavements in front, with shops as part of the total establishment, they are able to charge high rents; hence they manage to keep away people who are not respectable, families who have no furniture and bad tenants.[22]

As always, feverish business activity bordered on scandal and some-

times led to it. Hourdequin, head of department of highways at the
Hôtel de Ville under Louis Philippe, sold plans of projects which enabled the buyers to acquire buildings or land destined for fruitful
development. In the same way very substantial fortunes, like that of
Monsieur Dosne (or should one say of Madame Dosne?) were made
by speculation. Once more let us listen to Balzac:

> The prima donna, to use the humorous nickname given to her, is
> the daughter of an honest merchant in the Montmartre district. This
> woman lives in the Hôtel des Capucines[23] which Countess Molé and
> the marshal of Dalmatia previously found very much to their liking,
> but Madame thinks that it is not decorated lavishly enough and that
> it is not furnished with enough ostentation. Yet in her youth she had
> to sit behind the counter of a draper's shop where her mother kept
> the accounts. When she was at a marriageable age she was wedded
> to a young boy who had learnt stockbroking with a banking firm.
> This husband, Monsieur Dosne, obtained a stockbroking post
> through the favours of Madame d'Angoulème. He started entertain-
> ing; his wife opened her salon to visitors who came to talk about the
> latest novels, and she contrived to be invited by a few journalists to
> the great political receptions of the period. It was the age of the
> Restoration. She tried to mix with the St Germain set but failed
> to gain an invitation. Furious with the old nobility, she raised the
> flag of liberalism at her home ... It was then that the author of
> the 'History of the Revolution' was introduced to her.[24]

Indeed, the daughter of Madame Dosne married Monsieur Thiers,
the author in question. Thiers made his father-in-law a general tax-
collector, a regent of the Bank of France in 1836 and a director of
the firm of Anzin. But Dosne's main activity was his speculation in the
St Georges district then in course of construction. Among the important building firms which prospered under the July monarchy was
that of Lefaure 'the Red', a bricklayer like so many others from the
Creuse region; his success story was perhaps due to the fact that he
operated in Monsieur Dosne's district. During the same period the
Pavins of Lafarge, who were to experience lasting success, were already
working the quarries at Teil and sending their quicklime as far as
Algeria.

To satisfy the needs of the expanding city, new transport companies
were created at first in rather a chaotic way. In 1824 there were as
many as seventeen omnibus companies in Paris, poetic names such as
Atalantas, Zephyrs and Aeolians appearing alongside plain Parisians,
Gondolas, Tricycles, Dandys, Urbans, Lutecians, Vigilantes or, quite
simply, Omnibus. Here again, concentration was soon to bring order to
the situation; the banker Delamarre initiated it when he organised in
1838 the *Société des Voitures de Place*.[25]

The creation of new commercial methods typical of capitalist development was a response to the same needs. They were, like building projects, to be more fully developed under Napoleon III: *Charivari* called them the first 'giant stores'. During the Restoration the average small business in Paris was worth 1,000 or 2,000 francs. Yet in 1821 the *Belle Jardinière* appeared near the Quai aux Fleurs and in this venture alone Parissot earned 3 million francs, selling only underwear, fabrics and clothes, including ready-to-wear articles. The *Deux Magots*, established in 1813, was in fact the prototype of that kind of store. In 1829 Ternaux took the trade name of *Bonhomme Richard* and began 'the competition of the manufacturer who deals directly with the consumer'.[26] In 1845, at the Gros Caillou near the Champ de Mars, Bonnerot set up an important grocery shop which was soon to be accused of 'spoiling prices'. The grocery was taken over by Felix Potin five years later.

In time all these traders became both the customers and the beneficiaries of a modern type of advertising publicity that was beginning to influence the press. This development was influenced in turn by the changing nature of capitalism. In *Les Illusions Perdues* Balzac related how the bookseller Ladvocat[27] conceived the idea of adding eye-catching posters with 'fancy letters, strange colours, illustrations and, later on, lithographs' to editorial leading articles and to the few lines known as 'a puff'. Yet the appearance of the advertisement in newspapers, 'accessible to all who could pay, turning the fourth page into a fertile field for the Treasury and speculators alike' was certainly a more important tendency. In 1835 the *Journal des Débats* was earning only 20,000 francs from its publicity but on 1 July 1836 Émile de Girardin, a pioneer in the field of modern journalism, launched *La Presse* at a yearly subscription rate of 48 francs, soon to become only 40 francs for Paris. Other papers charged 80 francs. *La Presse,* of course, sold its fourth page to advertisers for 150,000 francs in 1838 and 300,000 francs in 1845. But since publicity only paid if it reached a wide enough public it was necessary to attract more readers. *La Presse* therefore launched a campaign of serial stories, creating in the course of it Eugène Sue and Alexander Dumas. Like its rivals the *Constitutionnel* and the *Débats* it signed a contract with the *Société Générale des Annonces,* the first publicity agency set up in 1845 by Duveyrier, Péreire and Arlès-Dufour. Like so many others later to be found in leading capitalist circles, this agency was a team of St Simonians. Yet already well before this the more old-fashioned journalism had been bringing in substantial profits to its owners. The firm publishing the *Constitutionnel*, created in 1817, had a capital of fifteen shares. In 1823 each one was delieved to be worth between 80,000 to 100,000 francs and yielded a dividend of 8,000: understandably the shares. In 1823 each one was believed to be worth between 80,000 to from wealthy Thiers. acting only as a nominee, wanted to buy one for 100,000 francs. In order to do so, he had to utilise the funds of three men: the German publisher Cotta, the journalist Cauchois-Lemaire and the Parisian deputy Gévaudan who managed the *Messageries Royales*. The share of the *Constitutionnel* yielded 23,400 francs in 1825, 27,000 in 1826 and 32,000 in 1828. Undoubtedly few investments at the time were as profitable.[28]

3 CAPITALIST TYPES AND CAPITALIST CIRCLES

Newspapers were extreme aspects of a business movement which in the last analysis rested on a basis of accumulation of capital. The lower level of capitalist society consisted of savers of money. They were passive capitalists one might say, yet their dormant wealth was induced little by little to participate in the great game of investment and speculation.

Savers, stock-holders and stockbrokers

Thrift was the traditional virtue of the French. There is no more commonplace theme. One might argue about that 'virtue' and about its economic, social and psychological associations, yet there can be no doubt of its importance. In old France it took very varied forms: the accumulation of movable property, of jewellery, of cloth and of lace and, especially, of hoarded money in the legendary woollen stocking under the bed. This accumulation was slow and for a long time inactive because the saver made no use of it until he found an opportunity for suitable investment. In the countryside the acquisition of land was the fixed aim, a point already mentioned but one to be emphasised.[29] The peasants, as Gasparin acknowledged, 'keep amassing their savings until they have enough to be able to pay for a coveted field near their property. Considering the great number of people with small resources one can say that enormous amounts of money must be kept out of circulation and their owners obtain no interest'. Capitalism lost by the practice and so did savers, for it led them to pay far too much for available land since they had no other way of using their money. In this way they secured only a meagre income relative to the amount of capital which they had invested. So many land-hungry peasants risked contracting mortgage loans when they wanted to purchase more land, and such loans were often too heavy for them to repay. Hence they risked expropriation and descent into the ranks of the wage-earners.[30] Yet it seemed very difficult to break old habits and 'to give our farmers the taste for investment in movables'—as Gasparin wanted. Pozzo di Borgo pointed out in 1816: 'In reality France's total income is considerable yet it is subdivided into small almost imperceptible fortunes. They are a source of revenue to the state for they are subject to taxation, but not a source of credit. Credit needs a great amount of available capital to be concentrated in the hands of a small number of men.' This scattering of French savings, combined with the traditional preference for secrecy and for certain types of investment, explained why it was so long before savings could be mobilised.

Nevertheless, there were agencies existing to promote the mobilisation of dormant savings: among them were the notaries who retained their place as advisers and intermediaries.[31] They guided people in investments and undertook to make the investments themselves; they pointed out good opportunities and brought together capitalist and borrower. It was through their mediation that le Rouget in *La Rabouilleuse*, the son of a doctor from Issoudun but himself a sluggard, caused his capital to grow. He lent money at the rate of 5 per cent which was pushed up to 7½ per cent by means of various tricks. He made certain of securing a first mortgage and never gave out more than one-third of the actual value of property.

> These were the rules which his father had told him always to follow. Usury, the stumbling-block of the peasants, was crushing the countryside. A rate of 7½ per cent seemed so reasonable that Jean-Jacques Rouget could pick up the business transactions he wanted. The notaries who received big commissions from the people for whom they procured money so cheaply would contact the old fellow.

Yet the part played by notaries did not end there. They also invested funds available to them in the interval between the signature of a contract and final payment; funds were entrusted to them specially for such use, against a receipt, at a rate varying between 3 and 5 per cent. They lent the funds against credit notes, an obliging clerk acting as creditor. Sometimes investments were made in concerns of a dubious nature: for example, the notary Roguin went bankrupt through fraud and his failure ruined Birotteau. The importance of notaries remained considerable until branches and agencies of credit houses appeared, and it has not entirely disappeared today in rural districts.[32]

Thus the most common types of investment remained the purchase of land and of property and loans on mortgage guarantee—which were sometimes not guaranteed. Doctor Labat, who in *l'Ame Paysanne* provided an interesting description of rural life in Gascony in the nineteenth century, described the account book of a village capitalist from 1810 to 1845:

> He had only 100,000 francs which he put simply into bonds, invest-
> ing small or moderate amounts at a reasonable rate which was not
> usurious. He did not hold a single certificate and sometimes he would
> lend a sizable amount of money without any security, relying on the
> man's honour if he was dealing with someone from the bourgeoisie
> and on the man's word if a peasant... Our capitalist lost almost
> nothing.

However, savings were also directed, even if still faintheartedly, towards fixed-interest stock. Government securities had the advantage of being perfectly safe, and the Restoration government accepted the debt burden, in any case rather a slight one, left to it by the Empire. These securities were completely free from taxation. In 1793 Cambon, the stock-holders' menace, created the National Debt Register and put a charge equal to that of land taxation on coupon bonds. But in 1797 the Directory, as if to compensate for the liquidation of two-thirds of the public debt, promised to exempt permanently from taxation the consolidated funds which were soon to enjoy complete immunity from seizure.[33] The actual rate of interest had gone down, however, for although the Chamber of Peers did not allow any conversion, apart from one in 1825 which was rather limited and not compulsory, the high prices fetched by securities—up to 126.5 in March 1844—had reduced the interest from the nominal rate of 5 per cent to an effective rate of about 4 per cent. Overall they remained in very few hands. In 1830 there were some 130,000 holders of stock. A large portion of the securities was held by institutions: the Bank of France, the savings banks (and the *Caisse des Dépôts et Consignations* which managed their finances) and the insurance companies. Another portion was the subject of speculation, and the remainder consisted of personal invest-ments which were usually very stable. Stocks were assets included in the family inheritance to be kept and handed down with it. They were almost always registered. Bearer-stocks were introduced in 1831 but in

1848 there existed fifty-four varieties of certificate for a particular bearer-stock at 5 per cent and thirty for one at 3 per cent. People were becoming accustomed to them in the provinces. The law of 1819 set up in each *département* a local copy of the National Debt Register to facilitate 'temporary investments and it enabled savings to be directed towards the purchase of land; but it aroused quite an amount of opposition. Many deputies, obstinately attached to the land, feared, as Pierre de la Gorce saw only too well, that certain rural landowners would give up their family holding of land in order to acquire bonds. To exchange land for a certificate was regarded as forfeiture, since wealth once made liquid was considered as second-rate, as degraded, so to speak, and inferior to land from a social point of view. Nevertheless, the law of 1819 did bring some success. The provinces were practically unaware of what the National Debt meant in 1815, but in 1830 10 per cent of that debt was held by the provinces and nearly one-third of the entire debt ten years after that.

The fortune of old Grandet could be taken as a perfect example, for Balzac assembled real characters from wealthy provincial origins, characters found here and there in historical sources. At the beginning of 1789 Grandet was by no means poor. 'He was a wealthy master-cooper knowing how to read, write and count who, early in life, married the daughter of a rich timber merchant.' The dowry and his inheritance were to bring him well over 300,000 francs. In fact, the revolutionary bourgeoisie came from a class which was already rising socially rather than from dispossessed classes. At the time of the sale of the national lands Grandet was worth 2,000 louis d'or through his wife's dowry and his own liquid wealth. He bought the most beautiful vineyards in the district, together with an old abbey and a few small farms, by means which were legal if not legitimate. Then he supplied white wine to the republican armies and received in payment magnificent pasture lands on which he planted poplars. Inheritances added to his fortune. He spent a short period under the Consulate as mayor of Saumur before Napoleon replaced him by a nobleman: it enabled him to have excellent roads leading to his estates 'laid out for the town's benefit'. He also obtained a very favourable classification for his houses and his lands in the land register. There is no need to talk about the wisdom of his management for Balzac pointed it out clearly enough. Balzac even mentioned the privileged position of the large-scale producer of wine who could afford to keep his harvest in the cellars and to wait until large casks could be sold at 200 francs each while the small growers were having to sell theirs at five louis. Grandet invested the revenues he amassed with the help of two accomplices—the notary Cruchot who was entrusted with his speculative investments at 11 per cent, and Monsieur des Grassins, the richest banker in Saumur, with whom he secretly shared profits when it suited him. He bought 600 acres of woodland. In 1818 he took advantage of the young Marquis de Froidfond's financial difficulties to buy his castle and estates, said to be worth 3 millions, at an advantageous price. In this way he made sure that he had invested his money at a 5 per cent rate. Yet he still had some liquid money because when his coffers were almost empty he had had his woods and forests completely chopped down, as well as his poplars, precisely at the moment when they were short of white wood in Nantes. He now had the great amount of 900,000 francs at his disposal. Yet government bonds were not highly priced and one could obtain a 20 per cent capital gain from them in a short time without counting a substantial yield of more than 7 per cent. Grandet, of course, was not unaware that there were favourable moments for buying: 'There is a drop in the buying pressure at the end of the month', he said. When he learnt that 'the price of gold had doubled because of numerous armament projects undertaken at Nantes and that speculators had arrived at Angers to buy gold', Grandet hurried to Angers to sell his own gold. He brought back bills 'issued by the receiver-general for the Treasury. They represented a sum—inflated by his speculation—exchangeable for purchase of stock. Des Grassins advanced him some extra money and he was soon registered as possessing 100,000 livres of stock bought for 80 francs net'. Some years later 'when the stock went up to 115 old Grandet sold out and withdrew from Paris approximately 2,400,000 francs in gold which he collected in his kegs together with the 600,000 francs of compound interest which his registered stock had given him'. Thus he had secured a safe income for himself 'without taxes, need for repairs, hail-storms, frost, tides or any of the risks associated with other forms of income'. He had understood the advantages of holding stocks, an investment for which provincial people usually showed an unwavering dislike. On his death in 1828 he left 300,000 francs of income from landed property to his daughter, 6 millions invested in 60 franc stocks yielding 3 per cent, 2 millions in gold and 100,000 francs in 5 franc pieces. 'His total assets were estimated at 17 million francs'.

Old Grandet would certainly not have bought any form of transferable property other than government stock.[34] Shares and debentures were not yet very common although they were on the increase. The quotation list of the Paris Stock Exchange contained 7 securities in 1816, 38 in 1830 and 260 in 1841. The list contained government stock, municipal loan stock and after 1823 loan stock for foreign countries like Naples, Spain and Haiti. Insurance, building construction and canals, ironworks and concentration in coalmines after 1835—all these were activities in which company issues began to accustom the public at large to the idea of shares. Yet the vital part here was played by railways. Besides, there were not many shares of a denomination lower than 1,000 francs, whereas from 1822 one could deal in 10 francs' worth of government bonds. The handling of shares involved high commission fees and only a small minority of people took an interest in share dealing. However, the Stock Exchange moved in 1826 into the palace which Brongniart had built for the purpose, the cost of which exceeded 8 million francs. The Exchange became not only a financial force but also a political one since fighting took place there in 1830. Its symbolic value can be exaggerated but it had its importance: it was one of the meeting places of Parisian life, being very close to the boulevards which constituted the city's vital centre. The unofficial but active outside market in shares operated nearby in the famous Café Tortoni and later in the passage de l'Opéra (rue le Peletier). During the twenties and thirties stockbrokers were active, their monopoly having been restored in 1816. They were the men who on their own initiative decided the admission of shares to the quotation list. Although forbidden by law, the market in options was regularly carried on. When legislation became too severe, especially between 1823 and 1832, the outside market undertook option dealing and was accordingly prosecuted in 1819, in 1823 and in 1840. Then from 1842 it was tolerated as a result of a report from Delessert.[35] The *Journal de la Bourse de Paris*, first appearing in 1828, paved the way for a whole series of specialised information sheets. The Stock Exchange's progress constituted a new feature of life. Share dealing was active enough already for public opinion to be concerned about it but activity was too limited yet to win general support. The treatment of this theme in the contemporary theatre under the Restoration showed its lack of appeal. In the one year 1826, writers now forgotten produced at least three comedies: 'The Speculator', 'Stock Manipulation' and 'Money or the Customs of the Century'. *Les Débats*, which reviewed one of them, criticised 'this frightful game of speculation. Cautious men are indignant that authority refrains from uttering the powerful word that would put a stop to so much misery and to so many disasters'. Such expressions of regret were in vain for better days were just beginning.

Capital and industrial ownership

Stock Exchange operations did not leave industry untouched. Certain firms already used them in order to accumulate needed resources, but these firms were still very few. In the same way the class represented by entrepreneurs and the owners of industrial concerns constituted an active sector of capitalism using and needing capital all the time, even if the need varied in its urgency and the use varied in its dynamism. These men represented a real cross-section of society as far as their origins or the scope of their activities were concerned. Equally diverse were their attitudes towards the new economic thinking.

There was no doubt that the entrepreneur was beginning to achieve social prominence. Roland de la Platière had already perceived it and had described the entrepreneur in the 'Encyclopedia' as 'the man who is at the head of a great enterprise where different kinds of raw materials are used, or at the head of a concern where the same material undergoes many different processes'. Jean-Baptiste Say, a theorist who had also been the owner of a spinning mill, described in full the entrepreneur's activities: he saw him as an owner and a manager as well as a creator and a supervisor, all at the same time. In 1834 Isoard glorified him: 'The time has come for our industrialists to take the place occupied successively, as one looks back to 1789, by the priests, the soldiers, the lawyers and the men of letters'. Another liberal economist, Dunoyer, enumerated in 1845 the virtues of the entrepreneur: they were ambition, moral integrity, business skills such as cleverness in speculation, knowledge of the market, commercial flair, a feeling for administrative work and for accounting as well as technical and even scientific aptitudes.[36] Yet this entrepreneur, so highly praised, had to make do with an instrument of production which was very unevenly developed. Only one sector of French industry was radically changed when the obstacles which had so long limited potential development were removed in the spheres of transport, supplies of energy and techniques of finance. A sector of capitalist industry came into being or was expanded along with the movement towards concentration, which itself occurred more swiftly and advanced more speedily in those areas where certain conditions prevailed: where the renewal of equipment was carried furthest, cost more, and where the growing disparity of cost prices eliminated the weak and backward firms, especially during the cyclical crises like those of 1816-18, 1825-32, 1836-39 and 1847-51. Concentration varied in the forms it took: sometimes the number of firms, sometimes the number of places of production, were reduced. In the Lille region there were 86 spinning mills in 1817 but only 27 in 1849. Out of 547 factories making sugar in 1838 only 288 were left in 1850. But often the relative importance of the larger units increased without their overall number being reduced. In 1846 there were as many, if not more, blast furnaces using wood as there were in 1819 but the proportion of cast iron produced by coke rose from 2 per cent to 46 per cent.

On the whole the concentration of companies—economic concentration—prevailed over concentration which was specifically technological. Thus iron and steelmaking remained geographically scattered but powerful interest groups were formed in the industry. At the end of the Empire ironmasters and iron merchants from the Châtillon-sur-Seine district formed an association. The merchants acted additionally in the capacity of bankers. Towards the end of the Restoration Marshall Marmont, an unfortunate entrepreneur, joined them. Gradually they selected their fields of operation, closed works which were unfavourably located, equipped others properly and bought or rented new ones as well. In 1845 they took over two other companies near their district with the result that they controlled nearly all the ironmaking in the Côte d'Or and some in the Haute Marne, in the Aube and in the Yonne. In the same year they merged with a company recently created with support from local and Parisian iron merchants to operate coal mines (belonging to the old Rambourg family at Commentry) and ironworks. The merger resulted in the powerful firm of Châtillon-Commentry with a capital of 20 million francs. A similar attempt at merger failed in Champagne where ironworks were in rapid decline and where family ties among the promoters of merger were not so close. Coalmining, which likewise required large investment for its operations, showed similar examples of concentration. In the north the Anzin company was responsible for two-thirds of the coal production and was obtaining three-quarters of the profits from coal in the region at the end of the July monarchy. In the Loire one of the most powerful economic concerns of the day was emerging: it controlled the majority of the coal seams in the field as well as the canal of Givors and the St Étienne-Lyon railway. As in this example, concentration was elsewhere sometimes accompanied by integration. Iron and steel works concerned about their fuel supply took over coalmines. Châtillon-Commentry—or the Terrenoire group—in metallurgy took over La Voulte for supplies of iron ore and Bessèges for coal. Mechanical engineering workshops were a new feature despite the achievements of forerunners like Périer de Chaillot. These workshops depended on a few major customers: Le Creusot for iron and steelmaking, Anzin for coalmines, Mulhouse particularly for the textile industry and not long afterwards the railways where the workshops of Batignolles supplied the *Compagnie du Nord*. The firm of Derosne and Cail which supplied the sugar industry—its owners being related to Lebaudy—and which retained its autonomy was an exception. The concentration movement also influenced the chemical industry. Kuhlmann benefited from it after he had commenced on a small scale at Loos in 1825 as a joint-stock partnership. Other beneficiaries were Saint-Gobain, reorganised as a joint-stock company in 1830, and its rival Saint-Quirin; they pursued a common policy of buying up competing firms and created a joint marketing organisation. With hindsight one can see that they were preparing the merger of 1855 when four main glassworks eliminated other firms and came together in a true cartel. The same tendency to concentration influenced the gas-lighting companies, with just one firm supplying Lille, Marseille and Bordeaux at the same time, and it affected the salt mines of Languedoc, breweries at Paris and distilleries in the north. In the textile industry giant cotton mills were making their appearance, bringing an impressive number of spindles into one organisation. There were 44,000 spindles at Motte-Bossut in Lille and 31,500 at Wesserling at the end of the July monarchy. Integrated firms were not unknown, particularly at Mulhouse where they were simultaneously spinners, weavers, cloth-printers and occasionally mechanical engineers.[37]

Yet once again the usual reservations applied. Concentration produced results which were spectacular but isolated and incomplete. In many sectors the unchanging nature of production (and even of the demand which it supplied) was a response to the relative stability of the industrial structure itself. In small-scale metal working, for example, the cutlery trade at Thiers remained a scattered artisan organisation. Tools changed little in the leather trade, and in places like Limoges, where it was in an initial phase, the shoe industry adopted the domestic system. The same considerations applied to the weaving of linen cloth and hemp, for in 1847 288 million units of fabric were produced at home as against only 62 millions in concentrated factories.

Besides, the textile industry generally remained under the control of commercial capitalism, and the concentration which it achieved did not always exclude a growing dispersion of productive units. Hence demographic concentration was retarded. In the silk trade at Lyon, for example, full control of the region's industry was exercised through capital, a control extending right through to the silk-throwing area of the Ardèche. Employers were looking for cheap manual labour as a solution to economic problems in the same way that the woollen trade of Normandy or Picardy had attempted a similar solution a century earlier to meet the competition of the cotton industry; when the additional problem of stable industrial relations appeared it was no surprise that the silk industry migrated to the countryside around Lyon. In the woollen industry based on Rheims a majority of the workers were rural, even though in 1834 some three-quarters of them worked for the large firm of Hanriot. A similar situation prevailed in the hosiery trade at Troyes and Balzac's famous description of it in 1847 in his *Député d'Arcis* was perhaps one of the best descriptions he ever wrote on economic matters:

> Almost all the considerable French hosiery trade is done around Troyes. For about ten leagues around Troyes the countryside is full of labourers whose looms in the villages can be seen through open doors as one passes by. The workmen produce for an agent who in turn works for a speculator calling himself a manufacturer. The so-called manufacturer negotiates with a firm in Paris or with a retailer, and both of these have a sign with the words: 'Hosiery Manufacturer'. None of them makes a single bonnet or sock ... This middleman who comes between the producer and the consumer is an evil not confined to the hosiery trade. He exists in most branches of trade and increases the price of goods by the profit obtained through his intermediate position.

Balzac hoped, without too much conviction, that 'the fraudulent business of those merchant bankers' would come to an end; in that happy event industry could charge at home the low prices essential abroad if France was to compete successfully in the export trade. Unfortunately speculators were still in control of the weaving industry, including the cotton industry. Overall, there is no doubt that concentration increased, that the average size of firm became larger and that domestic manufacture was declining. Although the number of domestic workers declined, their suffering became even greater for they managed to keep going often only by accepting a starvation wage. The overall picture of industrial size at the middle of the century was very uneven. In a census at Paris, in 1848, out of 64,186 'industrial entrepreneurs' there were 32,583 who worked alone or with only one workman, and only 7,117 who employed ten or more wage-earners. In the whole of France in 1851 there was the contrast of some 124,000 so-called 'large' industrialists employing no more than ten workers each on average with some 1½ million small employers providing work for just over 3 million people, most of whom were women.

Hence there was a variety of industrial structures and, in consequence, a diversity of types of industrialist and of industrial groups. In an industry like cotton there was an enormous contrast from one region to another. The industrialist in Alsace was a manufacturer or 'factory owner' and his counterpart in Haute Normandie was more a merchant than a true manufacturer. At Cholet, Flers or Tarare the industrialist produced almost on an artisan scale. In the north the spinning industry had assumed technical superiority over weaving: that superiority, as Lambert-Dansette has shown, reflected a more progressive type of entrepreneurship consisting of truly capitalist manufacturers who had been in the region from the beginning of the century. Around 1860 the weaving industry, however, was still in the hands of the dominant class of traditional 'merchant manufacturers'.

Entrepreneurs also varied greatly in origins and in length of dynasty. Some dynasties and firms lasted for an astonishingly long time. In 1927, 62 out of 289 metal firms existing in that year were founded before, and sometimes long before, the Revolution. The de Wendel family was a good example. After a setback during the revolutionary crisis they commenced their rise once again during the Empire and especially after 1815. They used the English techniques of smelting with coke, and employed puddling and rolling mills; and they bought or founded new works. François de Wendel who died in 1825 left a business worth more than 4 million francs and was a distinguished personality: he was a field marshal, an inspector-general of the Moselle National Guard and a deputy of liberal views, besides being an industrialist. In his will there was nostalgia and pride: 'I, François de Wendel, former cadet in the royal navy, officer in the regiment of hussars and in the light cavalry, and now the owner against my will of ironworks and of several firms which have prospered in spite of all circumstances...' After his death the firm was controlled by his widow, by his sons (the fifth generation of the dynasty) led by Charles de Wendel, a graduate of the *Polytechnique*, and by his sons-in-law led by Theodore de Gargan, a mining engineer. They retained a strictly family ethos in the firm but expanded it by the manufacture of steel plates and rails and by coalmining, the Petite Rosselle coalfield being discovered in 1847. The de Wendel firm produced 1,370 tons of iron or cast iron in 1767 but by 1825 the amount had risen to 5,000 tons of 'English iron' and 6,000 tons of cast iron (600 being made by coke); in 1847 production was at the level of 23,000 tons of cast iron (17,000 of them by coke) and in 1850 of 19,000 tons of iron.[38]

Another long enduring dynasty was that of Peugeot in the Montbéliard region but its final sphere of economic specialisation took longer to evolve. In the fifteenth century the Peugeots were farmers, in the seventeenth they were influential innkeepers and in the eighteenth they were millers. In 1759 they commenced industrial activity by opening a workshop for making printed cloth at Hérimoncourt, and became associated with the Japy family, their neighbours. Under Louis XV Frédéric Japy began the clockmaker's shop at Beaucourt which was to make their fortune. As 'patriots' they bought 'national lands'. Founding a cotton-spinning mill in 1805, they also became mechanics and began making their own spindles. But in 1832 they gave up the textile industry, for in the meantime, in 1810, another branch of the Peugeot family, the branch from which the 'great dynasty, was to come, launched out as steelfounders at Sous Cratet. During the Restoration they made finished goods such as saws, springs and corset busks, receiving support from the Bâle bank in the crisis of 1816. The firm diversified, occasionally taking foreign partners like the Jacksons of Assailly who supplied steel to Peugeot. Unlike the de Wendel family, the Peugeots suffered from family disagreements and divisions, but on the whole their business flourished and under Louis Philippe they developed in due course their own speciality, the umbrella frame.[39]

For a whole industrial 'patriciate', however, one has to look to textiles at Mulhouse where there was an outstanding example. Among the cotton industrialists there were the old bourgeois families of Koechlin, Dollfus, Mieg, Schlumberger and Blech. In the sixteenth century they were already well known, perhaps partly because their conversion to Calvinism resulted in their becoming the social and political élite of the Mulhouse republic. They were a strongly established homogeneous group, and among them ran a whole network of family links founded on internal marriages like that which provided the name for the famous firm of Dollfus-Mieg. They were motivated by common traditions, religion and way of life, in which simplicity bordered on austerity. Their strong professional conscience, strict morality and self-fulfilment, justified in their eyes by divine favour, resulted in worldly success. They were a true caste although also a numerous and prolific one;

G

closed and exclusive, they were described as 'monolithic' because of their lack of contact with other classes and their inability to pursue interests other than business. Yet their business activity was widely dispersed in an international setting. With the expansion of Mulhouse they were involved in constant travel and distant ventures, export of products, changing techniques and a commercial policy of free trade.[40] They also became involved in politics and social problems and they practised philanthropy and paternalist social welfare schemes. Economically, they created their wealth by cloth printing in the second half of the eighteenth century, and in the nineteenth they added spinning and then weaving, creating great manufactories, yet in a way compensating for large-scale concentration by a new specialisation which allowed autonomy to chemical and machinery sections.[41] This 'manufactocracy' of Mulhouse was a rather astonishing and humane group, 'a race of men apart' as one sub-prefect wrote in 1821. Their wealth was explained less by a series of local circumstances than by many links with a whole series of great historical episodes: the Reformation; the upsurge of the countries of the Rhine, from Holland to Switzerland; the Revocation of the Edict of Nantes; the rise of business centres at Neuchâtel, at Bâle and at Zürich and, finally, the Continental System, yielding profits from contraband. Furthermore, the so-called capitalist 'vocation' of protestantism was associated with human qualities and aptitudes characteristic of this severe, frugal and hard-working bourgeoisie, bold in its time.[42]

In other instances industrial activity sprang from merchant origins. Certain dynasties that established themselves during the economic prosperity of the eighteenth century remained in existence by changing with the times. The Morin family of Dieulefit moved from commerce into manufacturing, and the Latune family of Crest, formerly merchants in silk and ratteen, became paper manufacturers. A goodly proportion of the average textile millowners was composed of former merchants, manufacturers or wholesalers who, as Claude Fohlen notes, were merchants as long as work was done by hand but became industrialists once machinery allowed mechanical spinning or weaving to be installed without great expense.[43] Among many such firms were those of Toulemonde-Destombe at Roubaix, Lemaître-Demeestère at Halluin, and Méquillet at Héricourt.[44] Elsewhere, without any necessary continuity of firms, the industrialisation of numerous towns appeared to benefit from the redeployment of capital formerly accumulated and employed in commerce. Capital might arise from port activity or from internal distribution centres which created a replacement economy after the ruin or decline of the great trade of the old régime. There was porcelain at Limoges, conserves at Nantes, chemical products, seed mills and food pastes at Marseille. At Bordeaux the Balguerie family, formerly powerful ship-owners, turned to the hinterland where between 1818 and 1824 they founded an insurance company, a bank and a savings bank. They also founded a gas-lighting company, paper mills and a metal works (which was a failure), and they had interests in river navigation and, a little later, in the Bordeaux-La Teste railway. In the same way the great capitalists of Strasbourg—Saglio and Humann, wealthy as a result of the blockade—bought in 1808 the ironworks of Audincourt, formerly the property of the dukes of Wurtemberg, and made it in 1824 into a limited company with a capital of 4.4 millions. It was extended and re-equipped under Louis Philippe.[45]

Entry to industrial entrepreneurship was open, therefore, to those who possessed available capital acquired from other sources. The Dansette family, coming to Houplines from Halluin where they were sheriffs, stud breeders and managers of a great domain belonging to the Duke of Orléans, were an example of the rural bourgeoisie who became spinning masters. A more vivid example is that of the lawyer Woussen, adviser at the Court of Douai, who was a magistrate for one part of the week and a cotton spinner for the remainder. Another avenue of recruitment, besides money, was technical competence. This seems to have played an inferior and rather occasional part in textiles, where overseers who became owners, like Thiriez at Lille or Herzog, were the exception. Herzog was first a workman and then an overseer for Dollfus and a director of spinning for Schlumberger at Guebwiller; around 1830 he finally became a spinner on his own account and a member of the bourgeoisie. His son became a student at the École Centrale and joined a 'good family' at Colmar. More frequent examples of rise through competence occurred in more technically sophisticated industries. Baignol, who founded a porcelain factory at Limoges in 1795 was a turner in the machine shop created in 1771 by Turgot. One of his turners, Tharaud, set up his own factory in 1817. In Dauphiné large-scale industry owed a great deal of its development to entrepreneurs who were formerly artisans or small-scale hand workers, truly self-educated employees who had broken away from their trade. There was Charrière at Allevard in steel, Kléber and Lafuma in papermaking and later the Perrins in glovemaking. Their generation was followed, under the Second Empire, by superior technicians educated in the *Écoles*. Pinat, son-in-law and successor of Charrière, was an engineer from *Les Ponts et Chaussées* and Bergès from the *École Centrale* was the 'father' of hydraulic power. During the Restoration it was a student from the first *École Polytechnique* of 1794—Georges Dufaud—who was responsible for the new importance of Fourchambault as a metalmaking centre and introduced puddling there, initially on behalf of the Parisian iron-merchant firm of Boigue. Under his initiative Fourchambault adopted a new policy and turned towards mass production and securing a national market. The capital of the Boigue family came originally from commerce, yet systematic reinvestment of profit allowed expansion by purchase or merger. Integration with iron mines at Berry, with collieries, and with basic and specialised metalmaking occurred to achieve a range of industrial plant giving real primacy to the enterprise for twenty years.[46] As another example, the Jackson brothers from England began production of crucible steel at Assailly near St Étienne and joined with the Coulaux, metallurgists from Alsace, and with Peugeot. The necessary competence was shared between the four of them: the eldest one William was at the head and in charge of the office, John and James possessed technical skill and Charles was the marketing and sales expert.[47]

In any case, even in those heroic times of industrial adventure a certain base of capital or an initial amount of assets, whether personally owned or supplied from outside, was the limited but indispensable condition for success. Social mobility and the possibilities of climbing from rags to riches must not be overestimated. In Paris a majority of the dealers and manufacturers active under Louis Philippe were men from families who had long been wealthy. They were often the inheritors of an existing business but rarely sons of small shopkeepers. Sometimes they came from moderately affluent rural origins. Yet a brewer in the rue Mouffetard who left a fortune of 1,400,000 francs on his death in 1835, was certainly a self-made man. He was the son of a day labourer in the Pas de Calais who left him nothing, and was himself only a workman to begin with; one might almost say that he started from nothing except that he did have an 'initial push' from his father-in-law, a merchant fruiterer, who left him an inheritance—though a rather slender one—of 7,000 to 8,000 francs.[48] The capitalism of this first period of nineteenth-century France was modest in scale and without overmuch rigidity. Yet it was not the kind of social democracy founded on universal recruitment to entrepreneurship which the *Constituants* or later the *Montagnards* had envisaged. In that respect 'the ephemeral and prophetic year II' had not lived up to expectations.

Whatever its origins—whether it was of recent emergence or grown from deeply embedded roots—the entrepreneurship of the period remained, in general, dominated by an archaic routine conservatism which marked its economic attitudes and its financial organisation. It remained attached to an individual and family framework that was almost universal in the textile industry and common elsewhere. The Giroud family at the La Mure collieries repurchased in 1810-12 the shares of the firm of La Mure, founded in 1806, and remained substantial majority shareholders until the reorganisation of 1857. The appropriate legal form was a firm under a collective name grouping parents or friends usually with modest initial capital. For example, the Mequillet-Noblots began in 1802 with 45,000 francs supplied in equal parts by the father, the son and the cousin. Sometimes the amount was larger; the capital of Allevard in 1831, for instance, exceeded 1,700,000 francs. Finance was assured by the regular reinvestment of profits.[49]

Yet it often became necessary to call for greater amounts of capital. In 1837 the ironmasters of the Landes, still landed proprietors in the old style, brought in supplies of capital from Liège. Simple limited liability was usually imposed in such instances but it made little difference since the suppliers were from the family or were local merchants or bankers. They were less frequently the latter but the distinction between types of supplier was not always clear; they might even be capitalists who took part in financing an enterprise by taking a requisite mortgage guarantee. The true call for external credit began with limited liability by shares, a practice which was increasingly used under Louis Philippe as far as it could be, but the progress of limited companies was always fettered by legislation. Indeed, the *Conseil d'État*, whose advice was always followed by the government, gave the necessary authorisation for the creation of joint-stock companies only with extreme reluctance. Around 1830, apart from banks in the *départements* and eight insurance companies and gas-lighting companies (gas being a new technique encouraged by the state), only the *Compagnie des Salines de l'Est* and some metal firms adopted this type of structure. A banker who was a shareholder in one of them—the *Forges d'Alais*—declared in 1834 that 'this form is inherently disastrous. One has to recognise that every joint-stock company manages its industrial business badly'. The alternative of partnership by shares, not quite so hampered by legislation, was often preferred; this was especially so after 1835-39 although before then and even afterwards it also was faced with some legal difficulties. The difference between the two forms was seen in the relative statistics: between 1826 and 1837 there were 157 authorised joint-stock companies with a total capital of 393 million francs whereas 1,039 firms in share partnership were created with a capital of 1,200 millions.[50]

Overall, entrepreneurs were not supported by a credit system adapted to their needs. The textile industry of Mulhouse had some assistance from bankers in Bâle but it was an exception; and, even so, capital at Bâle was still recalled in bad times, as it was in 1826. Parisian banking became involved at Mulhouse only once, when in 1828 a syndicate inspired by Laffitte advanced 5 million francs to Dollfus, Koechlin and others. Yet the historian has to ask whether entrepreneurs requested more capital. Were they aware of the 'needs' which we ascribe to them? On the contrary, they seemed to prefer their independence with its sacrosanct aura of 'business secrecy' and preferred stagnation to the influence of outside capital with the risk and opportunities it involved. A spinner from Lille rejoiced in the situation under Louis Philippe: 'We do not live on bearer bonds and we do not wish to throw to the dogs a name that already counts honourably among industrialists'. The Chamber of Commerce at Lille congratulated its supporters on being hard-working people and not 'speculators'. The great men of Mulhouse readily explained their reluctance to borrow by instancing occasions when they had unwisely accepted money, and in 1828 Jules Albert Schlumberger, then twenty-four years old, drew object lessons from the crisis and proposed rules of conduct embodying a rather short-sighted wisdom. These rules revealed the typical austerity of Mulhouse: 'Have neither carriages nor horses for private use at the firm's expense; pay for everything that is taken: oil, vinegar, wood, coal, sugar; borrow no outside capital but, if you are obliged to do so for a while, repay it as soon as you can'.

It was wisdom with some merit, yet it was associated with that lack of drive and timidity so characteristic of the development of French capitalism, and revealing already the Malthusian tendency which was to become one of its dominant features. For the immediate moment there were other rather important results. Self-financing required substantial profit margins, especially during a time of technical re-equipment, and hence a relatively high level of prices. Here was part of the explanation for the determined protectionism of French entrepreneurs, which was one of the causes of long-term stagnation. No businessman escaped the influence of protection except for those groups specialising in exports: groups found in the silk industry at Lyon, in cloth printing at Mulhouse and in large-scale overseas commerce—the ship-owners and merchants of Bordeaux, for example, or those in charge at ports like Marseille which depended on external trade (the railway linked Marseille to inland France only in 1849). The merchants of Marseille traded in the hard wheat of the Black Sea and the sesame plants of the Levant, and they fought to retain the privilege of temporary import admission, secured in 1836 partly by their own efforts. In the elective Chamber ironmasters and textile manufacturers joined with the great landed proprietors in defending and consolidating a protectionist or even prohibitionist situation. This constraining of the French market into a closed system was itself an element in the high cost of living. In addition, the employers' need to make sufficient profits in difficult circumstances implied a policy of low wages. Hence the financial structure of industry carried a share of responsibility for the working-class misery which reached its worst depths under Louis Philippe. To tighten the circle, industry only geared its production to an inadequate consumer market.

In these conditions it was not surprising that the first producers' agreements had a typically Malthusian aim: the ironmasters of Ariège organised limitation of production between 1825 and 1836 under the pretext of avoiding serious deforestation. It was only natural for them to hold the view that coke gave inferior results in smelting. A different reason for some producers' agreements was protectionism, for at each threat of lowering the tariff technical innovators seemed to have no inhibitions about joining traditionalist groups. Hence the Boigue family of Fourchambault, the Marquis de Louvois and the great Schneider dynasty joined the *Comité des Intérêts Métallurgiques* and the *Union des Constructeurs de Machine* founded in 1840. Other associations were those of textile employers, of mine owners (the first *Comité des Houillères* also dating from 1840), and of sugar refiners among whose members were Lebaudy, Sommier and Say, and Morny as president. By contrast, associations of free traders carried little weight except in ports like Nantes, Le Havre and especially Bordeaux.[51]

Industrial capitalists, however, felt that they were pursuing the right policy. It was a time of firm, definite thinking on social questions and problems of political economy. Theories were based on the laws of economic liberalism put forward by J. B. Say—a writer, professor and cotton spinner, whose family was to become one of the great sugar-making dynasties. Say believed that economic laws were in no way the work of man but 'derive from the nature of things'; hence one never violated them with impunity. Those laws brought about a wage level which hardly rose much above basic subsistence requirement in any region, but they did allow the wage level to rise as the economy progressed. Say agreed with a number of earlier writers that 'the well-being of the lower classes is not at all incompatible with the maintenance of the social framework' but his optimism was not general. Others agreed with Dunoyer that poverty was a hideous evil, yet necessary since it was beneficial to society that there were inferior positions into which families leading unsatisfactory lives might be allowed to fall. The majority of writers were not quite so extreme, but they conveniently persuaded themselves that 'whatever the fate of the workman it does not depend on the manufacturer to improve it'. The poor should help themselves and their first priority, according to Destutt de Tracy, should be to try to restrict their fecundity. Malthusianism applied to men as well as to the production of goods.

Some entrepreneurs, however, showed a deeper appreciation of their social duty, especially at Mulhouse where they were influenced by protestant Christian socialism. Nicolas Schlumberger and Frédéric Zuber were two employers to show concern. It was possibly due to their activity that Léon Faucher could meet workmen in 1845 who were 'in good health and probably happy'—employees in a firm in Mulhouse where there was a family, if paternal, atmosphere. Paternalism was equally a feature of the mines at Rive-de-Gier; there social security funds were administered by the employers because they believed that the position of workmen in respect to employers should be the same as that of children in respect to the father of the family. It was a policy of provision for basic need—sometimes for lodgings—which scarcely went beyond charity. Even the *Société Industrielle* of Mulhouse threw out interventionist measures proposed by Gérando on the grounds that they would injure individual liberty. Liberal dogma justified non-intervention except, as we have seen, in external commercial policy and in that sphere the intervention of the 'tariff state' was desired and even exhorted. No doubt this was a logical contradiction and thoroughgoing liberals like Bastiat came to insist that it was. Yet the capitalist bourgeoisie was not enamoured of theory; it made its decisions in every case according to its own interests or what it believed to be its interests.

The bankers—kings of the age?

The industrialist, however, was not the keystone of capitalist society of the time. Under the Second Empire Eugène Schneider was to preside over the *Corps Législatif*, but under Louis Philippe Laffitte and Casimir-Périer were presidents of the *Conseil*. 'Banking', wrote Stendhal, 'is at the head of the state. The bourgeoisie has replaced the faubourg St Germain and bankers are now the nobility of the bourgeois class.' Banking triumphed in 1830 after being held back during the Restoration by a last fling of the aristocracy at supremacy. Balzac rightly described the balls which Nucingen gave around 1819 as 'insolent festivities', where the world of 'new wealth tried to defy the drawing rooms of the aristocracy. The aristocrats of the faubourg St Germain had their fun without foreseeing that one day bankers would invade the Luxembourg and sit on the throne.' The accession to power of the new régime in July 1830 truly foreshadowed the accession of bankers to the peerage in 1831. According to Marx, the new régime was one of financiers and not of industrialists. His analysis was undoubtedly forced but it had some basis in fact in that it classified as one entity a financial aristocracy consisting of 'bankers, kings of the Stock Exchange, kings of railways, owners of coal and iron mines, owners of forests and the group of landed estates linked with them'.[52]

When Toussenel, a disciple of Fourier, denounced 'the Jews, kings of the age' he was really denouncing all principal bankers, among whom the Rothschilds now took a foremost place. Baron James was the head of the Parisian firm and in close contact with his brothers in Frankfort, in their birthplace London, and in Vienna and Naples. Following family custom he married his niece Betty from Vienna in 1824. From 1823 he had a monopoly over state loans. Even in 1832 he was granted a loan without tendering for it although it is true that he offered 98.50. Already under the Bourbons, and more so under Louis Philippe, he was a political power and an adviser to be listened to. In 1840, for example, a Rothschild influenced events in the cause of peace against the warlike zeal of Thiers. For several generations the family name became a very symbol of wealth. Less known by the general public, other Jewish families like d'Eichthal, Fould and Heine also directed important banks. Yet protestant banks from Switzerland, whether under the old régime or afterwards, played an equally important part in the commercial life of Paris. They included Delessert, Mallet, Hottinguer and André, the last named merging in 1847 with

Poupart de Neuflize, a merchant at Sedan, and under the Third Republic giving his family name to the Banque André. Other bankers were Vernes, Pillet-Will, Hentsch and Paccard (the latter was taken over in 1855 by Mirabaud, another protestant family from Geneva, to absorb the d'Eichthal Bank). Laffitte was the son of a carpenter from Bayonne and showed precocious financial genius first with a merchant banker in his native town and then with the firm of Perrégaux. He became Perrégaux's partner and after 1808 his successor, entering principal banking in a similar fashion to firms that began in provincial industry or in merchanting. The Périer and Davillier families were examples of such firms—the latter being successful Montpellier merchants who became manufacturers at Wesserling with business interests in Alsace, at Lyon, at Gisors and at Bordeaux. Another banking group was the Seillière family, who were first of all clothiers and ironmasters in the Ardennes and then contractors.

This world of high finance was linked by marriage with numerous industrial dynasties: Mirabaud-Paccard with Dollfus and Koechlin, for example, and Mallet and Vernes with Oberkampf. Marriages also occurred with the new or the old nobility: the daughter of Laffitte became princess of Moskova; a Fould married a marquis of Breteuil; and a nephew of Richelieu, count of Rochechouart, married the daughter of Ouvrard. Successive boards of the Bank of France were full of financiers and were to remain so. Without interruption from 1800 to 1936 four generations of Mallet officiated as regents. Their record was unique in continuity, but there were also, at fairly close intervals, four Hottinguer, four Davillier, three Périer, three Pillet-Will, two d'Eichthal, two Rothschild, two Heine, two Vernes, a Mirabaud, an André and a Neuflize. Laffitte, regent from 1809 to 1831, functioned as governor between 1814 and 1820.[53]

Some of the same men were at the head of insurance companies which reappeared during the Restoration. Their activities were given a firm base by regular payment of coupons of government stock which allowed them to build up reserves in state funds. In 1816 the *Assurance Mutuelle des Immeubles de Paris* and the *Compagnie Royale d'Assurances* were launched by Delessert, Laffitte and Périer. The latter company was a revival of the company of 1787-93 and was to be renamed *La Nationale* in 1848. In 1819 the *Compagnie d'Assurances Générale* and the *Phénix* appeared and became rivals of the *Royale* after the failure in 1820 of an initial attempt to bring their respective premiums for fire risk into line. In 1834 they brought their tariff rate war to an end by an agreement covering the majority of risks insured. Other companies were the *Union*—associated particularly with Benoît Fould, Paccard, d'Eichthal, Davillier and Guizot—and the *Soleil*. After the life and fire companies there appeared the *Automedon,* insuring against accidents, and others covering such things as the risk of hail or of legal expenses. It was a new aspect of capitalism closely linked with principal bankers and based on a widespread advertising campaign in which the famous publicist Gaudissart was active.

As we know, Jacques Laffitte and Casimir Périer succeeded as presidents of the Conseil at the opening of the July monarchy. Their temperament and policy were in complete contrast and each showed himself as a quite different type of principal banker. Laffitte was a self-made man but his rival came from an old-established family. The family of Périer, originating in Dauphiné, began its rise in the eighteenth century. The founding father installed himself at Grenoble around 1730 as a cloth merchant and married a daughter of a former consul of the town. He became consul himself in 1760 and invested part of his profits in land and in property, distributing 128,000 livres between his three daughters and leaving a fortune of 600,000 livres in coin. His sons were already in a transitional stage between medium-scale commerce and big business. The eldest, Claude Périer, called 'Périer-Milord', controlled almost all the cloth trade from Voiron and supplied funds for a firm from Marseille which traded with the colonial islands. He went into banking and made big advances to the excise administration. While remaining a merchant, he was speculator and banker much more than manufacturer. He financed various industries, setting up a factory to produce printed paper and cloth at the château de Vizille which he bought in 1780 for 1,024,000 livres from the Duke de Villeroy. He married a daughter of the general trustee for the merchants of Grenoble who was a colonel of the bourgeois militia, and himself acquired a position as chief registrar for the *Chambre des Comptes* in Dauphiné. The Revolution, with its famous prelude at Vizille, seriously hit his commercial business and caught him burdened with stocks bought at too high a price. He contrived to repay his creditors in *assignats*, set up a huge arms factory in 1794, and bought great national estates and the larger share of the *Compagnie d'Anzin* in 1795, which was to prove the most fruitful element in the family fortune. Overall, during the revolutionary period his capital undoubtedly increased tenfold. He was one of the capitalists thought to have financed *Brumaire*, and was a founder of the Bank of France; when he died soon afterwards in 1801 he left an inheritance valued at nearly 6 million livres. His sons shared and developed the family enterprises. Augustin, who passed through the *Polytechnique* and married a wealthy woman from Mulhouse, occupied himself with the factory at Vizille, became a deputy in 1827 and a peer of France in 1832.[54] Antoine-Scipion and Casimir founded the Périer bank at Paris in 1801. The former recommenced operations at the foundries of Chaillot (created by another Périer) and installed steam power in the mines of Anzin. On his death in 1821 Casimir succeeded him as regent of the Bank of France and President of Anzin and added the lease of the mines of Denain. He remained a well known commercial figure with many business interests while forging a prominent political career. Camille Joseph, also a student of the *Polytechnique* and of the *École des Mines*, was an auditor at the *Conseil d'État*, a prefect of Napoleon and of Louis XVIII and, like the eldest son, became a deputy in 1828 and a peer in 1838. Finally, Alphonse remained at Grenoble as merchant, banker and industrialist. The following generation broke with the original provincial ties and leased out the declining factory of Vizille in 1839. Yet they provided a counsellor to the *Cour des Comptes*, a third regent for the Bank of France and a minister for Thiers in 1871 in the person of Laurent Casimir-Périer, the eldest son of the president of the Conseil in 1831; Laurent's own son, Jean Casimir-Périer, was to become president of the Chamber, president of the Conseil in 1893-94, president of the Republic in 1894-95 and always held the principal shareholding of Anzin. Yet the family role in business, by this time largely indirect, was scarcely a diminishing one. The Périers financed and controlled numerous mining, metal and banking firms and were truly one of our finest 'banking dynasties'.

In the banking world of the provinces or among the small bankers of Paris, life was not quite so spectacular. In 1826 there were some 220 banking houses in the capital but their banking function was by no means separated from other lines of business. In *Illusions perdues* Balzac wrote of the firms of Métivier in Paris and Cointet in Angoulême who combined their activity as bankers with their business as agents in the paper trade and as printers and stationers. There were other numerous and well-documented examples of the same sort of thing. The Mennet family of Strasbourg, before their demise as a result of the financial crisis of 1826, speculated in real estate, in landed income, in public funds, in merchandise, and in finance for the alum mines at Bouxwiller. After 1838 at Mulhouse the Oswalds carried on both credit and transport business. At Le Mans in 1833 Trouvé-Chauvel began as a merchant in sheets, muslin and lace and dabbled at the same time in fixed income stock, land and buildings; later he became a minister during the Second Republic. At Valenciennes the bankers were the principal sugar refiners of the region. At Lille the families of Pollet, Cuvelier-Brame, Scalbert, Beaussier, Verley and Rouzé-Mathon were merchants, industrialists and bankers, and at Boulogne the Adam bank was grafted in 1784 onto an armament and commission business—a business liquidated to the bank's profit in 1839. Even when specialising in banking, the provincial bankers were often former merchants who remained men of repute and a source of money for traders and manufacturers in their old line of business. At Lyon, Morin-Pons was just such a link for the silk trade and Gautier for cotton, and at Bordeaux Samazeuilh did the same for the wine trade. At Lille bankers tended to give credit to beetroot growers and to grain merchants rather than to industrialists; at Nevers they counted agriculturalists and breeders among their clientèle; at Grenoble they had interests in ironmaking, the cloth trade and building speculation.

Private bankers, then, put their own capital to fruitful use but deposits were rather slender since they received contributions from only a few suppliers of funds. Beneath them were a host of discount agents who were difficult to displace since their activity was limited to discount itself and to recovery of funds in a very limited sector. By degrees they were to disappear during the Second Empire. Overall, it was an extremely varied banking world in which the brilliance of the Rothschilds should not blind us to the mediocrity of local manipulators of money. The French banking structure remained fragile, rigid, and insufficiently organised to fulfil its proper function. It was so haphazard that the Bank of France and the great credit houses as yet unborn in the thirties were going to take it under their wing and reconstruct it in conjunction with their own networks. In that decade, those who dreamed of future miracles in the credit system were rare. Under Louis Philippe banking services were not in overmuch demand. Clapier, a banking specialist, wrote in 1844: 'Printing does not create thoughts, it gives them wings; railways do not create movement, they speed it up a hundredfold; banks do not create capital, they promote its circulation'. It was a modest statement of intention but its aspirations were by no means fulfilled. We can repeat our questions: were bankers kings of the age? Perhaps they were, but they were niggardly rather than really ambitious, inclined to favour safe securities rather than great plans—just like the Citizen King.

4 NEW PERSPECTIVES

Yet not all the capitalists of the July monarchy could be constrained by the rather faint-hearted wisdom of the age. Some of them had detailed the principal themes of a great economic programme, with social considerations as a first priority, but designed, in fact, to assure the triumph and expansion of capitalism. Indeed, a certain quickening of progress noticeable around 1840 seemed to suggest that the programme was well on its way.

Saint-Simonianism supplied formulae, enthusiasm and personalities in a far more influential way than the liberal school which was only capable of delineating an ideal framework for the working of 'natural laws'. For Saint-Simon himself it was the great dream of a total rebirth of mankind that led him to frame his well defined plans. His cult of organisation served as an antidote to the liberal tendencies of the time. In seeking to improve the moral and physical existence of the most numerous class in the population, he proposed two instruments of economic expansion which seemed to him connected with his great social aim: full employment and a programme of public works to be financed by private capital, thus reconciling (in modern parlance) public and private enterprise. His disciples developed the master's suggestions in all possible ways, ranging as was typical of Saint-Simonian fanaticism, from the most cranky to the most positive—and Saint-Simonians could be positive, however extravagantly they showed themselves in the opposite direction. Among them were Enfantin, a graduate of the *Polytechnique*, Olinde Rodrigues, and Émile and Isaac Péreire. Coming from a Jewish background they were all bankers or connected with banking. As Jules Simon has said: 'There is in every Saint-Simonian a dreaming poet and a very prudent business man'.

Hence, around 1830 the *Exposition de la Doctrine* and the *Globe* foreshadowed investment planning by a central bank and special banks for each industry, as well as transfer to the nation's capital of resources affected by debt amortisation. The group finally broke up after 1832, and its technocrats became most influential once the movement virtually lost its social conscience. Michel Chevalier, a typically successful Saint-Simonian, opened his course at the *Collège de France* in 1841 with the declaration that it was no longer necessary 'to worry about the distribution of wealth but only about its growth'. Previously he was top entrant to the *Polytechnique* and then top among the graduates

of the *École des Mines* and having participated ardently in all the
activities of the Saint-Simonian group he extricated himself from it
rather quickly to begin a career as engineer, economist and later as
adviser to the government. Chevalier was a member of the brilliant
team—all of Saint-Simonian origin—which did so much to bring
about a dynamic French capitalism. In 1832 his 'Mediterranean System' set out a detailed picture of the 'revolution' which railways and
steam shipping were about to accomplish. Enfantin himself between
1833 and 1837 began work on the vast Suez project which de Lesseps
was later to realise, and the Talabots again made a study of Suez in
1846 without any more success. Their failure at least paved the way
for the final achievement. Enfantin, the 'father' of the movement,
having abandoned his intellectual and mystic pursuits for business,
was to end as a company director and a pioneer of the P.L.M. Émile
Péreire, for his part, proposed in 1834 a new system of banks, which
was another of the group's essential aims. Like Enfantin, they wanted
to transfer the tools (which were capital) in the most convenient way
possible from the hands of those who owned them (without having
the will or the capacity to make them work) into the hands of those
who knew how to operate them but did not possess them. Thus the
main objective of practical Saint-Simonians became capital formation
in national transport and in credit operations.

Before 1848 tangible progress was achieved in the two spheres of
credit and transport. As always, doctrines of expansion like Saint-
Simonianism assumed genuine historical importance only as circumstances made expansion possible and predictable. Doctrine was effect
as much as cause. General conditions—that is, primarily the growing
wealth of the country—changed slowly but were obviously improving
around 1840. One indication of this, among people who were generally
not wealthy and who were not in any way the principal beneficiaries
of the growing national income, was the accumulation of capital in the
Caisses d'Épargne which had mushroomed since the first one in Paris
was founded in 1818. The *Caisse* at Paris was the creation of Delessert, Pillet-Will and their team of the *Compagnie Royale d'Assurances*,
and lasting links were forged between the two institutions. There were
241 *Caisses d'Épargne* in 1837. Active propaganda combined with
clever measures like the suppression of the royal lottery in 1836 facilitated their success. In 1844 the total of deposits reached 393 million
francs contributed by 150,000 savers, and their number increased
every year by between 12,000 and 14,000. On two occasions, in 1835

and again in 1845, the state became anxious about the swelling mass of deposits since it was under some obligation to use them for state borrowing and hence to pay heavy interest. In these circumstances a limit was placed on the maximum amount of individual deposits.

There were occasional hints that public authorities themselves might undertake to influence the way in which these growing national savings were used. Authorities had ample potential sources of funds now that the endowment of the *Caisse d'Amortissement* had become available; the state no longer had any interest in buying fixed income stock back well above par price when it had sold well below par. There were a number of possible investment projects. Although the administration of the *Ponts et Chaussées*, inspired by Legrand, continued to carry out the programme of roads and waterways inherited from the old régime, it now conceived a plan for a railway network radiating from Paris. The state, however, soon met competition from private entrepreneurs. Railways aroused not only the romantic enthusiasm of those eminently curious men the *polytechniciens-mystiques* as they were described by the great railway historian Jouffroy, but the interest of the capitalists and notably of the principal bankers as well.

The readiness of banking to provide finance for social overhead capital was no small feature of the period. In spite of that readiness, the state had less need than formerly of banking assistance, and to provide assistance to the state had become less rewarding for the banks; thus if the government continued to borrow it did so on more favourable terms. Assistance for commercial and industrial enterprise in which, as we have seen, principal banking had always taken a meagre interest tended now to become the sphere of action for institutions of a new type. Here again, decisive changes were made around 1840. The *Caisses* were more or less inspired by the ideas of Saint-Simon, and Laffitte had dreamed about the *Caisses* for a long time. He was an inconsistent politician but a first-class financier capable of assimilating the most 'reasonable' elements of doctrine. Like other liberal bankers of the time—Casimir Périer and Hottinguer for example—he promoted some of Saint-Simon's publications. In 1826 he had tried to create a 'company for supplying funds to industry' with an enormous capital of 100 million francs, but the government of the Restoration—in part motivated by distrust of liberals associated with banking—brought about its demise. In 1837 Laffitte revived the scheme. He was no longer the highly wealthy banker that he had been in the period before 1830, when he claimed to possess 20 million francs: the political and economic crisis and his unhappy time in power had greatly weakened him. He had been obliged to sell the forest of Breteuil, to split up the immense park belonging to his château of Maisons (it became the divided estate of Maisons-Laffitte) and to wind up his business out of which he realised only 4 millions. Only a national subscription enabled him to keep his mansion in Paris. It was then, at the age of sixty-five, that he made his comeback to the scene by founding the *Caisse Générale pour le Commerce et l'Industrie* in association with a young merchant by the name of Lebaudy. It had a capital of 55 million francs but only 15 millions were called up.[55] The Bank of France prevented him from designating it a *Banque* and from issuing proper notes, but there remained this original concept of a bank of deposit capable of 'putting all idle capital into circulation' by opening current accounts and of redistributing them in the form of discounts, loans and so on. The formula was that of Saint-Simon and was to apply to the great credit houses from their commencement, with no clear distinction between commercial credit and investment. The *Caisse Laffitte* outlived its founder, coming under the direction of Gouin in 1844. Other similar institutions appeared: one in 1843 was promoted by Ganneron, and others in 1846 by Baudon, Béchet-Dethomas and Cusin-Legendre. In 1847 the five *Caisses* of Paris had a capital of more than 53 million francs and the turnover of their portfolio exceeded 1,600 millions. Numerous similar institutions appeared in the provinces, the majority of them in 1836-38 and in 1845-47. The success of the *Caisses* in the sphere of short term credit resulted in principal bankers turning to other lines of activity and prepared them to be sympathetic with the plea of Michel Chevalier in 1838 that national or local budgets were insufficient to provide appropriate support for the 'material needs of France' if private capitalism did not turn its attention to those needs.

Both the state and the business world contributed to railway capital formation. The parliamentary debates of 1837 and 1838 outlined state projects. The 'charter' of 1842 left the heavy burden of expropriation and of infrastructure to public finance and entrusted concessionary companies with the laying of track, the purchase of rolling stock and the burden of maintenance and running expenses. Then, during a period commencing just before the law of 1842 was passed, and marked especially by the spectacular inaugurations of the Paris-Orléans and the Paris-Rouen lines on 2 and 3 May 1843, there began an infatuation which was soon to turn to 'railway mania'.[56] The Saint-

H

Simonians in particular—Péreire and Talabot at their head—promoted company after company, some of them purely speculative since concessions had been acquired only for reselling when prices rose on the Stock Exchange. Capital was raised by powerful banking groups in which the Rothschilds were associated with Bartholony, Fould, Pillet-Will, and others, and at the time there was even some collaboration between the Rothschilds and the Péreires. A good part of the capital was supplied from England through the agency of the groups Blount-Charles Laffitte (the nephew of the great financier), Hottinguer or Mackenzie, since English promoters were interested in continental extensions of their own railway network, and also found themselves diverted to European investments because of American setbacks in 1837 and by a conversion of government stock. England also supplied technicians, workmen and locomotives. The new *Caisses* of Gouin and Ganneron were persuaded to participate and the commitments involved stretched their resources. At the end of 1847 the network in course of construction did not exceed 1,830 kilometres, involving an expenditure of 967 million francs—a third of it by the state—and almost as much money was committed for further expenditure. Railway development was definitely backward by comparison with other countries of western Europe because French banking had committed itself late in the day.[57]

The formation of railway companies was promoted in a business climate which gave a new look to the capitalism of the forties. At every level conflicts and jockeying for position occurred; there were clashes of local interests, with every *département* and every town claiming a railway and its benefits. Rivalries arose among landowners who calculated the profits of development or who insisted on changing an already planned route or on moving a station. Speculations by founders of companies and by the first shareholders were common since speculators made only a part down-payment and resold to realise a substantial profit. There was collusion between 'rival' firms who came to an understanding before public auctions and falsified the bidding. There were knowledgeable exchanges between boards of directors. technicians, financiers and prestige personalities: marshals like Soult and Gérard, aristocrats like the Duke de Doudeauville or the Duke de Caumont-La Force and the Count de Ségur were involved along with ministers, peers of France and deputies, the latter being useful as representatives. The opposition had an impossible task in denouncing the links between private interest and the political world in all these subjects for scandal. They were the themes of successful publicity campaigns in the press

and in news sheets. Similarly, in another sector—that of mining concessions—the corruption affair of 1847 discredited two peers of
France: Teste, who was attorney general at the *Cour de Cassation*
and a former minister of Public Works, and General de Cubières,
president of the Compagnie de l'Est. More important than these various episodes, however, was the change of scale in capitalism that
showed itself with the first railway upsurge. Never had such capitalist
syndicates appealed for savings and so stimulated the Stock Exchange.
Le Nord, founded with a capital of 200 million francs by the groups
Rothschild-Péreire, Hottinguer and Laffitte-Blount in 1845, had 25,000
shares of 500 francs between 120 initial or intermediate subscribers
among whom Fould had 15,000 shares and Rothschild 14,000. The
'prosperity' or speculation based on railways profited metalmaking by
the enormous orders which it stimulated;[58] furthermore, the transport
facilities being provided gradually benefited the whole of industry. A
new overall equilibrium of the economy tended to appear in which industrial, commercial and financial sectors weighed as much as agriculture, the traditional source of influence. Already the economic crisis,
which exploded in 1846 and lasted until 1851, seemed to be caused at
one and the same time by bad harvests—as in all previous crises—and
by industrial overproduction as a new factor, by Stock Exchange
speculation and by banking weakness or, in short, by features properly
described as capitalist.

Public opinion hardly approved of these new capitalist features. In
particular the first large industrial concentrations, which led even
among the bourgeoisie to a division between high capitalism—with its
eye on monopoly—and a lower type of capitalism devoted to 'free
competition', caused concern and scandal. Lamartine and Ledru-
Rollin inveighed against 'the feudalism of money' and railway companies and coalmines in the Loire region provided them with telling
examples. Their fears were no doubt premature, but we know what
strength was retained by old economic structures in France in the
middle of the century. Yet, paradoxically, the debate was also a rear-
guard conflict or rather the contemporary expression of a persistent
and unheeding hostility to be found in the middle sections of French
society (bourgeois, and attached to private property) towards progress
and capitalist dynamism. The new tendencies contrasted with bourgeois routine methods of work and patterns of thought. In any case, the
protests were those of defeated men, for in the Second Empire this
dynamic capitalism was about to experience its finest years.

3
The Great Upsurge: 1848-82

The central years of the century, 1848-51, were years of a major breakthrough both in the history of French capitalism and in political history. For once a major political turning-point and a change of economic structure coincided. Towards the end of the July monarchy the economic machine was turning more and more quickly and probably too rapidly; suddenly it went out of control. That economic reverse played its part in the complex of causes producing the Revolution of 1848, a revolution which brought a sharp setback to and appeared to threaten the very basis of the economic system. The social danger was, however, very quickly resolved but business activity continued to languish and atrophy set in. The fears of the bourgeoisie persisted after the danger was over and helped an authoritarian government to assume power, but the new government was also helped by favourable circumstances of new economic recovery and the beginning of a phase of prosperity. Everything was now set for a decisive upturn.

1 THE DECISIVE TURNING POINT

'48: Crisis and restoration

The crisis, then, was itself a sign of the growth of the capitalist sector in the French economy but for the moment caused stagnation in that sector. The nature of the crisis should not be exaggerated. Traditional factors—agricultural under-production, high living costs, under-consumption of industrial products and unemployment—were combined with new elements—over-provision of railways and over-capitalisation in iron and steel, downturn in profit and loss of confidence, and whether these occurred simultaneously or separately they certainly had a cumulative effect. The Revolution of February 1848 gave new momentum to the crisis and aggravated it. Being a social revolution, it terrified property owners. Business activity, demand and employment were at a standstill, or at least, contracted sharply. Bank deposits were withdrawn and the banks found no security in their portfolios since transferable securities were affected by the panic on the Stock Exchange and commercial bills were affected by the suspension of maturity dates. Dealings in Treasury bonds were suspended or the bonds were amalgamated with other issues of depreciated government stock. Parisian finance houses collapsed and disappeared and major banks found themselves in serious difficulties. Rothschild, for example, was deeply committed in railways, and besides this he had tendered for enormous public loans in Austria, Prussia and England and, as usual, for the entire French loan of August 1847, amounting to 250 million francs. The revolutions of March 1848 in Vienna and Berlin added to his embarrassments while popular opinion unleashed itself against him as the incarnation of financial cosmopolitanism and he was accused of cornering in the grain market. The mob pillaged his château at Suresnes. He was unable to supply the government with the 168 million francs outstanding of 250 millions envisaged although the first Finance Minister of the provisional government, the exchange merchant Goudchaux, had supplied him with the interest beforehand. Yet Rothschild met his most pressing commitments by selling government stock at 33 francs and by liquidating his foreign holdings at any price in London, Antwerp and Amsterdam. The Delessert bank was less fortunate and was obliged to amalgamate with the firm of Hottinguer, which itself had come near to failure.

The capitalist world was heavily shaken and seemed to be threatened even more seriously by the socialist direction which the Revolution took in its early stages. The fear arose that the recognition of the right to work and the attempt to give employment to all would put a stop to the free play of the laws of liberal economy or would completely undermine existing arrangements. An even more precise cause of fear arose—the nationalisation of railways. Railway shares were dragged down in the general débâcle and lost 316 million francs in value between 23 February and 12 April. Nationalisation might give employment to workmen of the national worshops. Railway and insurance nationalisation, both envisaged by Garnier-Pagès as Goudchaux's successor, was formally proposed in May in the Constituent Assembly and the principle of progressive taxation was retained.

In fact, capitalism was to benefit by the social fear that these very threats inspired in the majority of Frenchmen, and the threats were exploited by clever propaganda. The fear of communal sharing won over all property-owning interests, even quite modest ones. The government's measures, taken under the stress of circumstances, affected interests that were smaller and more widespread than those of high finance. A supplementary tax of 45 centimes was levied; a tax of 1 per cent was raised on the capital of mortgages; a partial default consisted of repaying Treasury bonds at par in depreciated government stock (5 per cent stock standing at 116.10 on the eve of the revolution had fallen to 97.5 on 7 March and to 50 on 5 April); and depositors in small savings banks were repaid for the most part in stock and in Treasury bonds. Moreover, by a rapid ebb of the revolutionary tide forces of conservatism benefited from massive reaction. The great army of property owners, of small savers, of *rentiers*, and of heads of firms closed their ranks. They were drawn together by that fear of 'Reds', which, in the dictum of Georges Lefebvre, 'the high bourgeoisie and others experienced and, sustaining thoughts of the darkest kind, exploited for their own ends'. The bourgeoisie triumphed in the days of June. Goudchaux returned to the Ministry of Finance and announced 'the end of nonsense and of presumptuous deviations from normal life'.

The traditional social order had won the day. The structure of the liberal economy remained intact and the policy of nationalisation was abandoned. Without any difficulty, Montalembert saved the railway companies in the name of 'true democracy', contending that democracy must be 'the enfranchisement of the individual and not despotism exercised in the name of the masses'. The problems of the right to work and of a coherent plan of public charity were no longer matters for discussion. The crisis worked itself out and turned to the advantage of capitalism in many ways. The Bank of France remained an unbreached fortress. The decree of 15 March which pegged market prices saved its reserves which had been menaced by the monetary panic following the Stock Exchange débâcle, bank failures and social disorder. It emerged from the Revolution with renewed strength, and the issue of small denominations of 100 francs tended to familiarise the public with more of its notes. Above all, the crisis brought a successful conclusion to the campaign waged under the direction of the regent Pillet-Will for a 'unique bank'. This meant that the bank's monopoly of note issue was extended to the whole country. At the high point of the crisis in April and May 1848 banks in the *départements* that were also in difficulties were absorbed in its organisation; their shareholders incurred no loss since certificates were exchanged at par against shares of the Bank of France. Thus monetary unity was accomplished and the Bank of France remained the sole regulator of note circulation. It substantially reinforced its provincial network, adding six more branches in 1848-51 to its previous offices, and nine subsidiaries resulting from the take-over of the banks of the *départements*. Moreover, another chance decision arising from the crisis—although dimly foreshadowed in 1830—paved the way for a lasting improvement in the country's banking structure. The general failure of commercial banks had blocked the entire credit system since it prevented those demanding discount from finding the third signature required by the Bank of France; hence a number of national discount banks and trade branch banks were created to provide the signature, and, additionally, receipts of general stores representing stocks in warehouse were valued as transferable and discountable commercial effects. The state in Treasury bonds, the municipalities in communal liabilities, and the capitalists in shares wholly paid, provided capital in equal thirds. In this way sixty-seven discount houses appeared between March and May 1848. Once the state withdrew, leaving the discount houses in private hands, this temporary expedient was transformed into one of the typical banking institutions of the Second Empire. Appropriately enough, Émile Péreire and Achille Fould drafted the statutes of the *Comptoir de Paris*.

Another important episode was the debasement of government stock resulting from the successive manipulations of financial policy in 1848. Firstly, certificates were distributed in repayment for Treasury bonds and deposits in savings banks; then other certificates were added and were given to certificate holders and to small savers in compensation for losses suffered by them at the time of repayment, which had been carried out when conditions were unfavourable to them. The government distributed these certificates to property owners injured by social disorders and even to shareholders of the Paris-Lyon railway when it was necessary for the government to take the line over temporarily. In March 1848 Garnier-Pagès launched a National Loan which returned only a derisory capital of 441,000 francs but after 'the victory of order' Goudchaux was able to issue another loan in July which was much more successful: it allowed the subscribers of 1847, who had paid over only deposits of guarantee, to regain the credit of which they had been deprived. In this way, the state had to support an additional burden of 54 million francs of *rente* above the 175 millions left by the monarchy, but the number of *rentiers* between 1848 and 1850 rose from 292,000 to 824,000 and public funds were no longer reserved for a minor section of French society. Here again, Napoleon III took advantage of the situation when in 1854, on the advice of Mirès, he made a direct issue of a loan to a public by now aware of the state of affairs. Napoleon's action avoided the need for the costly services of a major bank.

Very quickly, then, the Second Republic was able to reassure the French bourgeoisie and to grant substantial favours to capitalist interests. Yet full satisfaction was given to neither section. In spite of Cavaignac's show of strength in June 1848 the régime seemed a feeble enough guarantee against the recurrence of social danger. The Stock Exchange remained nervous. In April 1850 government stock lost 7 francs in one day following the election of Eugène Sue, who inspired inordinate fear among the bourgeoisie. The law of 31 May—which purged the country of universal suffrage—sent it up again 4.75. Business activity continued to be sluggish in mining, in metallurgy and in building as well as in agriculture. If the year 1849 saw a containment of the crisis, the stability which followed also signified stagnation. 1,600 kilometres of railway track were constructed in four years, but these were fragments of line rather than through main routes. Negotiations between the state and financial groups—all with loyal representatives in the Legislative Assembly—dragged on without end. A general resumption of work did not occur even when financial arrangements were ready. The government practised a policy of strict orthodoxy: it attempted to balance the budget by reducing expenditure and thus gave up all serious attempt at social betterment and at economic recovery. The budget for public works expenditure of 216 million francs in 1848 fell to 167 in 1849, to 66 in 1850 and to 64.5 in 1851. The majority of the Constituent Assembly, as of the Legislative, followed Thiers who was a passionate defender of protectionism and of classical fiscal policy. They were opposed to those who, in the manner of Peel in England, wished to broaden the horizons of the economy by flexible customs duties and to make up the consequent fiscal decrease by a tax on income. These proposals were put forward without success by Léon

Faucher, an administrator of the Paris–Strasbourg railway, a liberal economist and twice a minister of the Republic. His supporters were Girardin and a group of businessmen who seemed to be tempted by the idea that capital, in conceding a prior tax deduction to the state, was negotiating a kind of contract guaranteeing and legitimising their controlling position. The proposals were renewed in 1851 by some business groups in silk export and printed cloth in answer to the appeal of Sainte-Beuve, deputy for the textile district of Picardy, but their support brought no positive results.

The Bank of France played no very active role in the renewal of business. At the height of the crisis it did render valuable service by maintaining some discount and even allowing, against the trend, 34 millions of credit advance to carefully selected firms. Those firms were metal companies recommended by the Seillière Bank (Schneider, de Wendel, Commentry-Fourchambault), mining firms (like La Grand'-Combe controlled by the Talabots and underwritten by the Roths-childs) and banks like the *Caisse de la Sarthe* whose dynamism was inspired by the minister Trouvé-Chauvel. Overall, the Bank paid cautious attention to a rule of banking which resulted, in fact, in a contraction of credit: note circulation—even after the law of 6 August 1860 abolished the fixed amount imposed hitherto as a legal ceiling—was no more than 529 millions in September 1851 against metallic cash holdings which were then 620 millions. Its cover was more than assured. In addition, discount hardly progressed. It stood at 1,030 millions in 1849 and at 1,245,000 in 1851 against 1,817,000 in 1847. Such a credit policy gave no base for the renewal of general economic activity.

French capitalism had suffered no great harm during the republican episode, and had even become stronger in some respects, yet a new régime was needed before it could be provided with all the conditions necessary for its full development. In turn, the Second Empire—'the political economy of 2 December'—often acclaimed by official publicists and more recently analysed by Louis Girard, was to reap the benefits of capitalist development, whether the régime deserved those benefits or not. Did, then, the business world deliberately provoke or support this advent of a strong political régime? The question remains open, in particular over the provision of 25 million francs which the Bank of France allowed the Prince-President on 27 November. One interpretation—put forward by the official historian Gabriel Ramon— was that the Bank was bound by previous agreement; another line of thought—that of writers like Dauphin-Meunier—was that the Bank's motivation consisted of a rather suspect willingness to oblige a new pretender. Émile Péreire related how he found some of the principal banks of Paris around the bed of invalid Baron James on the morning of 2 December. 'We did not really blame Louis Napoleon for deciding to take decisive action before 1852; we looked on it as virtually inevitable and we were worried only about the risks involved in the adventure.' When Péreire explained that the seizure of power was probably going to be successful, 'the great financiers heard this reassuring news with pleasure'.[1] The news quickly spread to the provinces and on 4 December Frédéric Zuber noted in his journal: 'Mulhouse remains calm. People prefer dictatorship to anarchy'. Whether the occasion was one for joy or resignation the choice was in any case uncontroversial. In six months, prices quoted on the Paris Stock Exchange rose by 4 milliard francs.

Opportunities and advantages of the Second Empire

Primarily the Empire provided capitalists with a set of circumstances favourable to their enterprises. This was certainly a coincidence but it could be turned to advantage. The *Revue des Deux Mondes* of 15 November 1865 noticed clearly the factors—and the extent—of the general upsurge which marked the period: 'Railways and gold mines are the two secrets of the industrial and commercial prosperity of Europe'. Gold flowed from mines discovered in California in 1848 and in Australia in 1851. These mines yielded in twenty years almost as much as the amount extracted since the sixteenth century. Under Napoleon III France minted 6,164 francs, or more than four times the amount minted between 1799 and 1851. This inflation of gold soon put bimetallism in difficulty but a far more important effect was to give a significant stimulus to the economy in general. Inflation is usually considered one of the causes of the prosperity which expressed itself in a long wave of rising prices; prices rose by about one-third between 1851 and 1873. In its turn the rise in prices stimulated production, thereby causing the profits of entrepreneurs to rise to four times their original amount according to the calculations of Simiand.

Nevertheless, the government was determined to make the most of this opportuninty presented by external circumstances. Firstly, there was the personal policy of the Emperor, who believed in government

action and was opposed to the liberal view that deplored it. As a distinguished economist said, 'A government is not an inevitable disease
but rather a vital part of every social organism'. The Emperor, therefore, had in mind an ambitious policy since his government's primary
concern was to promote the greatest possible degree of economic expansion. Yet he wished to preserve the essential feature of liberalism
—private enterprise. Indeed, he wanted to avoid the unfortunate inclination of the state to devote itself to activities which could be performed equally well or even better by private businessmen. His policy
was favourable to capitalism since it proposed to stimulate its expansion
without undermining its structure. There was also the policy of the
advisers to the new régime, among whom were the former Orleanist
groups. Associated with them were ex-deputies—supporters of Guizot
like Achille Fould who represented the Jewish Bank but was now
converted to protestantism, the lawyer Magne, the engineer Bineau,
and Morny himself. Morny was half-brother to Napoleon III and the
most brilliant symbol of imperial business manipulation, a principal
controller of refineries and even president of the sugar works of France.
A useful deputy to Guizot, Morny used the money of his mistress, the
Countess Le Hon, for playing the Stock Exchange before breaking
with her in rather sordid circumstances. He was involved in all the
political-cum-financial intrigues, receiving his share from even the
most dubious of them, like the shady credit transactions of the Swiss
banker Jecker in Mexico, with the support of the French armies. He
was, moreover, intelligent and shrewd and completely convinced that
'politics is only the outward show of great public problems'. More than
any other imperial adviser he was capable of leading a government preoccupied with business problems. In the same tradition there was
Rouher. Coming into active politics only in 1848, Rouher was anxious,
as Blanchard has pointed out, to renew the practice of Louis Philippe's
reign by creating political groups linked with business interests. Rouher
was better, however, as the efficient servant of a grand strategic plan
than as the originator of one. The most vigorous drive, especially at
the beginning, came from another group who were followers of Saint-
Simon and included financiers and technocrats, unrivalled business
initiators and general entrepreneurs. Among them were Péreire and
Talabot, Enfantin, Chevalier, Didion, Dubochet and Arlès-Dufour,
and it was their personal influence that sustained the rapid expansion
of the first years of the régime. Their ideas and their enterprises best
expressed the distinct policies of the Second Empire. The Empire

declined along with them when Orleanist finance, helped by turncoats like the Talabots, triumphed over Saint-Simonian finance—when the Rothschilds were on the winning side against the Péreires.

One can hardly say that this period of great upsurge came to an end in 1870. Neither the change of political régime nor even the supposed turning-point of 1873 which began the period of the 'Great Depression' immediately after imperial prosperity marked a decisive break. If, in this nebulous area, one really had to suggest a limit and to fix a date, the best choice would be around the years 1882-3. Those were the years marked by a number of significant events: the cyclical crisis in the economy (in which the crash of the *Union Générale* was only the most spectacular episode); the adoption by the deposit banks of a more rigorous credit policy; and the aggravation of financial conflicts—in Switzerland or the Middle East—which denoted the approach of the era of imperialism. There were railway agreements negotiated which transferred to banks and to companies already in existence the burden of carrying out the Freycinet Plan, denoting the victory of liberal capitalism over the state which made a last attempt to play a role of general economic initiator and to direct—in the words of Freycinet himself—'not only the balance sheet of the government but also that of the nation'. There was even the beginning of the 'second industrial revolution', as Georges Friedmann called it. One could easily lengthen the list of events occurring together at this time and, diverse though they may be, they are a good enough general indication that here is the convenient terminal date required.

2 MONEY

The mobilisation of capital

The great progress made in the accumulation of capital, in its outlets, and in its economic utilisation was the essential basis of the imperial upsurge, in contrast to the slow improvement of the preceding period.[2]

The wealth of France possibly doubled and its composition to some extent changed. According to some estimates, it rose from 105 milliards in 1853, of which 15.5 were in movable property and transferable securities, to 209 in 1878, of which 64 were in this specially significant category. A more reliable statistic—bearing on a social circle less connected than others with the upsurge of capitalism—was that of the

Caisses d'Épargne: in 1849 they had 97 million francs of deposits made by 730,000 subscribers, but by 1869 the figures rose to 765 millions made by 2,400,000 subscribers.

This growing amount of savings found its way into investment and was attracted there by distribution of dividends, by instances of rapid rise to wealth and by the propaganda of the great interest groups. Each group had its specialised organ. There was *Le Journal des Chemins de Fer* for Mirès and *La Semaine Financière* for the association of major banks. The Péreires controlled *La Liberté* and the leading newspapers began to publish daily Stock Exchange lists. According to an English author in the 1860s the outlets for savings were henceforth more extensive than they were across the Channel. 'All the small capital hitherto inactive was now put into circulation. While in England the average denomination in shares was a value of 2,500 francs, in France the average was a value of 500 and even shares of 1,000 francs were very rare.'[3] Stockings under the bed were indeed being emptied! The transferable security that attracted a wide range of small savers in preference to the share was the bond with fixed income, and it became the great instrument for collection of capital and thereby for national savings. It was made safer by the guarantee of minimum interest given by the government, and it was also favoured by the railway companies after their privileges had been lengthened to 99 years to spread the burden of amortisation more evenly. Financing of railways by bonds was in a proportion of 20 per cent after 1850 and of 60 per cent in 1855.[4] The bond had also become an investment to be handed down by inheritance and for that reason enjoyed equal favour with government stock. In 1854 Bineau, Minister of Finance, sought to place the loan of 250 million francs necessary for the Crimean War; disappointed by the offer of Rothschild—the usual agent—he let himself be persuaded by Mirès to issue it directly. It achieved a real success within eleven days and the Empire proclaimed 'the universal suffrage of capital'. 99,274 subscribers came forward, 7 out of 9 from the provinces and 2 out of 3 to buy less than 50 francs of stock yielding altogether 468 millions. This democratisation of public credit was noisily publicised and, as we shall see later, the episode was not without abuse. The reign of the great bankers in this domain was not yet over, even if they compromised in their methods. Between 1851 and 1869 the capital of the public debt climbed from 5 to more than 11 milliards. This easy financing of expenditure also enabled the state to refrain from increasing fiscal pressure. Instead, the government relied on the general climate of expansion to bring an increase in fiscal return which moved, in fact, from 42 to 57 francs per inhabitant. A systematic policy of budgetary deficit was even practised, in the manner of the July monarchy, and helped to promote the great public works.

New role of the classical banks

Denominations of stock, of shares, and of bonds were ways of raising money that were increasingly adopted and they resulted in a growing integration of capital for business purposes. Associated with this development of movable capital there was an extension and development of banking institutions which then came to assume an importance and character hitherto unknown.

Banking creations were so numerous and innovations in this sphere proliferated to such an extent that the role of the major banks, which had become more discreet, might well be underestimated by the historian. In fact, it remained essential. The great Parisian banking houses were not content with just managing the interests of their own select and chosen clientèle. In spite of the blow of confidence in 1854 they remained privileged if not essential intermediaries for the placing of public loans. The point was well shown in 1871. Alphonse de Rothschild, junior, who had become head of the Rothschilds of Paris on the death of Baron James in 1868, was then held in considerable favour. He was powerful through his contacts with Léon Say, a grandson of the great economist and son-in-law to Bertin of the journal *Les Débats*. Alphonse was to become a future minister of the Third Republic but, for the moment, was prefect of the Seine and a counsellor well regarded by Thiers. He had contacts with the German banker Bleichröder who was an agent for Rothschild in Frankfort and in Vienna and a financial adviser of Bismarck. Alphonse, however, derived his main strength from the financial power, from the social contacts, from the activity, and ultimately from the name of Rothschild. He made the deposit banks and the new commercial banks pay dearly for attracting to themselves, in the words of Jules Favre, 'the large profits which our public misfortune allowed them to realise'. He gained the lion's share of the issues of 1871-2 which were made necessary by the conqueror's requirements. The 200 millions imposed on the city of Paris and the 5,000 millions imposed on France brought profits for the Rothschilds. Those profits came from underwriting commission (which was unnecessary in view of the eagerness of the public) and from commission on placings. They came also from various agency functions, from the supply of specie and of promissory notes payable in Germany, and from differences between the rate of purchase and the rate of resale (82.50 francs against 77.50 francs being considered as 5 per cent commission in 1871). The Rothschilds' overall profit was 75 million francs, at a low estimate. It was not their last success in spite of the counter-offensive led after August 1871 by the rivals they had either ousted or held in thrall. Yet public loans were no longer the sole long-term investment which the major banks undertook after the decade of the forties. Their industrial investments enabled them to exercise extensive control over enterprises benefiting from their finance. This control was due to the fact that they granted credit, that they took their share of the risk involved and that they issued stock and distributed it under their own aegis. From 1863 the Rothschilds held 27 seats on various boards of directorates, the Mallets 22 and the Hottinguers 10. The whole air of traditional discretion surrounding these banks—conveyed so well by the subdued, quiet, padded atmosphere of the offices where they reigned supreme—began to make bankers feel ill at ease. The narrow rue Laffitte, for example, was the seat of the Rothschild bank and yet it was so near the new department stores built on the Boulevard by the credit houses. Consequently, to fit in with the style of the age, the major banks adopted many guises. As we shall see, they inserted numerous tentacles into the credit houses and into the commercial banks. They refused neither the tainted associations nor the seductions of share capital. They did not spurn the connections which the formation of bank associations and of financial groups imposed on them. These groups, in which bankers often occupied a predominant place, differed considerably in organisation and in length of existence.

The Bank of France was always controlled by regents recruited from members of the major banks and its successive governors served as president. Between 1836 and 1857 the governor was Count d'Argout, formerly a minister under Casimir-Périer, and between 1857 and 1863 the Count de Germiny who was a former receiver-general, a minister and a regent, and then governor of the *Crédit Foncier*. Next came the lawyers: Vuitry, a section president in the Conseil d'État (his daughter married Henri Germain) and, in 1864, Rouland who had just left the Ministry of Education. The renewal of the Bank's privilege in 1857, together with a doubling of capital, assured its future. As we shall see, it knew how to defend itself against the Péreires. Naturally, it continued to perform its essential tasks—discounting (which surpassed 6,600 millions in 1869) and note issue. France became more and more familiar with its notes and in 1865 the small denomination of 50 francs appeared. In accordance with the law of 1857, its network of branches was extended to meet the demands of local business all over the country. As Labasse notices, in many cases 'the opening of a branch was due not so much to the commercial potential of the town involved as to the quality and influence of the bank's agents'. There were 74 branches by the end of the Empire. The Bank, following the example of the great Parisian financiers, became much more actively involved in the business world. After 1852 advances on public issues were extended to railway stocks and municipal bonds of the City of Paris. This enabled companies to find purchasers more easily for their stock, which could not be sold off entirely to speculators buying only in order to resell. In 1857 the *Crédit Foncier* benefited from the same procedure. In 1858 the Bank came to the aid of the Railway Syndicate in the role of a true investment bank; it allowed the Syndicate important advances (245 millions in one year) and undertook to place stock which it underwrote. Protests came from business houses and this use of its funds obliged the Bank to raise the rate of discount. Discount was, however, its primary function and, in fact, it changed the rate fairly often, raising it to 8, 9 and 10 per cent during the crisis of 1857. Yet the Bank stuck to its new policy and simply asked 1 or $\frac{1}{2}$ per cent more for its advances than for discount, not hesitating to double advances in 1862 in order to facilitate the redemption of government stock. The functions which it assumed towards the state and the railway companies brought it to play a wider and more diversified role.

New types of bank

There is no doubt that banking institutions better suited to the new demands and objectives of capitalism were now required. The new institutions came into being under the Second Empire, sometimes with the cooperation of the major banks and sometimes in competition against them.

The creation in 1852 of the *Crédit Foncier*, consisting of three distinct institutions at Paris, Marseille and Nevers which soon merged into one, had no hostile intention. It aimed at filling a serious gap in the French banking structure by offering to the rural population a method of borrowing money other than traditional usury. According to the enquiry of 1845, usury was practised at 9 per cent on average and sometimes at as much as 20 per cent.[5] In practice, however, the *Crédit Foncier*—which was organised on the same lines as the Bank of France and connected with the state in a similar way—had to sacrifice its original intention in order to assist in financing property construction and great urban projects. Between 1853 and 1908 it was obliged to pour $4\frac{1}{2}$ milliards into urban investments—either on mortgage or on loan to the municipalities—and it put less than 1,900 millions in rural property. Firms created afterwards to revive its programme of agricultural assistance fared no better. The *Crédit Agricole* (1861) plunged into the loans for the Khedive of Egypt which were to cause its failure in 1876. At least the *Crédit Foncier*, besides participating in the development of towns and especially of Paris, also played a great part in the diffusion of the concept of movable capital. Its shares of 500 francs were a much-prized investment. The liabilities of the *Crédit Foncier* were guaranteed by mortgages taken in exchange for its loans and its shares returned an interest related to government stock, thus making them very popular among modest small savers.

The *Crédit Mobilier* presented an entirely different picture. It was primarily an instrument of expansion for which both the government and Saint-Simonian finance felt a need. Almost an instrument of combat, it aimed at discouraging recourse to the traditional banks, which it soon outflanked. It saw itself as the Bank of France of the Second Emperor. In fact, it was born from an early disagreement between the new régime and the lords of the business world who were anxious about the boom of the year 1852. Stockbrokers were mindful of these fears and on the day following the 'Senatus-Consulate' which restored the Empire—some days before the second plebiscite—they decided to ask for a down payment of 150 francs per share negotiated for a fixed period. That was on 8 November 1852. Émile and Isaac Péreire then proposed the foundation of a new establishment capable of restoring the inflation now in jeopardy and—in the words of Girard—of 'taking the Empire out of the hands of the Stock Exchange in order to put the Stock Exchange into the hands of the Empire'. There was an immediate rupture between the Péreires and their former employers the Rothschilds. Other major banking houses, however, shared in the creation of the new firm. The decree of 18 November 1852 authorised the inauguration of the *Crédit Mobilier* with a capital of 60 millions divided into 120,000 shares of 500 francs.[6] 40,000 shares were immediately subscribed by 12 initial shareholders. Among them were the Péreires, with 11,446 shares, and other Saint-Simonians (Rodrigues, Lesseps),

J

some representative officials or personalities like Morny, the Duke de Mouchy, who was a spokesman of great railway interests, Daru, the Duke de Galliera and some great Paris bankers like Fould—Benoît Fould, the eldest brother of Achille Fould and head of the family firm as chairman of its board had 12,804 shares. Then there were Mallet, d'Eichthal, Seillière, Cahen d'Anvers, and their correspondents from the Jewish Bank—Torlonia from Rome, Oppenheim from Cologne and Heine from Hamburg. But it was the Péreires who came to exercise control over it, and to guide its path—often in competition against rival concerns from the major banks—towards far more ambitious ends than the mere maintenance of high prices on the Stock Exchange.

We have already mentioned the two Péreire brothers: Émile, the elder, full of ideas, of projects and of policies, and Isaac who was less extrovert but perhaps cleverer. They were close partners and were the best representatives of Saint-Simonian dynamism in the service of the imperial economy. Their concept of the *Crédit Mobilier* was not new: the formula of 'financing of national works' had already been adopted by Laffitte.[7] Enfantin, in his book *Le Producteur* in 1825, had proposed that shares issued by different business houses could be merged into an overall holding company which would give riskier shares the support of those considered to be blue chips. The idea was put into practice in the railway mergers which the Bartholony-Mouchy group for Orléans and the Rothschild-Talabot group for Lyon-Marseille brought into being. However, the idea was applied only in a limited sphere and successful enterprises only were chosen, whereas the Péreires wanted to operate on a much larger scale from the beginning. They were quick at defining their methods and at putting them into practice. Their aim was to create the bank conceived by their predecessors—a very powerful bank capable of regulating national investments. They wished to remedy the shortage of credit that was hindering the development of the nation's business life and they also wanted to end the isolation of the great financial houses. For that purpose, they decided to create a centre 'powerful enough to bind together the enterprises which in isolation would experience great difficulties in the process of formation'. The *Crédit Mobilier* would thus take over the finances of the large firms, bring them together into a common organisation and prepare their general fusion. It was an anticipation, and possibly a more thoroughgoing and advanced form, of what were later to be known as holding companies. As for the means of accomplishment, the *Crédit* was able to supply this, thanks to its own capital and to the deposits received in current accounts. French small savings were organised on a vast scale by an appeal for a 'plebiscite' of capital. As bankers of the Empire the Péreires derived their power from a plebiscite in the same way that the Empire itself derived its power from the electors' plebiscite. Here again the instrument was at hand: preference shares were issued in massive quantities, at a rate obviously inferior to that of the negotiated loans of the *Crédit*, so as to yield a profit. The shares were easy to sell since the public no longer had to calculate the risk involved in this or that particular business. Public confidence was unquestioned in view of the imposing collection of solid joint-stock enterprises. An additional point in favour of the *Crédit*—another idea of Enfantin—brought more popularity: already an enormous commercial and investment bank, it became also an issuing bank. Some of its bonds, while remaining shares at 3 per cent, circulated as 'portable money', as bank notes, for they were divided into small denominations and repaid at very short notice of 90 or 45 days. In the final analysis, the *Crédit Mobilier* managed to transform completely the role played by capitalists in the financing of enterprises. Out of shareholders who speculated and were interested in business trends it created bond bearers and sleeping partners who had security and received an income but had no active part to play. The mass of capital holders became entirely distinct from the active general managers. Later on, the nationalisation of the railways in 1937 and of the banks in 1945 was to have the same result. The *Crédit Mobilier* had to act not only as a lender but as a go-between. The policy was to resell stock at a profit and, while waiting for the price to stabilise, to manipulate dealings by Stock Exchange speculation. Risks had to be spread and balanced by organisation and control of enterprises.[8] Such were the great expectations of the Péreires when, in the euphoric days of 1852, they outlined their ambitious plan.

It is usual to distinguish the *Crédit Mobilier* of the Péreires from the great 'credit houses' which also appeared under the Second Empire. It is true that they managed to outlast the *Crédit Mobilier* and that, after 1880-90, they became clearly specialised in their own sphere which was distinct from that of the commercial banks.[9] They changed considerably. At the beginning they were little different from the rest and were no better than the *Crédit Mobilier* when it came to finding the right use for their resources which they acquired haphazardly. They opened long term credits, made industrial investments and created financial offshoots. They organised foreign loans—thus exporting a part of their resources. In short, in the initial phase they behaved like 'commercial banks' strictly defined.[10] Obviously they sought, in this way, a greater return from capital than commercial credit would bring, but consequently laid themselves open to greater risks. 'Discount could not bring great profit and security together. The discount houses had to seek their profits in speculation. Like the commercial banks they became gambling houses which were badly hit by every crisis.'[11]

Yet the oldest of them, the *Comptoir National de Paris*, was the same concern as the *Comptoir National* created in 1848. Ceasing to be a national firm in its title in 1853 since neither the state nor the city of Paris had any dealings with it, it moved to the hôtel Rougemont and experienced modest enough beginnings. Then in 1860 its capital was raised from 20 to 40 million francs and a new foreign and colonial sphere of action was promoted. Agencies were opened in Shanghai, Calcutta (1860), Bombay, Hong Kong, Saigon (1862), and then in London, Yokohama and Alexandria, and the banks of the old French colonial territories were reorganised. Thus the *Comptoir* gradually became a financial house and fell under the influence of the major banks. In January 1874 its management was taken over by the former stockbroker Girod (who was subsequently to resign in 1883 to become one of the partners of the firm of Neuflize). The chairmanship of the board went to a great international financier, Edward Hentsch; he was the head of a private firm in Paris and founder of the *Banque de Paris et des Pays-Bas* in 1872 and brother of a powerful banker in Geneva. Hence the *Comptoir* became 'a great centre for the buying and selling of transferable stock' and represented a huge amount of available capital in the hands of private bankers. Between 1875 and 1879 it came to assume the responsibility for the conversion and consolidation of the Egyptian debt and agreed also to share a Russian loan with a Berlin group. In addition, it became the principal cashier of the Portuguese government and undertook to reorganise the Swiss railways on behalf of which it waged—and lost—a great conflict against German financiers.[12]

The *Société Générale de Crédit Industriel et Commercial*, founded in 1859, was clearly introduced as a deposit bank. At its head was the Marquis d'Audiffret, an economist and influential politician as well as a senator and a *membre de l'Institut*. It was explained to the shareholders that this new machinery, as yet untried in France, was organised on the same lines as the English joint-stock banks. The intention was to fill a gap in the functioning of French credit institutions. The principal function was to receive funds lying idle and sterile in private hands. Private holders could dispose of funds whenever they liked and would receive interest. The funds were speedily put into short-term commitments for productive uses in commerce and industry. The formula was perfect. The resources were supplied by idle savings accepted as deposits on immediate call. These deposits were then used for discount or for unsecured advances, but never for long-term commitments since, by their very nature, they must always remain sufficiently liquid. Yet the principles were not really put into practice. The *Crédit Industriel*—as it was to be generally known—commenced with an authorised capital of 60 millions which was reduced in practice to 40 millions. There were 80,000 shares of 500 francs, of which only a quarter were called up. Among the various subscribers were merchants from Lyon (like Arlès-Dufour) and from Bordeaux, the German financier Hansemann (founder of the Diskontogesellschaft), a London banker of the P.O. (Gladstone), and a Parisian banker in the circle of Morny (Armand Donon). Current accounts were opened for a minimum of 3,000 francs and branches were founded only in Paris. It was not surprising that the total of these deposits grew very slowly, from 17 millions in 1860 to less than 50 millions in 1872. In addition, the *Crédit Industriel* arranged loans for different companies even if it did not directly finance them.

The opening of the *Crédit Lyonnais* in 1863 and the appearance of Henri Germain on the scene were of greater importance for the financial world. The new firm operated in much the same way as the *Crédit Industriel*, using cheques and current accounts. Its object was 'never to let a fraction of capital, however small, lie unproductive in the hands of its holders'. Its funds came particularly from the firm of Arlès-Dufour (always on the scene), from steel groups like *Châtillon-Commentry* and *Forges et Aciéries de la Marine* and from Swiss bankers like Hentsch and Paccard. There was great economic potential in the region of Lyon, if one included areas which had industrial or geographical links with it, like the coal beds of central France and the Alpine region.[13] That potential explained why such an important banking concern should develop in the provinces. At the time, it was the only French bank unrepresented in Paris. However, it eventually opened a small branch there—in the rue de Choiseul—in 1864. Later, on the boulevard des Italiens, it built what has been described as a huge stronghold of stone. The bank's management moved there in 1882 but the head office remained in Lyon. The new building in Paris was later greatly deplored by those who felt nostalgically about the great days of the Second Empire. They could remember the boulevard in the days of its Chinese baths, before it was dominated by this edifice of a bank. By 1869 the *Crédit Lyonnais* had a capital of 22 million francs and its deposits and current accounts in credit amounted to 83 millions; it was a substantial advance on the *Crédit Industriel* or the *Comptoir d'Escompte* which had only 170 million francs of deposits to show for a capital of 100 millions. Indeed, it practised a better and more efficient policy in attracting savings, opening a current account 'to any person, no matter what his circumstances or station provided he would make a first payment of at least 50 francs'. After 1866 it abolished all charges for keeping certificates in safe custody and all broker's commission on Stock Exchange orders; this policy commended itself to merchants and industrialists who were only too pleased to economise on the always considerable commission fees for such services. Yet there was still hesitation about the use to be made of available capital. The bank acquired a substantial portfolio of shares and became rather unwisely involved in the *Société Foncière Lyonnaise* and in numerous industrial enterprises including *La Fuchsine*, a chemical dye firm which failed. Such enterprises were 'out of the ordinary' and when they succeeded, proved to be more remunerative than current commercial credit. Naturally, they were more risky. They were suitable for rapidly increasing the bank's reserves as well as for enriching a small number of interested managers. Thus a practical and daring approach, typical of the ethos of the Second Empire, marked the beginnings of the *Crédit Lyonnais*. It was a period of trial and error but valuable in the sense that it enabled the management to evolve their famous business strategy, which Henri Germain conducted with an even surer touch after the testing time of 1882.

The last to appear on the list of the great credit houses, the *Société Générale* (to support 'the development of commerce and industry in France', according to its full title) openly started as a business bank. The *Société Générale* was no other than the *Syndicat* or the *Réunion Financière*, founded in 1855—in opposition to the *Crédit Mobilier*—by the rivals of the Péreires. Their intention was to compete with the *Crédit Mobilier* since they wanted to prevent 'all business falling into the same hands'. Doubtless the Rothschilds supported it, and Swiss bankers like Bartholony, Paccard, Pillet-Will, Hentsch and others, together with the railway magnates Blount and Talabot,[14] provided finance. The group acted uncertainly for a long period, and pondered for a moment on a 'romanesque fraternisation' with the Péreires in a giant 'general company' which would have financed nearly all the French commercial system. They tried also to create a *Comptoir Impérial*—tending to specialise in short-term credit. In fact, it was only in 1864 when at last they obtained the authorisation to set up the *Société Générale* that they acquired a real identity. The *Société Générale* cut an imposing figure with a capital of 120 millions comprising 240,000 shares divided between 1,200 subscribers. The *Comptoir d'Escompte* applied for 20,000, a London firm, the *General Credit and Finance Company*, for 20,000 more and the *Crédit Lyonnais* for only 2,000. Eugène Schneider was chairman of the Board. Among the participants were bankers like Hentsch, Oppenheim, Davillier, Fould, Cahen d'Anvers and Laffitte; Saint-Simonians like Talabot, Enfantin and Arlès-Dufour; great industrialists besides Schneider like Darblay (from flour milling), Dubochet (from gas) and Sommier (from sugar); and finally, of necessity, some great names from the nobility. The *Société Générale*, like its rival the *Crédit Mobilier*, financed building speculations such as the Boulevard Magenta, mining enterprises such as iron ore at Mokta el Hadid in Algeria, and foreign loans. With 5,600 depositors and 88 million francs in deposits it made a profit of more than 10 million francs in 1869, which was five times greater than that of the *Crédit Lyonnais*. But it was soon to experience reverses that brought its operations back to the norm for a credit house which was unable to embark on long-term commitments because of the known extent of its debts.

At this initial stage of their history, deposit banks were acting both as investment banks and as commercial banks. Yet commercial banks already presented a different image. This was due to the nature of their resources—consisting essentially of their own capital—and to their indifferent attitude towards the average small saver. Such an ethos gave them greater liberty of action than other banks and explained their ability to play more boldly the role of economic pump-priming, a role not yet to be taken for granted. The Second Empire was an age of feverish creation which resulted in fierce competition between different kinds of bank and between bankers.[15] Yet in 1872 the *Banque de Paris et des Pays-Bas*—'Paribas' in specialist jargon—was born from a merger between two older establishments: one was directed by Hentsch and under the patronage of Fould, Germiny and Joubert (an adviser of Thiers), and the other was controlled by a less typical personality, the Milanese Cernuschi, a refugee in France after 1848 and a collaborator of the Péreires. Cernuschi was later forced into a new exile by the declining imperial government, a government which he fought both by money and by propaganda; he returned to his own country with very valuable collections acquired without much difficulty in Japan. Other new banks were the *Banque Parisienne* (the future *Union Parisienne*) founded in 1874, and the *Banque de l'Indochine* in 1875. The major banks were often in two minds about the creation of these new banks, and we know what rivalry existed between the Rothschilds and the 'Paribas' promoters in 1871. But it did not take them long to see the advantages brought by the existence of the new banks and to find out how this new instrument could be manipulated. If one of the newcomers tried to interfere with them, it did not take them long to get rid of it. The Belgian Philippart, who took over the former *Crédit Mobilier* from Haussmann and tried to cut a figure in the business world in the style of a Mirès, was soon crushed. On the other hand, an important man like Edward Hentsch, who was the manager of three banks— 'Paribas', the *Comptoir d'Escompte de Paris*, and his own—had all three at his disposal and used whichever he wished according to the nature and size of the operation.[16]

Regional banking and the birth of the great banking networks

Although the great deposit banks had hardly yet started to create their own special function, from before 1870 they began to gather in small savings hidden in the depths of the provinces. Their branches already influenced credit conditions wherever they were set up, and supplemented the branches of the Bank of France which were also increasing. One could hardly say that entire banking networks had yet been created. In fact, the provincial banking creations of the Second Empire often represented traditional activity in a new guise, and took the form of enterprises specialising in banking which had been built on the foundations of a previous business. From 1850 to 1865 Grenoble saw the appearance—or transformation—in this way of four private banks: Gaillard developed from a postal service, Charpenay from cloth and linen merchanting, Ferradou from a flour-milling concern and Lamberton from a grain business. Regroupings were also seen. Additionally at Grenoble other firms were founded in liaison with powerful groups from Lyon, like Pont who was connected with the *Société des Banques Unies*, and Jouvin who was supported in his early stages by the *Société Prost* which already had 100 branches, 40 millions of capital and an annual turnover of 3 milliards. Wherever the Bank of France was operating, credit began to be reorganised on different lines. According to Labasse, the whole banking network was entirely dependent on its branches for the operations of encashing or discounting bills of exchange, of providing ready money for cash balances or for commercial information required for the negotiation of credits.[17] The Bank of France had prepared the ground and credit houses could now establish their own system. The *Comptoirs d'Escompte* of 1848 returned to private hands in the manner of their Paris exemplar and operated numerous powerful establishments. The one in Lille was directed by foremost industrialists like Kuhlmann, the pioneer of the chemical industry and president of the Chamber of Commerce, by flax spinners like Catel-Béghin and by yarn and cloth merchants. In 1866 it became the *Société de Crédit Industriel et de Dépôts du Nord*, with a capital of 20 million francs: that capital was ten times greater than that of the Comptoir and was divided into shares of 500 francs each. The change was made with the support of the *Crédit Industriel* and of its subsidiary, the *Société de dépôts et de comptes-courants* created in 1863. These two banks had already encouraged the creation of similar establishments at Lyon and at Marseille in 1865. Likewise the *Comptoir d'Escompte de Paris*, while finding openings abroad, did not neglect the provinces and set up agencies at Nantes, at Lyon and at Marseille. The *Crédit Lyonnais*, born as a provincial bank, opened branches in Marseille and in Paris and even envisaged winning supremacy in the great French towns. It was soon to erect a whole array of regional agencies around its base at Lyon where it reigned supreme. The most recent of them all—the *Société Générale*—was the first to embark on a systematic coverage of the whole of French territory. It was anxious to secure the greatest number of deposits and to distribute risk as evenly as possible. By 1867 it had a foothold in St Quentin, in Marseille and in Limoges, and by 1869 in St Étienne, St Germain-en-Laye and elsewhere. In 1870 it had 57 agencies or branches.

Yet the 'modernity' of the Second Empire should not be overrated. The typical small-town banker, who derived his strength from his personal contacts and his knowledge of local circles, was far from extinct. For example, in the Nièvre where a branch of the Bank of France had been set up in 1854 thanks to the Regent Lafond (a former deputy for Cosne), the *Comptoir d'Escompte* flourished at first and then collapsed in 1864. A *Caisse* set up in 1857 did not survive although it was underwritten by the *Compagnie Générale des Caisses d'Escompte*. Two pri-

vate banks remained in existence at Nevers. Banking concentration
worked to their advantage and allowed small moneylenders to continue
in existence and even to multiply. There were over thirty of them, six
being at Clamecy, and all were capitalists who changed easily from one
kind of operation to another—from mortgage lending to discounting,
from the role of agents for the payment of dividends to banking proper.
In this region where bankers financed overheads for great landed property but not for industry, Fourchambault had to arrange its own deposits, its current accounts and its cash services. High interest rates
prevailed and with them went a taste for extra caution and for security
which were stronger than the urge to speculate. These were the charac-
teristics of a traditional banking economy, consciously Malthusian and
set in its ways and in its routine. Even here, however, a new age was
at hand. The *Société Générale* came to Nevers in 1869 and the influence of the great Parisian banks was about to make an impact.[18]

The financial market

Thus the years 1850-70 were marked by a great development of banking business, by an increase in the circulation of money and by the
growing power and diffusion of wealth. Concomitantly, there was an
enormous development of the capital market and a new upsurge of
speculation. Dumas *fils*, who was born in 1824, said that 'the Stock Exchange meant to the people of his generation what the cathedral
meant to the men of the middle ages'. The author of *La Question
d'Argent* was one of those playwrights like Ponsard or Émile Augier
who brought to the theatre some rather far-fetched denunciations
against the cult of the new god. However, it did not stop him from
'putting on a false nose in order to go to buy stock on the Exchange
with the money which the publication of his play had brought him'.
Yet, as one could see in the drawings of *le Charivari*, the real thing was
far from adequately represented in these comedies with their traditional
themes and rather thinly drawn characters. Undoubtedly Zola was
aware of the true state of affairs since in his novel *L'Argent* he gave
some rather astonishing pictures of the Stock Exchange, of its men and
its goings-on, though his powerful and overloaded descriptions were
not of the same quality as the evocative creations of Balzac. In this
novel, published in 1891, the action supposedly set around 1866 was
too plainly inspired by the crash of the *Union Générale* occurring in
1882. Balzac's infallible precision was missing; no literary work during

the Second Empire contained that admirable delineation of society and of reality clearer than life which is to be found in the *Comédie Humaine*. Yet, in Zola, the facts themselves were clear enough.

In 1851 the Paris Stock Exchange quoted some 118 shares representing about 11 milliard francs, of which rather more than 2 milliards was foreign money. In 1869, 307 shares were quoted with a portfolio of 31 milliards, a third of which was foreign. These reasonably accurate figures give an overall idea of the capitalist upsurge between the two dates, and show the kind of operation undertaken by stockbrokers. The asset value of a stockbroking business rose from 280,000 francs in 1818 to a value of more than 2 millions in 1856. When allowed to do so, the unofficial brokers, expelled from the *Casino de la Chaussée d'Antin* to the boulevard, operated in the open air; they had to leave the boulevard in 1859, but soon returned to the neighbouring square of the Palais where their officially recognised colleagues were working. To supply this market it was necessary to lift the fetters which hampered limited companies, and the laws of 1863 and 1867 met the need.

'Bastilles' and battles of finance

As we have seen, transferable shares were held by an increasing number of Frenchmen. Yet Georges Duveau notes that 'the Stock Exchange was a Janus with two faces. If securities were allotted in a more democratic way on one side, the great financial fortresses were growing out of all proportion on the other.' In 1869 Georges Duchêne, a disciple of Proudhon, claimed, before the idea of '200 leading families' became a subject of discussion, that 183 individuals were, in fact, at the head of an 'industrial empire'. They owned over 20 milliards in stocks and shares, either invested or in the course of being issued. 'Banks, credit houses, steamboats, railways, large factories, large-scale metallurgy, gas and all the firms of importance were to be found concentrated in their hands.' These financial groups were real enough even if their overall capital was grossly exaggerated by hostile propaganda. They themselves were divided by long and violent conflicts and the moment of great financial strife had come. There had already been rivalry among the bankers in bidding for public loans, and in the 1840s there had been arguments by the railway companies about the lines to be constructed, but there had not yet been any really major conflict before the appearance on the scene of the *Crédit Mobilier*.

James de Rothschild on one side and the Péreire brothers on the

other were the leaders and symbols of the two camps. Business competition in connection with the profits expected from this or that enterprise stood between them. But there were also other factors—the clash
of two powerful wills and the incompatibility of their respective tem-
peraments and attitudes. The Péreires embodied the genius of the
imperial age in its power and its disarray—popular because it relied on
universal suffrage or on small and medium savings, yet authoritarian in
tone. Duveau has correctly written that the Péreires showed democratic feeling and business dynamism simultaneously. They tried to
prise out from the country itself the means which would give it power
in vast international competition. Yet they went to excess and were
prone to trust to luck and to double their stakes in pushing their fortune. They possessed insight. 'In my thinking,' wrote Isaac Péreire,
'the luck and the power which God bestows on some men must be
considered by them only as an advantage which they are given in order
to accomplish greater tasks than those which are entrusted to others.'

Among the Rothschilds there was no messianism. One may speak of
the Rothschilds because the whole family supported the schemes of
Baron James which soon assumed European dimensions, for he had
resources which his rivals did not possess. Of Jewish stock like the
Péreires, they were firm in their views but of a conservative turn of
mind and with no other aim than to increase their influence—already
considerable. They felt that all they needed was a further expansion
of their business, but always along the same lines. They had little sense
of adventure. In spite of their enormous wealth and their giant enterprises, their outlook was rather narrow. Yet they were wiser than the
Péreires and better calculators of risk. If they had any ideal of their
own it was peace and not adventure. It is true that theirs was the peace
of well-gratified conquerors, in the style of Bismarck, and in their own
way they wielded formidable power. One may read in the *Mémoires
d'un Coulissier*, by Ernest Feydeau, the description of the huge office
where the Baron James and his three sons worked in their large building in the rue Laffitte. They clearly inspired Zola for the background
to Gundermann, a leading character in his novel *L'Argent*. 'Through
an unbearable din and in the middle of chaos and disorder' the Baron
received, all day long, brokers, courtiers, bankers, general investors—
'a crowd of people belonging to the three sexes—masculine, feminine
and beggar . . . dealers in precious stones spread their caskets of jewels
under the baron's weary eyes; dealers in pottery and pictures came to
offer their rarest items; and people in droves came to solicit inform-

ation'. The horde pursued James de Rothschild into the nearby room where he took his meal with his family. 'Occasionally, in spite of his natural gaiety and his good fellow feeling he was exasperated.' Then he would address one of his agents in an angry voice: 'Buy me 5 Nord' or 'Sell me 3 Vieille Montagne' just as one might throw a dog a bone to gnaw. The agents withdrew after a deep bow.

One can easily understand the antagonism that existed between James de Rothschild, 'a tough, strong banker with set ideas, who would see in railways only an opportunity for profitable issues and other financial gains' and Émile Péreire, 'a romantic entrepreneur who could foresee the improvements the railways would bring'. While Péreire was full of enthusiasm and anxious to start, to spend, to build, or to expand, Rothschild proceeded cautiously and was prepared to wait. Where the one wished to leave a monument the other wished to leave a fortune. Moreover, Péreire was too strong a personality to be content with a subordinate position and Rothschild was not a man to tolerate equals. For Rothschild the setting up of the *Crédit Mobilier* was a personal affront. In his eyes the Péreires were intruders. He did not resent them for being newcomers; indeed, there was always room for new respectable firms ready to play the game according to the rules. Rather, he felt that the Péreires undermined his personal hegemony and he was needled by the insolence of Émile Péreire. This former subordinate, this man whom he had trained, had the impertinence to offer him a tiny share in the new concern as a favour. Worst of all was the consideration that, given the almost infinite possibilities of limited companies, the Péreires might well realise their aims. The entire wealth of the Rothschilds, no matter how large, could hardly compete with the savings of the whole of France. Was there, then, a clash of personalities rather than a conflict of ideas? It was true that the Rothschilds—and all the major banks—had since the forties adopted the practice of making investments especially in railways and, in respect of those operations that linked them to the capital markets and to the Stock Exchange, they were obliged to sell some of the issue to a difficult and changing public with the possibility of making a fortune but also with the risk of losing money. Hence they adopted a practice of adjustment, of making some room for other firms, of sharing opportunities and risks in the expectation of similar treatment in return. Their motto was 'live and let live in mutually benevolent neutrality' and their symbol was 'the small allowance of shares, customarily reserved in any issue, for friendly firms not participating'. Thus the 'reputedly old bank' was capable of adapting itself to the new requirements of capitalism by creating 'an unwritten code of conduct, designed to ensure the maximum of security and to limit the harmful effects of competition'. We have already mentioned that several important Parisian firms helped to establish the *Crédit Mobilier*. They saw it as 'a great bank', yet less 'refined and specialised' than themselves; it was admirably organised to attract the savings of modest capitalists without assuming any responsibility towards them since it was a limited and anonymous company. To consider the conflict between the Rothschilds and the Péreires as a confrontation of 'old versus new bank' would certainly be an exaggeration. The Fould family, for example, were divided. The family bank directed by Benoît Fould supported the *Crédit Mobilier* whereas the minister Achille Fould—who had been a joint partner in his brother's firm and was still a sleeping partner—supported the other side. The Rothschilds were considerate in their treatment of the Péreires at least until 1855, and later there was one occasion when they managed to co-operate with them in an exceptional Spanish enterprise. The Rothschilds were being true to their character—stifling their feelings and setting their mind on the gain expected from a short term association. But, on the whole, the Péreires certainly had the goodwill of the Emperor and serious claims to his gratitude, even though his marriage had brought him closer to the Rothschilds, who had already been long connected with the Montijo family. The hunt at Ferrières which Napoleon III attended with the Baron on 17 December 1862 was an event which infuriated the Péreires. In the Emperor's entourage opinion was divided. Morny and Persigny—the men of 2 December—supported the masters of the *Crédit Mobilier* on important occasions. According to Girard, Michel Chevalier was for a long time their associate, sharing the same ideological origins and a common dream of an imperial 'New Deal'. Yet the 'specialists', the 'budget balancers'—men, like Fould, opposed to abnormal expenditure—were attracted by the cautious financial policy of the Orleanists. Morny, sensing what was coming, was to join them in 1860. The Civil Service, too, mistrusted the Péreires who readily denounced the collusion between the Talabots (their enemies) and de Franqueville, the influential director of the *Ponts et Chaussées*. The latter was one of the *polytechniciens* whose esprit de corps was even stronger than among the Saint-Simonians. The support of the Empire had contributed to the success of the Péreires and protected them for a while, but it was not to save them.

Splendour and downfall of the Pereires

The challengers in this great duel were the Péreires themselves, for the *Crédit Mobilier* had a flying start.[20] Its shares—500 francs at par—opened at 1,100 francs on the Stock Exchange at the end of November 1852 and reached the record point of 1,982 in March 1856. The dividend rose from 13 per cent in 1853 to 40 per cent in the distribution of 1855, to yield the enormous net profit of 28 million francs. Enterprises launched or taken over by the *Crédit Mobilier* multiplied in France and beyond its frontiers. There were transport concerns like the *Compagnie du Midi* promoted in 1852 (which controlled both a railway and a canal), the *Compagnie de l'Est* founded in 1853 and the *Compagnie de l'Ouest* resulting from a merger effected in 1855. Some railway lines were promoted in the north of Spain and in Andalusia, in Switzerland, in Austria, and even in Russia. Other projects were the *Compagnie Générale Maritime*; heavy industry such as steelmaking in the region of St Étienne and mines in Galicia and in Leon; property companies like the Rivoli buildings; and banking firms like the Crédit Espagnol and many others.

Nevertheless, the financial basis of the operations was by no means sound. Although it was rather partial to the Péreires, the imperial government refused them permission to issue bonded notes in 1853. The issue was an innovation which was technically questionable and obviously regarded with disfavour by the Bank of France. In 1855 the *Crédit Mobilier* produced a more reasonable request: it wished to launch a long term loan of 240,000 bonds worth 500 francs each at 3 per cent interest, redeemable at par in 90 years, and offered at 280 francs. Yet Magne, the Minister of the Interior, was worried by the 'wild impulses' resulting in recklessness on the capital market and forbade the loan. On 9 March 1856 a decree prohibited the issue of all new shares. Hence the *Crédit* was obliged to operate with its capital—wholly subscribed by then and amounting, it was true, to some 60 millions—and with its deposits, which continued to flow in to the extent of 103 millions in the balance sheet of 1855 but which were payable on demand or on short term. These resources could fail them at a time of crisis, thereby lowering the price of shares and unleashing a wave of withdrawals. Some commitments entailed the payment of fixed interest, and others involved the payment of attractive dividends so that dividends were distributed recklessly in order to promote confidence and no provision was made for the building up of reserves. The

Péreires made use of these resources to meddle in dangerous operations and they held a portfolio of shares, subject to all the fluctuations of the Stock Exchange, which could not possibly yield a steady income. Inevitably, the enterprises they financed were not always the most rewarding. The *Ligne du Midi* received great publicity and an inauguration marked by the ballyhoo on 22 April 1857 when two trains met at Toulouse, one arriving from Bordeaux with Émile and the other from Cette with Isaac, the two brothers embracing to the cheers of the crowd. Yet the line yielded only a meagre profit. The Péreires' rivals often secured stronger positions in the network of the 'great industrial points of control'. The Rothschild group acted against the Péreires at every opportunity. In Austria, where the Rothschilds had many advantages since they were well known, they constructed a railway network by the Semmering line when the Péreires sought to control the Simplon in Switzerland. The Rothschilds gained possession of one of the Péreires' projects by founding the Kredit-Anstalt bank at Vienna and in Spain they acquired the mines of Huelva and the coalmines in the Asturias. In France itself the Péreires failed to control the main route, the 'great isthmus' through which the P.L.M. was to go. Already under the Second Republic attempts to gain the concession for it had come to nothing. In January 1852 Paulin Talabot organised the great ironmasters of central France against them—Schneider of Le Creusot, Émile Martin of Fourchambault, Drouillard of Alais and Jules Hocher of Saint Étienne—and obtained the concession for Lyon–Avignon which soon became the Lyon–Méditerranée. Meanwhile the Paris–Lyon line fell into the control of a powerful Anglo-French syndicate. It consisted of the London and Paris Rothschilds, the Barings, Devaux, Masterman, Hutchinson, and all the major bankers: Mallet, Hottinguer, Bartholony, Paccard, Pillet-Will, Dassier and even Isaac Péreire. But the latter was dwarfed in this coalition of interests which was soon to turn against the *Crédit Mobilier* once the *Crédit*'s promoters had broken their agreement with Baron James. The *Nord* remained a fief of the Rothschilds, and Léon Talabot, Paulin Talabot's brother, was one of the great ironmasters: these were further factors to the disadvantage of the Péreires.

In their fight for control of the railways the Péreires were unsuccessful. However, the idea of the Grand Central remained to be exploited. The construction of a railway in the central mountainous region was technically difficult and from an economic point of view it would bring uneven returns. Yet it seemed justified because of the region's wealth of coal. At the time the mines were certainly the foremost in France but their importance had been grossly exaggerated by propaganda and they were presented as the source of fabulous treasures—as a future Swansea or a future Charleroi. In 1853 Seraincourt (of Aubin-Decazeville), the Delahantes (of the *Mines de la Loire*), and English bankers (like Masterman and Hutchinson, who were investing in several French companies in the hope that they would be a better proposition than new ventures in their own country)—all participated with the *Crédit Mobilier*, under the patronage of the dukes of Morny and of Mouchy, to undertake the operation. At first the enterprise was given much publicity. Since the name of Morny was associated with it, it could be presented as an undertaking approved by the Emperor. Perhaps the Emperor attracted the subscriptions of people in 'high society', including well-known dancers and comedians. In fact, the difficulties inherent in the enterprise—the adverse circumstances and all the rivalry it had to face—hastened the collapse of the Grand Central. In 1856-7, according to Audiganne, 'the scattered bones of the giant' were shared between the Paris–Orleans line—synonymous with Bartholony—and the P.L.M., which was the result of the 1857 merger under the aegis of Talabot.

1857 was undoubtedly a bad year for the Péreires. The economic crisis meant that the shareholders of the *Crédit Mobilier* received only their statutory 5 per cent, and the dividends of the early years were far from attainment. More serious yet were the difficulties experienced by the railway companies still anxious to issue their shares, since less profitable secondary lines were now being opened and they could not distribute inflated dividends as they had done in the early days of the Empire. Consequently measures were taken towards reorganisation but the Péreires did not benefit from them. The direct intervention of the Bank of France in the finance market operated to the advantage of the 'antisystem' of all their opponents. That intervention also emphasised the excessive ambitions of the *Crédit Mobilier* in its assumption of the role of principal if not sole supplier of funds for French social overhead capital. Then, in 1858, the Franqueville Conventions laid down a new order for the railway companies. Its complex rules need not detain us here but they mark a date in French history. They virtually reduced railway shares to preference stock. The future of railways was no longer in the hands of the government or the Stock Exchange but in those of the small saver. From then on the companies would have to depend on him for their loans and on his ability—or lack of it

K

—to absorb them. As Girard has pointed out, railway shares became an 'institution' and were no longer the subject of speculation. Great capitalists lost all interest in them after the Conventions were passed. Enfantin wrote on 3 March 1858:

> I am assured that the Péreires have completely given up railways and that they are only concerned now with acquiring plots of land included in the imperial development scheme for the boulevards. Indeed, that is the only activity left for those who cannot remain without doing anything... We have seen the end of normal business, of the kind of business which has been so profitable. One has to face the facts.

Even though the *Crédit Mobilier* still had under its control all the networks which it had floated or taken over, it went through a phase of relative idleness and of slender returns in 1858-59. The sixties saw a return to activity. Vast urban speculations were now added, but no new railway companies as it had not been able to acquire the Cette-Marseille line in 1863. The Rivoli developments had been turned, in 1858, into the *Compagnie Immobilière de Paris* and a merger was then created with two ventures at Marseille—the *Société des Ports* and *la Rue Impériale*—to form one property company with a capital of 50 millions. A number of concerns were floated or reorganised—the Omnibus Company of Paris, the *Entrepôts et Magasins Généraux de Paris* and the *Gaz de Paris et de Marseille*. The salt works of the *Midi* were taken over. The concessions for the steamship lines Le Havre—New York and St Nazaire—West Indies enabled the *Compagnie Maritime* (founded in 1855) to be converted into the *Compagnie Transatlantique* of 1861. Insurance companies like *La Confiance* and *La Paternelle* were founded and in Spain the *Union* and the *Phoenix*. Banking subsidiaries in London and in Amsterdam were established, and the Ottoman Bank and the Italian *Crédit Mobilier* were opened. In 1863, according to Duchêne, Émile Pèreire controlled nineteen companies with $3\frac{1}{2}$ milliards of capital. The good years seemed to have returned; if the profits were not so high as they had been in 1855 or 1856 they were still quite substantial.

Yet nothing had changed in the financial structure of the *Crédit Mobilier*. Its commitments remained very heavy or were even increased by advances made to new firms, and liquid assets were almost nil. The audacity and resourcefulness of the Péreires led them to a venture which would have given them more room for manoeuvre. Since Savoy was annexed to France in 1860 they thought of taking over the note-issuing bank at Annecy as a rival to the Bank of France. They would strike money themselves, be assured of unlimited credit, unleash an ample inflation to create a fall in the value of money and thus stimulate a rise on the Stock Exchange. All that would revive business. But the government gave them no support and the *Banque de Savoie* was absorbed in 1865 by the Bank of France which retained its monopoly.

On the morrow of this abortive operation, difficulties began to accumulate. Their new burst of activity brought nothing but trouble to the Péreires. Their creations of the sixties came at the wrong time: during the last four years of the Empire business became slack and the so-called 'money strike' immobilised an enormous amount of funds in the Bank of France. Their property speculations quickly turned sour. They were easily able to supplant Mirès at Marseille—a town which seemed to symbolise all their hopes even before the Suez Canal strengthened its position as the gateway to the East. Yet the failure to acquire the Cette-Marseille line prevented them from having a railway station in the port, and they were unable to exploit the economic possibilities of the harbour. It meant that they could not make the profit which they had anticipated on the land acquired there. Moreover, their property company was already heavily in debt to the *Crédit Foncier* for its property development in Paris, and had failed in the selling or leasing of the new buildings of the *rue Impériale*. The *Crédit Mobilier* continued to support it and lent it 79 millions. The railway enterprises in Portugal and in Spain were similarly in jeopardy. In 1866 catastrophes multiplied with floods, epidemics, the abandonment of Mexico and the 'thunderblow' of Sadowa. The atmosphere of general crisis was reflected even more acutely on the Stock Exchange. In the midst of growing disasters, nine government brokers unloaded their holding, and the manipulations of the Péreires—already in a bad way— aroused violent hatred against them. The doubling of the capital of the *Crédit Mobilier*, which the Emperor could not refuse to such old members of his glorious régime, excited 'endless curses' in January 1866. Determined to revalue their shares at all costs, the Péreires bought in the market and, thanks to the restoration of peace in Europe, the shares did achieve a rise in price. Having fallen from 880 at the beginning of the year to 420 in June, the shares recovered to 683 in September. But the government now abandoned them; Rouher, Fould, and Béhic, another friend of Talabot, imposed their will on Napoleon III and raised difficulties for each new issue. In December the *Crédit Mobilier* announced that it would distribute the statutory 5 per cent only to bearers of the new shares. At that point came collapse. After March 1867 the share fell for all time below par. It was to fall as low as 140. Émile Péreire turned in vain to the *Crédit Foncier* for help: its governor Frémy was connected with Péreire's traditional enemies and the deputy governor, Soubeyran—the natural son of Fould—sought only 'to tire him out in continual speculations on the Stock Exchange'. The Bank of France let it be known that it would intervene only if the Péreires resigned. The press was unleashed. Mirès, ready to retaliate, suggested that the directors of the *Immobilière* should be asked to offer their personal fortune as a guarantee. Boudon concluded that 'when the Saint-Simonian pirates can no longer speculate, they can no longer live'.

The Péreires handed in their resignation in December 1867, and in the new year they had to leave the *Transatlantique*. Pouyer-Quartier took the offensive to the Legislative Corps: 'The *Crédit Mobilier* is the trunk of a tree producing only poisonous fruit from its branches and one of those branches is the *Translantique*'. Certainly the Péreires did not retire altogether from the business world either in France, where the *Compagnie du Nord* among other concerns remained their fief, or outside France where their interests remained powerful—in Austria, for example. However, they had lost the great business campaign which they had waged with so much zeal following the coup d'état of 2 December 1852. They were to die—Émile in 1875 and Isaac in 1880—at about the time when the Freycinet Plan 'marked the end of Saint-Simonian France'. At least 'men like the Péreires had their moment in history. As pioneers, they gave a new ethos to the age-old phenomenon of the company promoter'.[21]

Mires—or the life of a gambler

There was a place for lesser personalities in the arena of the great financial struggles in which the Péreires, the Rothschilds and the Talabots tended to outshine others. Jules Isaac Mirès—previously mentioned—was one of these lesser men. Rouher said in 1856 'that he was a financial personality whose importance was of recent date. Mirès is to Péreire what Péreire is to Rothschild'. One can hardly avoid a mention of this highly characteristic figure of an age in which 'business is other people's money', as the younger Dumas wrote.[22]

He was a Jew from Bordeaux, like the Péreires (whom he met only in Paris) and like his partners Moïse Millaud and Solar. He was born in 1809, nine years after Émile Péreire and three years after Isaac, but he was not an educated bourgeois in their style, ready to take up any doctrine with enthusiasm. The son of a small watchmaker, he started his own career in a humble way as a contact man or solicitor for settling 'disputes' first in Bordeaux and then in Paris; it was a rather shady and dubious business in the course of which he incurred a sentence for wounding and fighting. He found the crisis of 1848 advantageous for he bought the *Journal des Chemins de Fer* with Millaud for 1,000 francs—a sum which the Péreires may have lent him. Then came *La Patrie*, the *Conseiller du Peuple* (Lamartine's news-sheet), *l'Evénement*, *le Pays* and *le Constitutionnel*. They were papers of different appeal which enabled him to influence various sections of society. Once he had gained control over those papers he was able to establish a *Société des journaux réunis* which had some influence on Morny. He was also in a position to advise capitalists badly hit by the crisis who were in search of more fortunate areas of speculation. Besides his press empire he opened a kind of stockbroking business-cum-deposit bank with a capital of 5 million francs. By playing a shady game on the Stock Exchange Mirès speculated in the shares with the money entrusted to him by the subscribers and so enhanced his fortune.

The coup d'état brought enormous profit to Mirès, who had committed himself to a rise in prices. Millaud pulled out after sharing a gain of some 8 million francs with his partner. Mirès replaced him with another publicist—Solar. Several of Solar's monarchist acquaintances were then appointed to what was grandly described as a 'watch council'. Up to this point Mirès had been in the wake of the Péreires but he now felt strong enough to spread his wings. He founded the *Caisse générale des Chemins de Fer* whose capital soon reached 50 million francs, almost equalling that of the *Crédit Mobilier*. He plunged into big business and was soon in competition with the most powerful financial groups. He obtained a Spanish loan from the Rothschilds and ensured railway concessions for himself in Spain, with the Pampelona–Saragossa line, and in the Papal States—for which he placed Roman railway bonds in France without worrying unduly about restrictive measures imposed by the government. It was true that he clashed, unsuccessfully, with the Péreires over the railway network in the Pyrenees, but at Marseille it was he who ousted the Péreires—a considerable achievement.

The creation of great steamship lines and of ancillary harbour installations seemed an indispensable adjunct of railway construction during the period of the Second Empire. This necessity was felt more acutely at Marseille than anywhere else. The importance of the port in-

creased greatly on account of the big boost in Mediterranean trade
which took place before the opening of the Suez Canal and was partly
associated with French settlement in Algeria and with active French
policy in Italy, in the Black Sea and in the Levant. The *Revue Contemporaine* wrote in 1865 that 'Marseille expresses the commercial
policy of the whole world'. Capital from Marseille played a considerable part in Algerian railways (with Rostand) and in the Suez Company.
Traditional port activity was in full expansion and Grandval the 'sugar
king' employed 1,500 workmen and realised 600,000 francs in yearly
profits. Plans for creating steelworks multiplied. Naturally, steamship
companies developed and increased, starting with the *Compagnie
Fraissinet* in 1836; there followed the *Compagnie de Navigation Mixte*
in 1850, *Messageries Maritimes* in 1851, the *Compagnie Paquet* in
1860-63 and the *Société Générale de Transports Maritimes à vapeur*
in 1865. A shipbuilding firm, *Forges et Chantiers de la Méditerranée*,
was founded in 1856. Perhaps there was something out of proportion,
something artificial and precarious in this exuberant prosperity. According to Edmond About 'the passion for personal enjoyment was stronger
than the desire to accumulate funds; there are not ten fortunes of 5
million francs in the town'.[23] Nevertheless, among the great capitalists
of the time there was a merciless fight for the control of Marseille.
Talabot with his Algerian mines and the P.L.M., the *Messageries
Maritimes* and the *Société des Docks et Entrepôts* seemed to have all
the necessary assets. Yet in 1856 Mirès, in his turn, obtained the gas
concession for Marseille and the land of the Joliette. He secured the
land by offering 50 francs per metre against 40 offered by Talabot. The
Péreires tried in vain to nullify the contract and to undertake development in place of Mirès. The latter, moreover, regarded it only a a pure
speculation. In order to take an immediate profit he put his contract
in the hands of the *Société des Ports de Marseille*, a company in share
partnership but lacking the necessary authorisation for a limited company. He allotted himself 5 millions of the capital supplied. The minister Magne stated:

> Monsieur Mirès will doubtless make a considerable profit but his
> profit, already partly made, does not come from resale of the land but
> from the speculative ethos which he has injected into the affair...
> That is the real concern of Monsieur Mirès. The interest of the
> share-holder comes afterwards; it is then that disillusionment will
> begin and dreams quickly vanish.

Meanwhile, Mirès prospered and founded a *Société des Gaz et Hauts
Fourneaux de Marseille* operating coalmines at Portes in the Gard. He

reached the high point of his career in 1860 when his daughter married a Polignac. In September of that year the Emperor came to his stronghold of Marseille to decorate him with the Légion d'Honneur. He was then said to control 350 millions of capital.

In actual fact, his fortune was fragile since it was based on the assumption that new speculations would come just in time to provide the funds necessary for supporting previous ones. From 1854 Enfantin suspected him of selling for his own account shares deposited in his bank, and in 1855 Rouher suggested that 'close investigation of his books and accounts would provide positive proof against him'. This boundless activity annoyed the government, which wished to put a brake on speculation. The strong positions he had assumed at Marseille aroused the envy of the Péreires and the Talabots. But because of his lack of foresight he made a number of enemies in that same year of 1860 when he seemed to be triumphant. His projected Ottoman loan irritated the Emperor, whose troops intervened in the Levant to protect Christians against Turks, and irritated other high financiers who had their own issues of stock to place. A Republican deputy, Darimon, spoke of Émile Péreire embracing the author of a pantomime on 'The Massacres of Syria' and crying out: 'It is the last blow struck against the Ottoman loan'. With the treaty of commerce and the return to power of Persigny, the Péreires were then well in favour. The complaint of a dissatisfied partner was enough to provoke a lawsuit against Mirès (on 15 December 1860) who was arrested some weeks later, or as spiteful comments had it, when the high personalities to whom he had lent money had had the time to pay off their debt and to leave no evidence of it. Indeed, opinion was roused by the Mirès affair and people were generally on his side, especially so for female public opinion. In the whole he was regarded as having been too obliging towards high dignitaries of the régime rather than really blameworthy. One senator, Count Siméon, who was implicated in the affair, was asked to justify himself during one of the sessions of the Senate. Morny and several ministers were connected with Mirès through the *Constitutionnel* newspaper if not in any other way. Legal actions flowed in. The great barrister Berryer (a Legitimist deputy very much involved in the politics of Marseille and connected with the Rothschilds) turned the defence of Mirès into a charge against the *Crédit Mobilier* which he made out to be 'the greatest gambling house in Europe'. Yet Mirès was in disrepute. The government prevented him from floating a new loan to make a new start. In 1864 Morny failed to obtain permission for him to create a *Banque des États* which he wished to establish for the placing of public loans. He was successful only in founding a news-sheet —*La Presse*—in 1866. With some bitterness he observed the infiltration of Péreires into his own area of Marseille and then, as we have seen, rejoiced in their discomfiture. He died at Marseille in 1871, and there his memory is not held in bad esteem.

3 INDUSTRY

One can contrast the flamboyant and unsuccessful career of a Mirès with more lasting achievements. It was with the Second Empire that the great masters of industry assumed a social importance and a place of merit as supreme representatives of the capitalist world. Previously, the bankers had been the only ones to aspire to such heights. The typical case-study of this rise in status is that of the head of *Le Creusot* —Joseph Eugène Schneider. When he died in 1875 *L'Illustration* allotted him a page which was controversial in many respects but accurate on the following point:

> Until 1830 the great concentrations of social influence and material power had only one instrument and one source of supremacy—wealth and money. Besides the power of the state and the moral influence of intelligence and knowledge there existed only one material and tangible power—finance and banking. The Rothschilds were the kings of gold. Steam power came unexpectedly on the scene and other realms of power were organised and established—the realms of the kings of iron.
>
> This entirely new power, which was generated by a number of bold scientific schemes and by hard-working application of intelligence, was much more democratic and personal than financial power which was dependent on the fickleness of fortune and the hazards of speculation. Rising from humble levels, the Talabots and the Schneiders seized the great levers of this formidable power almost at once. At 30 years of age Monsieur Talabot, a small-time engineer, was drawing the plans for his first railway line. At 21 years of age, Monsieur Schneider, a humble assistant to the Baron Seillière, assumed the management of the iron works of Bazeilles. Thirty years later, having become railway king and machine king respectively, these two men dealt with governments on equal terms and turned upside down the economic organisation of France and of Europe. Masters in their own sphere, they virtually subordinated finance to industry, and gold to steel.
>
> By a significant wielding of power, Monsieur Schneider symbolised the intervention of industrial and economic influence in the political direction of society. With him large-scale industry took its place in the assemblies and counsels of governments and in the corridors of power in the state.

It was an apt description even in its exaggeration. Allowances may be made for the necessary superlatives of an obituary, and the chronology has to be altered—for it was after the middle of the century rather than in 1830 that large-scale industry really triumphed. The advent of iron kings and their political importance was not absolutely new for ironmasters had sat in the governments of the Restoration period, but that importance had multiplied and was symbolised by the presence of Schneider in the presidential seat of the Palais-Bourbon from 1867 until 4 September 1870. The important feature was the prevailing mentality. For his admirer in *L'Illustration*, as for bourgeois opinion overall, Schneider was the ideal type of entrepreneur, the new king of capitalist society. He was a self-made man through his personal merit, his competence, his character and his work. The same point has been made by Lambert-Dansette in a recent study on the dynasties of textile manufacturers in Lille. He stresses the fact that the age provided 'an ethos, an atmosphere of social opportunity and a set of circumstances particularly favourable to the replacement of an old élite by a new one'. Yet it 'only provided the primary conditions, the right setting for the ascent of the bourgeoisie. The fruits were yet to be reaped'; the new capitalists did not obtain their wealth by means of a passive yielding of power by traditional groups.

The 'iron kings'

To achieve success the new capitalists undoubtedly needed the support of older financial circles. The example of the Talabots may be mentioned again. The father, from peasant origins, was a magistrate at Limoges. He had three daughters and five sons, one of whom became President of the Tribunal in Limoges and the other four industrialists. Of the four, Jules had been an army officer whereas the other three were graduates of the *École Polytechnique*. Edmond was a visionary and the only one deeply committed to the Saint-Simonianism of heroic days, but he was carried off by cholera in 1832; Léon was a fellow student of Enfantin at the *École Polytechnique*; and Paulin, an engineer of the *Ponts et Chaussées*, was the most practical of them if not the most enlightened. 'If you had arrived at the point of achieving a possible banking system,' he said to his friends, 'you would have done more for the future than in converting 100,000 people.' They began their careers in the service of a group which included merchants from Bordeaux (like Garrigou), major bankers (like Périer and Delessert), and heroes of the Empire like Marshal Soult, Duke of Dalmatia, minister and president in the Council of Louis Philippe. Early in their career they showed cold accuracy of judgement and they eliminated concerns which had no future, such as the Bazacle workshop in Toulouse which made files and scythes, and consolidated those they considered promising: the steel works of the Saut-du-Tarn, the ironworks and foundries of Alais and the mines of La Grand'Combe. Odilon Barrot—another star of Orleanist politics—whose family had just repurchased the mineral lease of Castries, decided to join the group. Having gained the support of the Rothschilds in 1837, they were able to raise 6 million francs and then successfully put pressure on the government to let them have another 6 millions. The valley of the Rhône—the great axis of France—became the principal scene of their activities, with Mediterranean extensions at Marseille and in Algeria. Up to 1848, their plans were more spectacular than their achievements. But from 1849 onwards, the Talabots—with continued support from the Rothschilds —gained the collieries of northern France (where they organised the merger of Denain-Anzin) and various mines, ironworks and steamship companies in Belgium.[24] Under the second Empire their power became enormous by virtue of the P.L.M. and other business concerns which could perhaps be roughly described as the Rothschild-Talabot group. Their conflict with the Péreires showed how great their influence was, but it is a question whether or not that influence was entirely due to their financial and industrial genius. It was, if one takes into account their ability to take advantage of opportunities and to find the right kind of support and cooperation just when they needed it. The Soult family helped them to begin operations and then the Rothschilds were induced to give them further support.

The story of the Schneiders was equally illuminating. Adolphe Schneider (1802-45) and Joseph Eugène Schneider (1805-75) came from ordinary middle-class origins in Lorraine. One of their uncles had attended the *Polytechnique* and had been an army officer under Napoleon and the Bourbons; then he had become a deputy and, for a while, a minister under the July monarchy. Their own career began in the offices of the Seillière Bank. After the younger one had gone to Bazeilles for a period of specialised training, their employers put them in charge at Le Creusot. In 1836 they purchased it for 2,686,000 francs when the firm was in very bad shape. From the time of the Revolution it had experienced a series of failures, despite the injection of capital and the help of English technical experts brought over in 1826 by Manby and

Wilson. Thus, the Seillière Bank installed the firm of Schneider on the very site where it was to make its fortune; it was the same site which had already been connected with the experiments of François Ignace de Wendel, the other great name in French metalmaking.[25]

At the time exceptional opportunities were open to the new masters of Le Creusot, as they were to all those French ironmasters who could adopt the techniques of smelting by coke, of the Siemens oven (for iron) and of the Bessemer converter (for steel). The new techniques were gradually improved and more widely used during the Second Empire. The railway companies placed enormous orders for rails, for bridge framework, for railway stations and for locomotives and rolling stock. The first locomotive made in France was produced at Le Creusot in 1838. Demand was so great that ironmasters could fix their own prices and charge the highest possible transport costs. They could pick up business deals or reject them at random without having to fear competition. There were close links between 'iron kings' and 'railway kings'; as an example, Paulin Talabot controlled the P.L.M. and Léon Talabot was the master of Denain-Anzin. The industrial requirements of the country were increasing and ranged from engines for large steamships to war equipment—it was the war of 1870 which turned the Schneiders into 'cannon merchants'. In 1867 Le Creusot was an enormous works employing nearly 10,000 workmen. If its masters were powerful industrialists they were also influential in politics. Joseph Eugène Schneider obtained in 1845 the deputy's seat left vacant by the death of his eldest brother in 1842, and became president of the *Corps Législatif*. He exercised a heavy paternalism over the small town dominated by his own firm. He controlled the employment of men, the municipality, the police and a great number of lodgings. When his grandson Eugène was born in 1868 Le Creusot was covered with illuminations, poles and streamers dedicated to 'Schneider III'. He was caught unawares by the strikes of 1869-70 but his comment on them was: 'My workmen don't seem to think that there are already enough deaths as it is'. He decided to fight back and to meet the stoppage of work by a general lock-out, obtaining without difficulty from the government the despatch of a sizable army. Financial power followed on from his political power, for he was president of the *Société Générale* and a regent of the Bank of France.

The de Wendel enterprise was comparable in size with that of Le Creusot. The collieries of Petite-Rosselle and the Stiring works were added to the original de Wendel plants at Hayange and Moyeuvre. At the end of the Second Empire the de Wendels reached a production of 134,000 tons of cast iron and 112,000 tons of pig iron, against the Schneiders' figures of 130,000 and 100,000. They employed 7,000 skilled workers, 800 iron miners and 1,400 coalminers. In order to house them they built a model village at 'Stiring-Wendel' which the Emperor opened in 1857. Yet Charles de Wendel was not a very enthusiastic supporter of the imperial régime. He had married a Commingues-Guitant, who came from old Legitimist nobility—although the family was also related to an ambassador of Louis Philippe and to the Montijo family. He became a deputy in 1849, but in 1867, prompted by the jealousy he felt towards Schneider, he decided to resign. He had already shown his resentment at the time of the free trade treaty of 1860, but he was a businessman of great vision and had readily accepted the measure even if it was passed rather hastily. To quote his own words: 'I believe that it is impossible to stop the movement towards greater freedom of trade'. His objection was to the fact that Schneider had been consulted and he had not. The financial connections of de Wendel were less numerous and less important than those of Schneider, yet here again the Seillière Bank had contributed to expansion. Nevertheless, the enterprise kept its family character, remaining until 1871 the property of Marguerite de Wendel, widow of François, and herself a descendant of Martin the founder. Her legal status was that of a partner with her sons Victor (grandfather of François de Curel) and Charles, and with her sons-in-law Theodore de Gargan and the Baron de Coëtlosquet, who were all to die before her.[26]

Behind the Schneiders was a bank and behind the de Wendels was an old and solid family fortune. Many other steelmaking enterprises, even when they appeared to be new, were similarly linked with old family businesses. The founders of *Houillères et Hauts-Fourneaux de Commentry* in 1853 were the Boigues-Dufaud family of Fourchambault and the Rambourg family of Commentry and they were far from being newcomers. However, Commentry-Fourchambault did not have its exceptional standing of former days; general changes of industrial location were soon to shift the centre of French steelmaking towards the north and north-east. After the crisis of 1857 it entered a phase of decline terminating in the collapse of 1898.[27] Specialised metalmaking offered an alternative to the ironmasters of central France and Le Creusot took advantage of the fact. Similarly, the works founded by Petin and Gaudet at Rive-de-Gier and St Chamond—during the reign of Louis Philippe—and those founded by Jackson at Assailly were brought together under the name of *Les Hauts Fourneaux, Forges et Aciéries de la Marine et des Chemins de Fer* and the new name clearly indicated what their new activities were. The Dietrich family still managed their concern at Niederbronn and their steelworks was one of the first in France. Féray, a grandson of Oberkampf, owned several works at Essonnes—mechanical engineering, spinning and papermaking plants. Joseph Magnin was an ironmaster who became a sugar refiner at Brazey-en-Plaine (Côte d'Or), when the free trade agreement of 1860 brought a sharp setback to charcoal smelting; he belonged to an old family of timber merchants who developed small iron mines and smelted metal in the traditional way. Both Magnin and Féray went into politics. Magnin became a republican deputy in 1863 and a member of the government of 4 September 1870. As for Féray, he was at the head of a pressure group which played a decisive role in the National Assembly of 1871.

The Peugeots were another industrial dynasty. To their already numerous and specialised works they added the factory of Valentigney in 1846, with the help of the Japy family. As the crinoline came into fashion the demand for steel frameworks—each one taking from 200 to 400 grammes of steel—became so great that the factory was hardly able to meet it. Then they installed the mill at Beaulieu which produced 7 tons of steel every month. The Valentigney rolling mills turned out 8 tons a month. When, in 1866, crinolines went out of fashion in Paris they continued to receive orders from the provinces and from abroad. Moreover, the range of Peugeot articles became steadily wider. They started making coffee grinders in 1850, clippers for horses in 1869 (followed by clippers for soldiers) and pitchforks in 1878. In 1866 the firm employed 567 workmen. Twenty years later there were 600 at Pont-de-Roide, 700 at Valentigney, 400 at Beaulieu and 900 at Terre-Blanche. After 1885 the bicycle figured among their new articles. The Peugeot group was always aware of the advantages of innovation, but at the same time remained very much a family concern.[28]

Of course, self-made men appeared among the prominent figures in metallurgy. The most typical was Jean François Cail, son of a wheelwright from the Deux-Sèvres region; he had started as an apprentice brazier and a *Compagnon du Tour de France*. In 1836 he went into partnership with his own employer, the chemist Derosne, who had a works at Chaillot. Cail turned this firm, which made equipment for sugarmaking, into a very large engineering establishment with several workshops. It supplied 80 of the 450 locomotives built in France around 1860. Less typical was Gustave Eiffel. The building of the great bridge at Bordeaux in 1860 was a spectacular achievement which was certainly due as much to Eiffel's technical skill as to the enterprise of his employer Nepveu and to the capital supplied by the Belgian group of Pauwels. He came, however from a merchant circle at Dijon and not from a working-class family, and his success was a sign that professional men were beginning to play a major role in industry. Eiffel opened a firm of his own in 1866. But alongside these new men one may quote many examples of employers who belonged to the old school. The Marquis de Grammont, whose family had owned the iron-works at Villersexel for several generations, was a deputy of the left under Guizot but quickly rallied in 1848 and in 1871 to the 'party of order' or to 'moral order'. An even better example was the Baron de Lespérut, described for us by Georges Duveau as the head of 'a very old ironworks' of the Haute Marne which was still using wood and where iron was produced for the making of so-called artistic objects. His works stood on the banks of the Marne, of the Rognon, of the Blaise and of other rivers flowing at a gentle pace. Gardens of pentagonal shape surrounded the buildings. Lespérut had adapted the style of Le Nôtre—at Versailles—to the industrial world. This industrialist who worked at a slow rhythm—like the rivers flowing by his works— also had his moments of extreme discontent. In 1860 he made a violent attack in the Corps Législatif against the trade treaties concluded by the Emperor.[29] Protests against these same treaties came from the last controllers of the 'Catalan ironworks'. As local nobility or wealthy middle-class they had operated in the valleys of the Ariège for a long time but now they were condemned by the archaic nature of their techniques. What destroyed them between 1860 and 1870 was competition from blast furnaces installed at Pamiers and at Tarascon. Thanks to the railways those furnaces could now use coal brought from Carmaux, from Graissessac and from Decazeville. Old capitalists from the days when industrial wealth was based on the forest and the anvil were now supplanted by capitalists who owned local mines and railways.

Textile ownership: concentration and its limits

The effects of the progress of capitalism was similarly felt in other sectors of industry but it was not always followed by a renewal of managerial talent. The old families who survived by adaptation were in competition with the social climbers. The latter acquired their position by hard work, by technical merit and sometimes by luck. Often they relied on funds from outside sources, as though their rising destiny needed the support of well-established backers.[30]

In the textile industry, for example—now no longer a pioneer industry in the field of entrepreneurship as a result of the advent of the new steelmasters—concentration was at last triumphant and claimed its victims. The crises of the Second Empire—cyclical shocks, or cotton famines connected with the Civil War and the interruption of American supplies—put marginal firms out of business and caused the most backward forms of manufacture such as handloom weaving to disappear. Conversely, they strengthened firms which were soundly based or well managed. Fohlen has recently listed the pros and cons of the concentration movement, which was at once technical, geographical and financial. Yet the basic question was the extent to which textile capitalism underwent change. Its relative importance grew with the decline of artisan or semi-artisan competitors, but its structure was little changed. Some of the new firms set up between 1860 and 1870 adopted the modern form of companies owned by shares. Others, which were older, increased their capital by accepting support from banks or from commission houses. The tradition of family enterprise, however, retained its strength in this industry and companies with share ownership remained rare. The great Parisian banks played no part. Fohlen notes that

> the textile industry operated outside the normal capital market open to the public. The French bourgeois of the Second Empire bought state funds and railway bonds and, if they were daring, some shares in metal or mining companies. The public at large did not know about textile firms because the firms made no appeal to the public and were not quoted on the Stock Exchange ... Textiles formed a world of their own and their activities, instead of being known to the public, were conducted in very closed circles.

Not surprisingly, some textile capitalists represented long-standing traditional ownership. The active tenacious group from Mulhouse retained its importance and former prestige. The Second Empire encouraged the group's free trade policy and Jean Dollfus was an ardent defender and even an inspirer of the treaty of 1860. Nevertheless, the imperial government did not approve of their other views, which tended to follow those of English manufacturers. The men of Mulhouse opposed state interference in the national economy and their politics were close to an Orleanist form of liberalism, to put it mildly. In 1869 Mulhouse elected as deputy Scheurer-Kestner, a great industrialist of Thann and a republican. Social paternalism was still practised: employers at Mulhouse built houses for their workmen and encouraged them to save.

In the north, industrialists reached maturity at a later date. In general, they held protectionist views and their catholicism was as strict as the protestantism of Alsace. Nevertheless, they produced unusual personalities, one of whom was Alfred Motte. He was a supporter of free trade and an untiring general entrepreneur who set up various businesses managed by his partners but still under his ultimate control. If northern industrialists were traditionalists they were even more so at Lyon. Silk manufacturers there were a very close community and the concentration movement proceeded extremely slowly. There were 750 manufacturers in 1830 and still as many as 450 in 1860. They overcame the serious difficulties they were faced with by recruiting rural workers; such workers were less demanding since industrial wages constituted only an additional source of income for them. Manufacturers at Lyon were not very bold in their attempts at innovation. Georges Duveau has described them in appropriate terms: 'They were stiff and starchy, wrapped in tradition, and similar to English merchants in dress and appearance'. Elsewhere dynasties as old or even older were to be found. In the woollen industry around Elbeuf, for example, the Flavigny dynasty went back to 1652. Yet members of other old dynasties took an active part in the formation of up-to-date firms like the *Comptoir de l'Industrie Linière*, nominally founded in 1846 but not really making any headway until after 1850; the firm still exists under the name of *Comptoir linier*. It was a very large enterprise issuing 20,000 shares of 500 francs each at the time of its foundation. In its organisation it brought together two capitalist trends: the commercial trend represented by the merchant collecting linen made by hand in the Sarthe, Orne, Calvados and Somme regions; and the industrial trend represented by the owner of a modern spinning mill in the Pas de Calais. Cohin, one of these founder merchants, came from an old family of cloth merchants in the Haut Maine who were well known as early as the seventeenth century. They made a fortune in the eighteenth century by their overseas exports and became even wealthier during the Revolution. In his capacity as managing partner and shareholder Cohin earned an annual income of at least 63,000 francs from the *Comptoir*.[31]

Yet there were also newcomers who were self-made men in the textile industry. During the Second Empire, the economy in general was basically sound but it was prone to sudden bouts of fluctuation which put the talents of the most gifted entrepreneurs to the test. In a sense it was a golden age for the new men. One example of a new entrepreneur was Edward Vaucher, son of a small Swiss watchmaker. He was appointed by his employer (a commission agent in thread and fabric) as manager of a branch in Mulhouse; later, under Louis Philippe, Vaucher set up his own business and by 1857 he had earned a great deal of money which he put into takeover bids, into partnerships and into exclusive contracts. By then he was at the head of a real industrial empire and was readily accepted by the protestant upper class in Mulhouse. Another new industrialist was Pouyer-Quartier, whose success was even greater. Pouyer-Quartier was a self-made man who became one of the biggest manufacturers in Normandy. He owned *La Foudre* —a giant cotton spinning mill in the suburbs of Rouen—and woollen mills in the valley of the Andelle. His works contained combing and weaving sections. Under the Second Empire he began a great political career: from the municipal council he was promoted to the *Conseil Général* and then to the *Corps Législatif*. He became a deputy but fell out with the régime over the tariff question and was defeated in 1869. Nevertheless, he rose to power in 1871 on account of his obsession with protectionism, which he shared with Thiers. As Finance Minister he negotiated the payment of war indemnity with Bismarck, whom he astounded, it is said, by his hostility to beer and alcohol which was greater than the Chancellor's own. He was the image of the newly rich —energetic, vulgar and sure of himself. He bragged in 1869 about the deplorable fact that he earned no more than 800,000 francs a year when he had formerly earned 1,800,000. This was enormous wealth which had been quickly acquired and was precarious. Fohlen concludes that his great mistake lay in being over-impressed by titles, and in choosing for his sons-in-law men of good birth who led his enterprises to ruin and eroded his fortune.

Future pointers: the pioneers of the chemical industry

During the Second Empire, the arrival of new personalities into the business world was not confined to the steel and textile industries; it occurred also in newly growing industrial sectors. The future of the chemical industry, which was taking shape at the time, was to provide a new field of activity for enterprising capitalists.

A very old but active firm figured among the great names of the

L

chemical industry: Saint-Gobain. It merged in 1855 with Saint-Quirin and pursued its brilliant destiny—right up to 1959—under the title of *Compagnies des Glaces et Produits Chimiques de Saint-Gobain, Chauny et Cirey*. Its 3,264 shares were divided among 489 share-holders. Its directors were famous people from different walks of life and among them were Albert, duc de Broglie, the Marquis de Vogüé, the Minister Chevandier de Valdrôme, the Baron Roederer, Frémy, governor of the *Crédit Foncier*, and the chemists Gay-Lussac and Thénard. Management was discreet and accounts were divulged only to selected shareholders. The Board declared in 1862: 'We have always taken out of our reports everything which could lead to an assessment of our cost prices, for we believe that that kind of knowledge could be detrimental to our business'. This obsession for secrecy fitted in with their tendency to apportion profits to reserves rather than to dividends. As a result, the firm needed no loan capital before 1917. It was able to expand, to open a branch in Germany, to absorb in 1872 a great family business in Lyon—the firm of Perret-Olivier—and even to think of a merger with the firm of Kuhlmann.[32] The latter was more recent than Saint-Gobain but showed similar dynamism. Frédéric Kuhlmann, its creator, was a technician who had been a student of Vauquelin the chemist, and had become a professor at Lille. In the industrial environment of the north he found both capital and markets for the small firm which he had created in 1825 as a simple joint-stock company. Commencing with soda and sulphuric acid production he extended very quickly the range of his products. This type of unlimited extension was a feature of the chemical industry which was inclined to use its own by-products. It accounted also for the very powerful and rapid concentration which was forced upon it. Kuhlmann enlarged his enterprise, founded new works and turned it into a share ownership company in 1854, with a capital of more than 5 million francs, and in 1870 into a limited company. After Kuhlmann's death in 1881—followed shortly by the death of his son—the management of the firm was put in the hands of a technocrat by the name of Kolb. The chairmanship of the Board was entrusted to Crespel from Lille, a member of an old textile family. In 1897 it went to Agache, a son-in-law of Kuhlmann, who came from a family of linen merchants.

The firm of Péchiney was founded in 1855 at Salindres in the Gard, on the initiative of two technocrats—Henry Merle and J. B. Guimet—and with the help of capitalists from Lyon. It was a firm floated by shares, with a capital of 4 million francs. 8,000 shares in 1862 were held by 134 shareholders. Here again, the founding of new factories like that at Salins de Giraud in 1856 was soon followed by the launching of new products which were more and more diverse. Soda, acids, phosphate of lime, chlorates and copper sulphate were utilised by soapmakers at Marseille and by wine growers in Languedoc. The outstanding achievement of Salindres was the making of aluminium, which was developed by Sainte-Claire Deville, and for thirty years, from 1860 to 1890, its monopoly was absolute. The chairmen of the Board of Directors were respectively J. B. Guimet, Piaton the notary from Lyon and, after 1887, that strange man Émile Guimet. The latter kept up the dye works which his family owned near Lyon, and he acted as a 'model' employer anticipating, by his practice, laws concerning pensions and workmen's compensation. He also succeeded his father on the Board of the *Compagnie de Navigation Mixte*. But he had far wider interests. He administered the famous technical school of *La Martinière* at Lyon. A great traveller, he brought back from America and Asia the collections which were to constitute the Guimet Museum. He wrote oratorios and even an opera. The real master of Salindres was of a different stamp. Alfred Rangod was brought up by his future father-in-law, a small maker of toys in the rue Quincampoix. He assumed his father-in-law's name of Péchiney and became a chemist and manager of a modest phosphate firm in the Drôme. After being assistant to Henry Merle he succeeded him on his death in 1877 as manager of the firm and called it *A. R. Péchiney et Cie*. He was to rule over it until the early years of the twentieth century.

In the opinion of a friendly biographer, Péchiney was not a very great captain of industry.[33] He was little inclined to welcome innovations and preferred to stick to well-tried methods of manufacture and to improve upon them. He was very slow in adapting to the technical revolution of electrolysis, and after 1890 the aluminium of Salindres lost its outstanding position. He was an excellent businessman but held very strict ideas on the value of money and the sense of economy essential to good firms. Those ideas could be traced to his childhood in the rue Quincampoix and his modest beginnings. He delayed the change of the firm to a limited company until 1896 after proceeding in 1880-2 to a rather inopportune reduction of capital. As an employer he was hard to please, being both strict and interfering. Simultaneously he was director of his own company, a manager of each one of his factories, and general factotum. He was hostile to workmen's pensions because he thought they would destroy the sense of thrift among wage-earners.

He had hardly any other interests than the chemical industry. The sale, after his death, of furniture and toys accumulated in his villa at Hyères revealed no masterpieces. Madame Péchiney—widow of one of Péchiney's former employers—reigned over the *château* constructed near the factory; it was surrounded by a park designed to prove by the luxuriance of its vegetation that chemical products were not harmful. She received the préfet and the bishop there, as well as eminent personalities of the day. She treated partners in the enterprise rather disdainfully. One of them was a protestant who was assured of long favour because he played the organ in church. The virtue of bachelors was strictly watched over. Madame Péchiney took pleasure in marrying them off and it was worth their while not to throw aside plans which she held for them. When she went to Salins de Giraud to sail along the canals of the Camargue her whole entourage was quite ostentatious.

During the sixties a new product made its appearance—petrol. It was to play a vital part in the preoccupations and activities of capitalists of the twentieth century but in those days its importance was only secondary. In the beginning, nobody had any interest in its distribution arrangements, apart from the French firms involved. The first imports mentioned in 1863 by customs statistics, however, aroused the interest of speculators. Once more a Saint-Simonian was in the forefront—Alexandre Deutsch de la Meurthe. In 1843 he created a refinery for vegetable oil at Pantin. Then, in 1854, he opened a distillery for the treatment of colza oil, and this was one of the first to go over to mineral oil. His sons joined him as partners in 1877 and their interests ranged over various technical innovations from asphalt to airships; in addition, they practised a wide philanthropy to which the *Cité Universitaire* of Paris bears witness. An even more lasting future awaited the *Société Desmarais Frères*, founded in 1861, which installed refineries at Colombes, Le Havre and Blaye for oil coming from the United States, the Caucasus and Roumania. Right up to the present day it has remained a very large firm.

The coming of new industrialists?

Whether the French entrepreneur came from a traditional or from a new background, his organisation and his outlook were affected by the victory of capitalism. One feature was simply quantitative. The rise in each firm's profits—resulting from a favourable set of circumstances—and the concentration of production explained the considerable growth of wealth. One example of such growth is seen in the dowries given to the daughters of the Dansette family: 15,000 francs in 1830, 50,000 in 1856 and 300,000 in 1888. An archaic feature of entrepreneurial behaviour, the full economic repercussions of which remained to be seen, contributed to this rapid rise. The majority of entrepreneurs were rather careless about the volume of production and the level of cost and selling prices; in their management they were directly concerned with the amount of overall profit they could obtain. A magistrate declared in 1863 that

> the industrialists of the lower Seine, solely preoccupied in maintaining or accumulating unbelievable profits, maintain or raise the price of yarn and of cloth when they obtain the raw material for almost nothing. This or that manufacturer earns 2 million francs in a year without people paying one centime less for the cloth they are wearing.

New business connections arose between capitalists belonging to various sectors. Once they were no longer obsessed by self-financing of their own enterprises, employers tended to invest in other spheres of activity. Those in the textile industry in Lille became interested in regional banking, in insurance companies (like *Le Nord*), in the chemical industry and in mining (Agache-Kuhlmann, for example, sat on the board of *Anzin*). Nevertheless, they did not renounce their traditional landed investments. If land was no longer a matter for speculation, it was at least a guarantee against the precarious nature of transferable income and a symbol of more enduring values. In this respect, as in others, the capitalists felt a nostalgia for the way of life and the social role of the former nobility. In many cases, their landed possessions proved in the long run to be very profitable business propositions. The enormous increase in the value of land near large towns in course of expansion was greatly to their advantage.

If capitalist entrepreneurs had become a very close-knit community, this situation was partly due to their numerous intermarriages; the sharing of the same interests only reinforced their unity. Marriages were almost always within their circle: 'in order to marry one must own a smoking chimney'. Marriages did not necessarily take place between partners belonging to the same branch of industrial activity but their social background was the same and they belonged to the capitalist élite. The hierarchy of Mulhouse was a case in point. They formed a homogeneous caste as a result of their intricate family bonds. The drawing up of genealogies provides evidence of this state of affairs. The 'Cartulary of the Schlumberger family', undertaken at the beginning of the twentieth century, gives us all the names of industrialists in

Alsace. It starts with the pioneers like Koechlin, Dollfus, Mieg and Blech and then moves to the relatively recent ones like the Siegfrieds. The Siegfrieds only graduated into Mulhouse society when André Siegfried's grandfather married a Blech. The same state of affairs prevailed in the north. Once again, Lambert-Dansette has provided the evidence. Family wealth was consolidated but because of the nature of the line of succession part of the family inheritance was continually eroded; nevertheless, there was repeated interplay of inherited capital between families from dynasty to dynasty. As family ramifications became more widespread among the entrepreneurs—and they usually produced prolific families—they acquired more refinement, more culture and gradually became exclusive. The line of the Charvet family, which had its origins in the textile industry of Dauphiné (their subsequent activity was in the north) included around the year 1920 more than 2,000 descendants from their not-so-distant progenitors in the middle of the eighteenth century. The result of all this was the reinforcement of group solidarity.

Strengthened solidarity became the equivalent of a growing class consciousness, and the entrepreneur lost his former familiarity with the world of the working man. The evolution of techniques and of industrial organisation tended to make the daily contacts of the small workshop disappear. The new division of residence in the towns led to a stronger segregation between the working-class districts and the 'desirable' bourgeois areas. In the past, different social categories had often lived on different floors of the same building. Now the employer began to be 'depersonalised'. Divisions between the owners and shareholders became more and more frequent. Henceforth the workman was confronted no longer by one man but by a company. Undoubtedly all these features were noticeable only in major industrial concerns. Yet they tended already to set the employers' group apart and to emphasise class consciousness. In the fifties, when Kuhlmann decided to give his workmen a great banquet at which his daughters were present, it was such an exceptional event that the police became worried. The gap between classes continued to widen, for if the working class began to combine after 1860 the employers did so too, and with rather more success. Individualism among employers waned before a kind of capitalist trade unionism.[34] There was a growth of employers' associations in the textile industry, especially during the period of the tariff debates. In 1864 —a significant date—the *Comité des Forges* was born: its policy was to maintain existing arrangements, notably among rail producers, who had divided up markets between them for a long time.

The change in the capitalist outlook under the Second Empire must not be overrated. Many of the features indicated here developed only in stages and did not crystallise until well after 1870 or even after 1880. Social and economic mentality had not altered very much. More conciliatory attitudes towards improvement of working conditions and a greater tendency towards philanthropy might be noticed: practical examples were provided by the *Société Industrielle de Mulhouse* and by the de Wendels. It did not alter the fact that liberal policy had merely moved from strict non-interference to a kind of paternalism. Some signs of hardening, foreshadowing a certain maturity of outlook, might be detected already in the midst of the great capitalist upsurge. We might say, transposing a judgement which Labrousse applied to the European bourgeoisie in 1815: 'If the refusal to move with the times, the refusal to accept history, is a sign of ageing' then the French capitalist class around 1880 had already experienced inner deterioration. It had started to decline before reaching its climax.

4 THE CAPITALIST TOWN

For the moment, however, the success of capitalists manifested itself in the noisy activities of demolition, reconstruction and extension which were changing the entire layout of towns. They were undertaken on a scale and at a pace which still baffles Frenchmen of today, just as at the time it baffled poets like Baudelaire who wrote in 1857: 'Old Paris is no more. Alas! The shape of a city changes more quickly than the heart of mortal man.'

Besides the 'Haussmannisation' of Paris there were similar changes in large and small provincial towns, with Marseille, Lyon and Le Havre in the lead. Town change is a vast subject which cannot be dealt with here, but it is relevant to our study in many ways. An admiring Taine wrote about Marseille: 'Since the great days of Alexandria, of Rome, of Carthage, such a thing has not been seen on the shores of the Mediterranean. A city like this resembles a dynamic entrepreneur.'

Marseille was truly a capitalist town in the sense that building transactions, expropriations, concessions, allotments of land, as well as the work of demolition, excavation, construction, the supplying of material and the making of public highways, were all in their own way means of speculation. There were the vast overall operations of large companies (like the *Immobilière* owned by the Péreires) and the more modest activities of a landlord having a tenement house built. Speculation took all forms and resulted in the most diverse fortunes. Here was one of the best opportunities offered to capitalist investors under Napoleon III, and it soon became far more popular than investments in the great railway companies.[35] Among the artisans and beneficiaries of urban development we can single out Joseph Thome, a peasant of the Gard who became a building constructor at Chaillot. He was prosperous before 1848, was threatened for a time by the economic crisis but recovered, and became amazingly wealthy during the golden age of Haussmann by undertaking the construction of all the Champs Élysées district, the avenue Montaigne, the quais of the Seine and site clearing on the left bank. They were gigantic works, for which he raised enormous capital. The Duke de Galliera advanced him 20 million francs on one single occasion. Thome employed up to 700 workmen and turned over, on average, 125 millions of business a year. On his death in 1897 he left a fortune of 60 millions. Two of his granddaughters married the two sons of the President Sadi Carnot.[36]

The town of the Second Empire was also a capitalist town in the sense that, like capitalist society itself, it reflected a more clear-cut social cleavage than formerly. We have already noted the results of the residential division which discriminated between rich and poor, between employers and wage-earners. Though town building was not yet completed, Paris was already, apart from the somewhat mixed quarters in the centre, divided into a fashionable bourgeois area in the west and a poor working-class area in the south and east. Louis Lazare wrote: 'We have sewn rags on the purple robe of a queen. We have created in Paris two very different and hostile cities: the city of luxury surrounded and crowded in by the city of misery. The one is adorned with silk, velvet, and diamonds, and the other has only its working clothes.' There were all the city's luxurious attractions alongside its desperate needs, superfluity alongside poverty and satiety alongside hunger. It was Paris of the Commune.

And then it was a capitalist city in the sense that its new layout gave the wealthy inhabitants of the select districts the means of showing off their fortune both by the pomp of their residences and by their following a way of life based on that of the nobility. The bourgeoisie of western Paris, horse-riding in the alleys of the Bois de Boulogne or walking in the Parc Monceau, were caricatures of the old noblemen. The Bois de Vincennes and the Parc Montsouris were popular replicas of the Bois de Boulogne and the Parc Monceau (which had been designed by Haussmann), but Vincennes and Montsouris were not of the same standard and not frequented by the same people: segregation was not confined to living-quarters. The Countess d'Agoult well understood the social change that led to the laying out of the Bois de Boulogne. She had known the time when 'in any muddy or dusty weather sick and ageing and ailing aristocracy came by the great postal road into this pitiful desert'. Now, 'in wide, sandy, and well-kept alleys', and 'around large lakes, four or five rows of carriages passed each other during fashionable hours: phaetons, victorias, open carriages, go-carts, coaches with eight springs'. Here high society women ... and elegant young ladies ... brushed the ground with their long silk dresses. 'In the sidewalks rode horsemen, cigar in mouth, and horsewomen cracking their whips. Their loud voices, their noisy laughter and tittle-tattle in all the languages and slang of Europe seemed incongruous in those surroundings.' It was a 'meeting place for the vanities and insolence of the cosmopolitan merry-go-round'. It was the centre for *le tout-Paris*, so devoted to the power and cult of money, the setting for Daudet's 'Nabob' —though the novel gives only a pale description of the scene.

Paris—and French capitalism—triumphed with the Universal Exhibitions of 1855 and 1867. The witty stories, the visits of the sovereigns of Europe and of eastern princes, the choruses of Offenbach, the tumult and the glitter of the imperial festival, all this glossed over less agreeable but more enduring realities. France had come a long way since 1851. Thiers, who had been to the London exhibition of 1851, pointed to the superiority of England over France in one particular field—the manufacture of iron. France's display in 1851 was outstanding in its way but was confined to silks, painted cloths, lace, furniture, goldsmith's work, Gobelins or Sèvres manufactures and finely spun cottons. Thiers said that England had made the container for the exhibition and France the contents. Everything had now changed. The Gallery of Machines in 1855 and the Palace erected in the Champ de Mars in 1867, which was a 'Babel of iron and glass', strikingly advertised the success of French capitalists, at last bringing their country into the industrial age.

Even when the hubbub of the exhibitions died down there remained clear evidence of business development in Paris in the shape of the department stores. The achievements of a Parissot or a Bonnerot, whose importance in their time has already been mentioned, were now outstripped. In 1852 Aristide Boucicaut, son of a humble hat manufacturer at Bellême and section head of a novelty shop in the rue du Bac called *Au Petit Saint-Thomas*, went into partnership with the owner of a nearby shop called *Bon Marché*. The shop's annual turnover was less than half a million francs. But Boucicaut's commercial sense soon worked marvels. Fixed displayed prices replaced bargaining, profit margins were lowered and a slogan was adopted: 'We take back anything which is unsatisfactory'. These policies very quickly attracted the crowds. The *Bon Marché*'s annual turnover exceeded 3 million francs in 1857 and 7 millions in 1863. Boucicaut's partner was rather overwhelmed by this rapid success and retired after 1½ million francs had been invested by a Frenchman who had become a successful teashop and restaurant owner in New York. In 1869 the construction of the present shops began. When Boucicaut died in 1877 sales had reached 67 million francs. The business passed into capable hands, those of Margaret Guérin, Boucicaut's widow; she was a peasant woman from Burgundy, practical and hard working. She was to turn the firm over to her staff as the *Société du Bon Marché* and was to leave her wealth to charitable organisations like the hospital which bears the name of Boucicaut. The success of the *Bon Marché* was the result of new commercial methods: the limitation of profits around 5 per cent, the autonomy of each department, publicity achieved by widely distributed catalogues, the sending out of samples and the correspondence bureau which foreshadowed the practice of public relations. In 1893, six years after the death of Madame Boucicaut, annual turnover reached 150 millions. At the time it was a world record for a commercial enterprise.

The *Bon Marché* was the prototype of the modern department store, described in 1883 by Zola in his novel *Au Bonheur des Dames*. The Boucicauts had their emulators. Among them Chauchard, a humble shop assistant, launched *Le Louvre* with funds supplied by the Péreires, the Foulds and the Duke de Galliera. He benefited also from the exhibition of 1855. When he retired in 1891, sales were up to 120 millions and the firm's share price of 5,000 francs nominal value on its formation was quoted at 19,000 francs. Chauchard was a patron of art. He left to the Louvre numerous pictures of the romantics and of the painters of Barbizon, among them the *Angélus* by Millet. Yet according to the curator who received his collection: 'There was no sign of a connoisseur at work and the results were hardly those of a patient and watchful collector. Chauchard's technique when hunting for works of art was lacking in discrimination.' Let us say that he was a newly-rich.

Le Printemps was, in a sense, the offspring of the *Bon Marché*.

Jaluzot, its founder, had been a departmental head with the Boucicauts. A wealthy marriage allowed him to create his own firm in 1865, on the recently opened Boulevard Haussmann. His success was rapid and it inspired him with higher ambitions, especially in politics. He subsidised *La Patrie* and was to represent the *arrondissement* of Clamecy in the Chamber of Deputies under the Third Republic. Yet he lost control of *Le Printemps* because he put the considerable capital which he had acquired into chancy speculations, such as sugar refining and even banking. The sugar crash of 1905, which was serious enough to cause the suicide of the president of the refineries of Say, forced Jaluzot to hand over his position to the Laguionie family who were owners of a great silk firm.

The *Samaritaine* was the last to be added to the list of the great Parisian firms of the Second Empire (*Galeries Lafayette* did not appear until 1895). *Samaritaine* was founded by Ernest Cognacq, a self-made man like the others: the success of new men was becoming the norm in this sector of the business world. According to G. Duveau, his career was marked by the most determined willpower and he rose to the most astonishing heights; the dimensions of his activity were on the scale of a novel by Balzac. Coming from a bourgeois family fallen on evil times he was first a shop assistant in a novelty shop and then a hawker. This Napoleon of the hawkers' world leased a shop on the eve of the 1870 war, near the Pont-Neuf, which he called the *Samaritaine* (a picture of the Samaritan could be seen on a nearby fountain). During the war Cognacq supplied the army with trousers. Yet 'la Samar' began its real upsurge only after his marriage in 1872 with Louise Jay, a seamstress in the clothes department at *Bon Marché*. Like the Boucicauts, the Cognacq-Jays worked with a zeal which was rapidly rewarded. Their turnover was 840,000 francs in 1874, nearly 2 millions in 1877, 17 millions in 1888 and 40 in 1895. Francis Jourdain, who knew them well, presents them as withdrawn from the world, entirely absorbed by their enterprise. They had no need, and not even any love, for money. They preferred long days spent in the service of *la Samar* to idle luxury. To their mind, the money they earned belonged to *la Samar* and they felt uneasy when taking it and ashamed when spending it. However, this apparent meanness contrasted with their philanthropy, for they gave tens and hundreds of millions to charity.

The great newspaper concerns, which started their growth especially after 1860 when political censorship was relaxed, were also a sign of the increasing influence of capital over the urban masses. Girardin, who had always been in the foreground with his newspaper *La Liberté*, which was sold at 2 sous a copy in 1866 (instead of 3) and numbered 40,000 readers, was about to be overtaken. Moïse Millaud, ex-partner of Mirès, launched in 1863 the first paper ever to be sold at 1 sou a copy—*Le Petit Journal*. Its circulation attained 448,000 copies on the eve of the war of 1870. Villemessant, the founder of the *Figaro*, vied with Millaud in obtaining the services of the successful pamphleteer of the time—the terrible Rochefort. Undoubtedly, the most influential newspapers representative of average bourgeois opinion remained attached to less novel, less spectacular and more sober ways of presentation. The *Siècle*, under Havin, took the place formerly held by the *Constitutionnel*. But the Press capitalists who were inclined to value 'information' and 'sensation' above 'opinion' had already laid all the foundations of mass circulation. Until 1914 the press followed the path of Girardin, Villemessant and Millaud. Here, as in many other sectors of capitalist expansion, the Third Republic was to be an epoch of consolidation, of stabilisation and of maturity rather than of innovation.

5 THE EXTERNAL ORBIT OF FRENCH CAPITALISM

French capitalism can be said to have reached its apogee during the Second Empire. This was due to the emergence of new structures and of a new outlook, if not to the level of production and of business transactions. It was also due to the capitalists themselves, who abandoned their cautious attitudes and started behaving like conquerors. They made a striking and massive return to the international market, a market in which they had played a very small part in the first third of the century. Under the July monarchy their role had become feeble but now there was a more rapid upsurge. The external commerce of France trebled under Napoleon III and no country in Europe experienced such an expansion.

The widening of horizons

The gamble of 1860 was occasioned by the vitality of the capitalists. A section of the economic élite believed that France could compete with the most advanced economic power of the time. Many people contributed to the conclusion of the treaty of commerce with England. The theorists or popularisers of political economy (Bastiat formerly, and now Chevalier), administrators particularly concerned about the cost of living and its effects on the popular frame of mind and, of course, the Emperor himself—all these had done much to prepare the movement, to set it in motion and to produce results. Liberalism was not confined to professors and civil servants; it also existed among capitalists (or at least among some capitalists). Merchants, ship-owners and the bourgeoisie of the ports were its leaders. They were much more disposed towards free trade now that they no longer had any interest in competing against foreign sugar. Indeed, sugar production from the French West Indies had lost its former importance with the decline in the value of land and the emancipation of slaves in 1848 (additionally, the French West Indies and Réunion were freed in 1866 from the fetters of the old colonial system). The owners of the most progressive export firms and the representatives of trades which were practically untouched by foreign competition were also on the side of the free traders: winemakers from the great vineyards, silk manufacturers from Lyon, cotton merchants from Mulhouse and owners of luxury industries. The opposition included rural capitalists, coalowners, textile manufacturers and the majority of ironmasters—including those with the latest equipment which had to be paid for. This division was of a complex nature and genuine advantages could be overlooked through sheer force of routine or on account of conservative ideas or old-fashioned economic attitudes. The division was also a reminder where the strength and weakness of French production lay. In practice, the treaty of 1860 and the treaties which followed it established preferential tariffs with a large number of countries, as compared with normal customs duties. They were completed by measures designed to make national industry competitive. There was a lowering of duties on raw materials which, joined to the technical facilities due to the shortening of sea voyages (made possible by steam power and the Suez canal), gave to France the role of entrepôt or redistribution centre for cotton and wool. State loans were made available to individual firms to allow them to modernise. Overall, in spite of the outbursts of the protectionists and of those who felt that they had been cheated of their profits, it was a far-sighted policy. It was bound to encourage an increase in production and an attempt to reduce costs and, in the words of Marcel Blanchard, would put an end to 'the quiet exploitation of the native population in a closed environment'.

The lowering of freight charges contributed to commercial expansion. We have already noted the part played by the great pioneers of capitalism, Péreire and Talabot, in the founding of shipping companies and the close interlocking between their boards of directors and those of railway and steelmaking enterprises. Sometimes river companies, threatened by railways, undertook new ventures. The *Compagnie de Navigation Mixte* was founded by a group from Marseille—the Touaches and Louis Arnaud—with the help of capitalists from Lyon centred around the Gauthier brothers who controlled shipping on the Saône and the Rhône.

The opening of the Suez Canal was obviously undertaken with the same aim in mind. It was both a French and a Saint-Simonian triumph, rather belated, and largely achieved by de Lesseps alone. It was also the last triumph of the régime of Napoleon III. The Empress Eugénie presided over the inauguration festivities, which resounded with the trumpets of Aïda, for Verdi was asked to compose a pseudo-Egyptian opera for the occasion. To understand the opening of the Suez Canal in 1869 one must see it as the consequence of a great leap forward. It came as a result of the pressures of buoyant capitalists between 1850 and 1870 who were anxious to shorten distances. The great upsurge in Marseille started before the work of de Lesseps but benefits were anticipated from his work once it was achieved. In 1858 the Canal Company was able to find in France—since England abstained from participating—1,000 shareholders for 207,000 shares of 5,000 francs for 400,000 issued. The Khedive subscribed to the others but it was French banks who supplied him with the means. Suez was the most considerable and the most spectacular of the great distant enterprises which French capital and technicians of the age undertook, but there were many others. The story of the *Crédit Mobilier* has shown us the importance of public works, railway enterprises and urban construction firms—all of which proliferated across Europe. They constituted true 'industrial missions' and Blanchard rightly places them in the Saint-Simonian tradition. That is to say, they represented the most dynamic and the most ambitious tendencies of French capitalism.

French capitalists as world creditors

France came to assume the position of a world creditor and external supplier of money. This was proof that capitalism was becoming more vigorous and expanding its sphere of activities. The activity of Paris as a financial market became international and rivalled the older market of London. After 1855, when the government clamped down on Stock Exchange speculation and partly relied on the banks for placing its own loans, capital was increasingly turned towards distant investments. Some statistics are necessary for an assessment of the size of this movement, however approximate they may be. The foreign portfolio held by the French seems to have been worth over 2,000 million francs in 1850, 10,000 million in 1860 and 15,000 in 1880. In the one year of 1868 French capitalists were to invest 2,127 millions in fourteen foreign countries. Alongside this enormous expansion may be placed the relatively modest amount of French portfolio held by foreigners: 70 millions in 1850, 2,300 in 1860 and 4,500 in 1880. Nevertheless, its rate of increase was not proportionately slower, which shows that the different capital markets were closely tied together. The fact remained that France was overwhelmingly a creditor country.

This massive export of French capital was directed by preference towards Mediterranean countries and, in a sporadic way, towards the two Americas. Other continents were more or less neglected. The direction of capital investment seemed to be influenced by geographical proximity, by historical tradition and by cultural affinity rather than by commercial interest or by foreign and colonial policy. Securities considered to be safe were preferred, and more than half of French investments consisted of state bonds: Italian, Spanish, Portuguese, Russian (even before the alliance of the nineties), Austro-Hungarian, Ottoman, Egyptian, Tunisian, Greek and Balkan. Considerable sums loaned to the Mexico of Emperor Maximilian went by default. However, nearly 2 milliards lent to the United States government before the Civil War were repaid. French capitalists also played an essential part in railway investment in many countries. Railway constructors and suppliers derived large profits from railway activity but shareholders obtained scanty return. Among the beneficiaries of French finance were coalmines and ironworks, gas and water companies right across Europe, urban transport, property companies, and even the first international cartel in zinc (which included management of concerns in Belgium, Rhenish Prussia, Silesia, Sweden and Spain). Suez can be added to the list; so can the investments of the great French banks which amounted to a milliard between 1850 and 1860. In spite of a special liking for fixed income securities, French capitalists did not spurn more chancy speculations. The verdict of the most recent historian—an American—to write on the subject of French foreign investment is that 'French capitalists, as a group, seem to have been in no way less adventurous than those of other creditor nations'.[37]

However, those investments came, in larger measure than elsewhere, from average if not small savings, or, in other words, from a significant proportion of the French population. Yet it was not the mass of security bearers who determined the area of operation. The initiative of the receiving countries and the choice exercised by the bankers and the general contractors were the deciding factors. The government could intervene and could refuse to grant the admission of any foreign stock to a quotation on the Paris Stock Exchange but it hardly seemed to follow a systematic policy in the matter. When it tried to influence the decisions of capitalists it did not always succeed. However, if the political implications of external investments seemed to be limited and of little consequence in the first half of the century,[38] the time drew near when they were to become very intricate. To try to unravel them in order to estimate the relative importance of politics and that of economics or finance would be to start from the wrong assumption. Politics and economics were two closely connected aspects of the same question—the expansion of western Europe. In its mood of operation French capitalism anticipated the pattern of 'classical imperialism'— to appear later in the eighties and between 1890 and 1914—by reinforcing its positions of influence in the Middle East. Industrial investments were negligible except for Turkish railways, and among investors in those railways between 1869 and 1877 were the *Société Générale*, 'Paribas', Paulin Talabot and Schneider—all within the Hirsch group. Yet the public debt of the countries concerned always kept them in deficit, a state of affairs carefully preserved by the lenders to offer very attractive prospects for investors. At Constantinople the major French and English banks, who controlled the Ottoman Bank founded in 1863, withheld a floating debt and granted short-term loans varying from a month to a year at interest rates of 12 to 20 per cent and sometimes more. Working in close cooperation, they had no trouble in taking over Turkish finances in 1879. In the process, the interests of small savers in Europe—holders of consolidated long term stock—were sacrificed to the interests of the banks. Understandably the problem was not a political one at all. There was no Anglo-French rivalry but a conflict between two circles and two levels of capitalism in each respective nation.

If Egypt was, by contrast, a burning question, it was because of the clash between different traditions and strategies and because of the struggle for power. The problem was due to memories of Mehemet Ali and Bonaparte and to historic or present-day geographical realities— the Nile, Suez, the route to the Indies. Yet it was also due to the fact that the Khedive's floating debt was in French hands—in the *Crédit Foncier*—whereas his consolidated debt was held by British banks. The history of the Canal itself was changed by the financial situation. Ten years after the issue of its initial capital, the company floated a loan of 100 million francs in 200,000 bonds by ballot. In the following year— the year of inauguration—the Khedive, who owed 30 millions, returned the certificates for the 176,000 shares which he held and the Company realised them by issuing 120,000 *délégations de coupon*. The setback in the subsequent loan (only 20 millions of thirty-year bonds were issued in 1871), the small volume of traffic during the Canal's initial years and the heavy burdens imposed—all these features put the Company on the verge of failure. A principal shareholder—the sugar refiner Lebaudy—saved it by subscribing 7 millions of bonds. In 1875 the Khedive was in dire straits—a classical result of the relationship between European capitalism and the 'underdeveloped countries'. He put his shares up for sale and the French government let slip the opportunity to buy. Lionel de Rothschild—the London Rothschild, 'in his time perhaps the most powerful of the Rothschilds'—advanced Disraeli the necessary sum of 4 million pounds (almost 100 million francs). Disraeli immediately seized his chance to buy. French banks influenced the French decision not to intervene. They hoped that Egypt might keep its shares as an eventual consolidated guarantee against their claims on the floating debt. After this French setback the two groups—French and English—experienced alternate successes. They cooperated in throwing out Ismail, the 'execrable debtor', in 1879, but they came into conflict again over exploiting the inferior status imposed on Egypt. The definitive triumph of England in 1881-82 was facilitated both by the French political crisis, in which Freycinet was given the delicate task of succeeding in the wake of the great Gambetta ministry, and by the economic crisis which severely affected Lyon and Paris. Yet beyond these business and political squabbles it was surely European capitalism which triumphed under British leadership. In any case, the Paris Stock Exchange was confident rather than disappointed and greeted this promise of a 'return to normality' by a rise in the price of Suez shares.[39]

The economic consequences of these external investments can raise as many questions as their political consequences, since the problem

M

comes from the same controversies. In trying to resolve it one finds difficulty in avoiding value judgements. Cameron, at least, is inclined to be indulgent. In his view these massive exports of capital extended French influence in all fields, postponed her relative decline, and beneficially weakened the impact of cyclical crises while awakening a large part of Europe and the Mediterranean basin to a modern economy. His optimism seems amply justified, since French capitalism had just gone through a most creative period in every way. Yet one is tempted to believe that these large external investments were to some extent responsible for the underdevelopment of the country, which appeared, later on, to be very serious in certain regions and in certain branches of activity. Undoubtedly the slow rate of population growth from the middle of the century was part of the explanation. Overall, the demand for labour hardly increased, and consequently the internal demand for capital was not so pressing. It is a vain task to try to recreate history and to condemn the 'errors' of past generations. However, when one reflects that perhaps a third of French savings left France between 1850 and 1880, to be dispersed and drained in so many distant and more or less mythical Eldorados, it is not certain that the use made by our capitalists of the wealth they had collected was in the best interest of the national economy during those decisive years.

4
Maturity

If one had to give an accurate account of the history of capitalists and of French capitalism in the nineteenth century with an exact chronology and sharp demarcation of events, the problem would arise of determining when that account had to come to a close. It would be a difficult decision to make. Perhaps the terminal point should be well before the end of the century, around the years 1882-83: the reasons for this choice have already been stated. Perhaps it should be after 1900. Perhaps the nineteenth century only came to an end with the catastrophe of 1914, at the same time as monetary stability and the strength of the gold franc—together with so many human lives, so many material splendours and so many civilised values. In fact, the capitalist machine did survive the first world conflict, finding again in post-war prosperity a kind of new vitality. The fatal turning-point for capitalism is more likely to be found in the great crisis of 1929 and the thirties, which had an infinitely deeper and more lasting effect than the periodic downturns of the previous century. For example, it brought to an end the long career of so many provincial and local bankers who had weathered previous crises without too much damage.

Nevertheless, this idea of continuity must not be carried too far. There can be no question of writing a report that fits neatly between precise dates, and this is certainly true of the last episode of the economic and social evolution that we are trying to describe. Between the eighties, when the most noteworthy of the great capitalists were mainly men of the past almost at the end of their careers (Henri Germain, Ferdinand de Lesseps, Alphonse de Rothschild), and the years 1900-14 which saw the beginnings of Louis Renault, of André Citroën, of Horace Finaly and even of Marcel Boussac, one finds once more that complex and precarious equilibrium of old and new forces which provides so many historical episodes with the label of 'periods of transition'. One might say that capitalism at the end of the nineteenth century had reached a maturity which showed signs of exhaustion, despite the favourable years immediately before the war. This last phase cannot be summed up in a complete and systematic study. All that one can give is a few main pointers and a few brief significant individual examples—all necessarily treated much more sketchily than the 'undisputed' years of the nineteenth century.

1 THE FLOWERING OF CAPITALIST INSTITUTIONS

A study of French national income and of its development alone would show that capitalism had reached its maturity. The statistics we have may not be very reliable, but their import is clear enough. If Frenchmen in 1878 earned more than 3,600 million francs from their landed property and their houses and less than 2,500 millions from goods and chattels, these two main categories of income were almost identical by 1903—with 4,072 million francs for one category and 4,044 for the other. In 1911 the second category was in the lead with 5,300 millions against 4,700. The Frenchman henceforth held more wealth in his share portfolio than in landed property. One example of the men who benefited indirectly from this victory of liquid wealth over land was Fichet, the modest inventor of a lock which guaranteed the safety of strong-rooms. In 1825, he employed 25 workmen, but in 1910 there were 2,000 men in his firm. Between 1825 and 1910 all the institutions and features of the capitalist economy developed, multiplied and blossomed, offering a thousand new facilities to their users.

Firstly, one may consider the fundamental operation around which all their activities revolved—the handling of money. Metallic reserves were still plentiful (reaching over 100 milliards in 1913—double the English reserves) but there was not the same demand for them. Small transactions were still arranged in gold louis pieces or in écus—without distinction since 4 écus of 5 francs each were accepted for 1 louis of 20 francs. This state of affairs existed although the striking of money was no longer freely permitted after 1873, white metal being far too discredited. Notes of less than 50 francs did not exist. Important metallic reserves were dispersed, therefore, over the whole country, while the Bank of France held and increased a considerable reserve (1 milliard in 1868, 2 in 1882, 3 in 1894, more than 4 between 1909 and 1912). By 1912 bank-notes were taken for granted and were used instead of coin for substantial payments. Their circulation increased roughly at the same pace as metallic currency: 1 milliard in 1867, 2 in 1871, 3 in 1890, 4 in 1900 and 5 in 1909. Furthermore, the growing use of the cheque and of exchange operations reduced the uses of the bank-note. In 1913 the operations of the Bank of France consisted of 5 milliards of coin, 67 of notes and 310 of written bills. Much had happened since the time when crowds of men could be seen in the street, carrying bags filled with louis, on settlement days at the end of the month.

Principal banking concerns and commercial banking

The capitalist, therefore, now had a modern monetary system at his disposal and could ask his banker for wider and more flexible services than formerly. The banking structure itself had developed and diversified. After the Second Empire with its brilliant financial innovations, even if sometimes they were lacking in foresight, a need was felt for a more orderly system, for more specialisation and consolidation. As one might expect, the old families of the major banks remained rich, powerful and active. Yet the time of their pre-eminence had passed. One could even ask—to take the most striking example—if the Rothschilds were not on the wane. They appeared to embark on all kinds of activities—fashionable society, the turf, and public charities; some of them were involved in foreign travel, in political life, in scientific expeditions, in book collecting, in medical science, in the Zionist movement, in making collections of pictures and of precious objects. Nevertheless, there were still outstanding bankers among them who stayed with the firm. After the years 1895-1900 the bank experienced a recession and, 'while maintaining its liaisons with some large industrial organisations and its position vis-à-vis some governments, it appeared to have become more a respected partner of the organisations concerned than an initiator. Their financial pinnacle was a thing of the past'.[1] It was a relative decline and nothing more. Old private firms naturally retained their clientèle of solid and respectable holders of wealth, who trusted their experience, their discretion and their business contacts. Public loans, even when the stock was sold directly, as in 1878, on the Stock Exchange and at the Treasury offices, provided them with a way of making money. Their substantial capital reserves enabled them to obtain a large amount of subscriptions which, thanks to their financial knowledge, they were able to sell again very profitably. We do not know exactly what part they played in international trade and in sea transport, but it must have become increasingly important as world commerce and shipping developed. Their creations or their partnerships in railways and in industry remained under their control, at least to a great extent. Hence the Rothschilds retained control over the railway company of the north, over lines in Austria-Hungary and in Spain, the mines of Almaden, Penarroya, and Rio-Tinto, the firms *Le Nickel* and De Beers, and the Russian crude oil firm of Nobel. Hottinguer, Verne, Heine, Mirabaud, Mallet (whose activities were primarily in the East) and Neuflize (active in South America) were in the same position. Under the umbrella of limited liability organisation they were often found behind the commercial banks who acquired in the seventies a regular place in the commercial world. It was under their aegis that the *Banque Parisienne*, founded in 1874, was enlarged to become the *Union Parisienne* of 1904, the typical commercial bank of the new century. Their influence, even if not dominant, was still important in 'Paribas', which was managed in 1900 by Horace Finaly, son of a Hungarian Jew backed by the Rothschilds. He was a strange open-minded man of wide culture who had been connected in his youth with Proust and Léon Blum and had a passion for astronomical mathematics. In his capacity as banker he engaged in Russian loans like everyone else but he also appreciated the importance of the new Moroccan protectorate, where his bank was to gain a dominant foothold. On the eve of the Great War he became interested in the offensive directed by 'Standard' against the oil monopoly held in France by 'Royal Dutch'. Finaly acted as a leftist, upholding the cartel of 1924 and offending the catholic and conservative group of Émile Moreau and Laurent-Atthalin who expelled him from the bank in 1937.

Business and politics: Rouvier

La Banque Française pour le Commerce et l'Industrie, whose president was Maurice Rouvier, was founded later than other banks and it experienced slower growth. Yet with Rouvier we enter a world where business and politics were more and more closely interwoven. He was a southerner of vulgar appearance but of subtle mind, with a good training in banking and financial techniques, clever enough never to be blatantly indiscreet but involved in too many shady deals for his reputation to emerge quite unsullied. His period of training was spent at Marseille in the commercial and banking house of Zafiropoulo. There he met Eugène Étienne, another businessman of doubtful reputation, who was to become president of the *Tréfileries* of Le Havre and of the Omnibus Company, a leader of the 'colonial party', and was later employed in a shipping business. Although starting on a ministerial career under Gambetta who was ready to accept railway nationalisation, Rouvier very quickly became a champion of the railway companies. In 1883 he defended the Raynal Plan. David Raynal, a Jew from Bordeaux, an ex-employee of the Péreire family, had many connections with the high officials of the major banking concerns and of the railway companies. Raynal, Léon Say and Rouvier then drew up the Freycinet Plan with its greater advantages for private enterprise : the state left the railway companies with the task of running and developing the railway system, gave a state guarantee for loans to be contracted by the railway companies and guaranteed their dividends.

In 1887, with Étienne as Under-Secretary of State for the Colonies, Rouvier formed the first Cabinet of the Third Republic to enjoy the support of the monarchist right, even though the Cabinet members were all opportunist republicans. Yet it was as a specialist—in the Finance Ministry—that he won his reputation. In this capacity he saved the *Comptoir d'Escompte* in 1889. Profits were becoming increasingly difficult to obtain because of the general business depression and the *Comptoir* engaged in an unwise association with the Society of Metals, with a view to gigantic speculation in copper. The suicide of the director—Denfert-Rochereau—produced a rush on deposits which the *Comptoir* could not meet. At the time Rouvier was a minister in the government of Tirard. He asked for the help of the Bank of France, of the Rothschilds, and of the major banking houses. In consequence, the *Comptoir* was able to survive. It was reorganised and renamed the *Comptoir National* and put in the reputable hands of Denormandie who was a permanent senator and a former governor of the Bank of France.

Nevertheless, business deals had their risks. Rouvier, like so many others, was compromised in the Panama scandal. This affair had wide repercussions and revealed direct collusion between politics and finance. De Lesseps, overconfident from his triumph at Suez, plunged in 1880, at the age of sixty-nine, into a much more chancy undertaking—the piercing of the American isthmus. Besides being dogged by an unfortunate series of circumstances the Panama Company soon ran out of capital in its attempt to complete a project which had been insufficiently studied. The Company's loans were placed with difficulty even though they brought high returns to the banking syndicates undertaking their issue: four large credit houses, for example, obtained profits of more than 10 million francs. The Company sought to attract subscribers by making an exceptional lottery issue, equivalent to premium bonds, and in June 1888 obtained the legal authorisation to do so. It was all to no avail since the issue failed to save the Company, collapse ensuing in February 1889 with a deficit in excess of 1,300 million francs. Among the many creditors there was a multitude of small savers whose extreme anger found expression in the campaign launched by the ex-Boulangists. This group was only too happy to find fault with the politicians, their victorious opponents. In order to secure the vote for the premium bond issue the Company had substantially greased the palm of a good number of parliamentarians. The scandal broke in September 1892, to the accompaniment of sharp comment from the anti-government press and from the Opposition in the Chamber. Clemenceau was the most eminent politician to be attacked, since his newspaper was financially supported by Cornelius Herz—an intriguer who was at the heart of the affair. One of the cheques had been drawn by Baron Reinach, principal distributor of the Company's funds and a member of one of the most typical families of the new republican 'nobility' as well as a financial supporter of the opportunists (as Herz was of the radicals). The cheque had been endorsed by Vlasto, a man of straw close to Rouvier. Rouvier had paid Cornelius Herz a visit—in company with Baron de Reinach—a few hours before the Baron, beside himself with anxiety, committed suicide. Rouvier, however, was not easily put down. He left the Finance Ministry but at the Palais-Bourbon he defended himself vigorously; he had accepted money, he said, in order to increase secret funds—normally granted too sparingly—and in order to defend the régime. In other words, it was in the course of duty that he had let himself be corrupted. 'Money is necessary for government and when the Chamber does not vote enough one is quite happy to obtain funds by personal contact.' The charges were dismissed since there was an insufficient case against him to prosecute. Yet his position was undoubtedly affected. Moreover, he was involved in the scandal of the southern railways which had obtained grants of money and interest guarantees but had never built a single stretch of track. His involvement was indirect since he had

simply figured in the issuing syndicate that launched the affair. Yet he
made a comeback. His services were valuable and admirably met the
interests of the bourgeoisie. It was he who, in 1896, secured the failure
of a proposal for a tax on unearned income presented by the minister
Méline, even though the proposal was extremely moderate. In 1901 he
was one of the stars of the Democratic Alliance, a new political formation which brought together the right wing of the 'republican block'
—Étienne, Raynal, the great merchant Jules Siegfried (who was also
on the board of the famous metal firm Fives-Lille) and Christophle,
ex-governor of the *Crédit Foncier* (a firm which had been turned,
according to Barrès, into 'the Stock Exchange of opportunism').

The main triad of capitalist society—press, politics and business—
had the same objectives as Rouvier and the Democratic Alliance. The
controllers of the great popular newspapers were Charles Prevet, director of the *Petit Journal* (most popular in the world in 1900, with a
circulation of one and a half million copies), managing director of the
Forges de Montbard-Aulnoye and a senator, and the ex-bailiff Jean
Dupuy, also a senator. Dupuy was to achieve a new record with the
Petit Parisien—800,000 copies in 1900 and 1,550,000 in 1913—giving
it the same popular slant as the *Petit Journal* with varied new items,
rumours, titbits and cheap novels by Montépin and Richebourg. Other
press lords were Letellier and Bunau-Varilla, building contractors who
had made their money by supplying material to the Panama Company.
One of them took over the *Journal* and the other *Le Matin*. The latter
had a circulation of 700,000 in 1914 thanks to the detective novels of
Gaston Leroux and Maurice Leblanc and the motor races and aviation
meetings which it organised. *Le Temps* of Adrien Hébrard was a far
more serious newspaper though it dealt with topics of a similar nature.

The main influences on capitalism were politics, newspapers and
banking. In 1901 both the Democratic Alliance and Rouvier's Bank
were born. The government helped in the formation of the *Banque
française pour le commerce et l'industrie*. In the Waldeck-Rousseau
government of the day the portfolio of Finances was held by Joseph
Caillaux, Inspector of Finances, a protégé of Rouvier; he was the son
of a minister under Macmahon who had sat on the boards of several
railway companies. Caillaux hoped that the new establishment would
act 'against the tendency of French finance to direct capital too exclusively towards foreign investment, especially towards the purchase
of foreign funds'. In fact, Rouvier, who himself succeeded the young
Caillaux in the Combes ministry while remaining at the head of the

Bank, was too closely connected with the governing circles of French finance to break with their practice of external investment. His internal projects were few but it was not surprising to find at the head of one of them—the new *Société du Gaz de Paris*—the senator Adolphe Carnot, president of the Democratic Alliance. In reality, Rouvier was set on defending the traditional features of bourgeois strength in this ministry which had very strong leanings to the left. Combes prepared his Law of Separation but Rouvier, his Minister of Finances, once more evaded the question of taxes on income.

At length, in 1905, when the affair of the secret files allowed the Democratic Alliance to overthrow a cabinet which had become un-popular, Rouvier again became President of the Council with the 'Algerians' Étienne and Thomson in his team along with the radical Berteaux, a wealthy stockbroker. At the time of the Tangier crisis Rouvier—as a capitalist—was opposed to armed conflict and expelled Delcassé, the initiator of the affair, from the Foreign Office. It was significant that he used the banker Bertzold (among others) as a go-between in his diplomatic dealings with Germany and that on the board of his own bank two other German financiers were directors. Besides, it was at a moment when Schneider and Krupp were negotiat-ing a share of control over the Algerian mines of Ouenza. The busi-ness world, then, was conciliatory and preferred peaceful solutions which allowed the pursuit of activities yielding financial returns. The compromise of Algéciras, in fact, did not prevent the Bank of Paris from consolidating its foothold in Morocco. Under the influence of Rouvier the French money market advanced a new loan of 1,200 mil-lion francs to Russia—who had shown herself a loyal ally during the crisis and the conference.

The wisdom of Henri Germain

Some of the masters of French capitalism categorically refused to take part in the financing of French industry. In 1903, Henri Germain sup-ported them against the bank of Rouvier at a meeting of the *Crédit Lyonnais* when he replied to a question by a shareholder who was tempted by this type of investment. 'You are conjuring up illusions for yourself,' he said. 'The government itself has had the same illusions. Like you, it was convinced that we were not fulfilling our proper role and two years ago it wanted to create an establishment with a capital of

6 million francs. Do you know what this establishment has supplied in funds to commercial firms? Nothing; and it has my congratulations.'

The new rules of banking specialisation, indeed, influenced credit establishments towards short-term lending. We know that their policies had not always been so wise. The *Crédit Lyonnais* itself had only 2 million francs in value of share certificates in 1869 but held 61 millions five years later. If experience had taught it to keep away from industrial investments, it had not been able to resist the temptation to subscribe to the great public loans of 1871-2. Then it raised its capital to 50 million francs and began to extend its network of agencies on a national basis. When the boom of 1879-81 arrived the *Crédit* was already deeply involved in insurance, building speculation, lighting and water companies, and more and more concerned with foreign investment. It had started by granting short-term loans to Mediterranean states under French influence, and these were extremely remunerative at 10 to 20 per cent. In 1875—in spite of the Ottoman bankruptcy which intervened in that year—it opened a network of foreign agencies which were able to undertake a number of government loans that were considered to be better risks. Its relative foolhardiness seemed to pay dividends until about 1880. The *Crédit Lyonnais*, after eighteen years of existence, had at its disposal a capital of 100 millions paid up (half the nominal capital) and of 382 millions of deposits. On average it paid 9 per cent annual interest to its shareholders and some 15 per cent to its directors. If, at that date, a credit house like the *Crédit Lyonnais* differed from a commercial bank the differences were not so much a question of activities as a question of resources. A large part of the resources of the *Crédit Lyonnais* came from the savings of the masses, or of the middle classes. One might say it was the result of the democratisation of credit.

— Then came the crash of the *Union Générale*, which was not a straightforward case of bankruptcy. The *Union Générale* was a commercial bank founded in Lyon in 1878 (after an unsuccessful attempt in 1875) and patronised by members of legitimist and Catholic circles, among them the Vatican and the Count of Chambord. It was inspired by the engineer Bontoux, who had already worked under the auspices of the Péreire family and then of the Talabots on the railway installations of central Europe. If he was a good technician he was also an adventurous 'go-getter' and he became involved in too many risky enterprises that in size and recklessness recalled the activities of the *Crédit Mobilier*. The bank's interests included railways in Austria-

Hungary and Serbia, banks in Vienna, in Budapest and in Belgrade, gas at Bucharest and mines in Styria. It was in competition with powerful and firmly established interests like 'Paribas', the *Crédit Lyonnais*, the group succeeding to the Péreire interests, and the principal bank of Vienna (Wodianer) and of Berlin. Besides, the international circumstances of the eighties were unfavourable and the foundations of the Union were fragile even though it had the full support of respectable society. 'The provincial squire, the country curate, the old spinster, the small shopkeeper or the thrifty peasant' were favourably impressed by great names from the nobility or the diocese: these were the typical depositors but their resources were often modest. Because of its political colour the *Union* could not expect the main protestant or Jewish banks to make allowances for it. Moreover, this late counter-offensive of catholic finance was badly directed. In order to counteract the Stock Exchange moves of its enemies the *Union* had to buy back part of its own shares. The price mounted wildly from 500 (nominal value) to 3,400 francs. It was the episode which inspired Zola in *L'Argent*.[2] At that point the fall of an associated bank was sufficient to unleash the panic that engulfed the *Union*. Léon Say—the great financier of the moderate left, connected with the Rothschilds and a minister under Freycinet—did absolutely nothing to save it. Bontoux was arrested, accused of swindling and of bad faith, and the *Union* was put in liquidation (1 and 2 February 1882).[3]

The crash, which was only part of a more general crisis, affected millions of victims. The entire French banking system was more or less involved in it. The *Crédit Lyonnais*, for example, whose activities were geographically close to those of the *Union*, lost half of its deposits in a few weeks and its shares suffered a severe fall in price. This was the opportunity for Henri Germain to show his mettle. Not only did he restore the bank to its former status but he enunciated the golden rule which was henceforth to dominate the policies of the *Crédit Lyonnais*.

> There are certainly excellent industrial firms [he declared] but the best planned and most wisely administered enterprises involve risks which we consider incompatible with the indispensable security which a deposit bank must exercise in the use of its funds. Besides, in industry one must be prepared to wait for the time when a firm finally reaches its maturity and can yield the returns expected. Industrial assets cannot be relied upon to repay short-term deposits. Such deposits must have cover similar to that existing in the Bank of France. The active funds of the Bank of France consist of commercial bills and guaranteed credit, or forms of wealth which are the

safest and most easily realised assets. These must be the funds representing the deposits of the *Crédit Lyonnais*.

Henri Germain was obviously more cautious and less enterprising than the Péreires. His wisdom was that of the Third Republic and seemed rather limited and dull after the recklessness of the Second Empire. He was born at Lyon in 1824, and followed—along with Ozanam and Victor Laprade—the teaching of the Abbé Noirot who, according to Duveau:

> had managed to reconcile revelation and the natural light of reason. One might say that in financial matters Germain . . . put into practice the eclectic methods he inherited from the Abbé Noirot. The typical financier, under Louis Philippe and during the Second Empire, was often a hard character but yet a passionate mystic who dreamed of the resurrection of God. Germain did not come up to those standards. He belonged more to the bourgeois Republic than to the Empire. He was to contribute to the outflow of savings in foreign loans. He was more of a confidence trickster than a genuine rogue.

Even if one agrees that he was a trickster he was persevering and clever. If Noirot had achieved nothing else, he had certainly kindled Germain's energy. 'He could teach me nothing,' Germain would say, 'because philosophers know nothing, yet he gave me the taste for work.' In fact, Germain was interested in various branches of knowledge of a more concrete nature. With Rossi he studied political economy. As a stockbroker at Lyon he learnt about banking and securities, and then he worked for Arlès-Dufour and was connected with Enfantin. The influence of Saint-Simon was considerable. Germain even spent some time at the ironworks of Commentry in order to gain some initial experience in industrial management. As a liberal he was suspect after 2 December 1852, but in 1869 he was elected deputy of the Ain against the official candidate. In spite of his political views, he married the daughter of Vuitry; Vuitry was governor of the Bank of France, then President of the Council of State, a Senator of the Empire, a *membre de l'Institut* and President of the P.L.M. The *Crédit Lyonnais*, which was Germain's great achievement and which he directed right up to his death in 1905, was not his only interest. In Parliament he was one of the influential leaders of the left centre although his son-in-law— Baron Brincard, a sugar manufacturer—sat on the right. Yet he never became a member of the government. Thiers never forgave him his fiscal heresies—his idea of a tax on income, for instance. Rothschild preferred Léon Say. Yet Germain's financial and political power was considerable. In his mansion in the faubourg St Honoré he entertained the influential men of the capital—Gambetta, Renan, Hanotaux, Poincaré, Albert de Mun, Paul Bourget, Hébrard. In his self-effacing way he was one of the great men of the Third Republic just as Émile Péreire, a more vocal figure, had been one of the great men of the imperial régime.

The success of the credit houses

The *Crédit Lyonnais* showed the way for other credit houses, even though the policies of Henri Germain were not immediately followed universally. The *Comptoir d'Escompte* was in dire straits in 1889 with the collapse of the Society of Metals. The *Société Générale* took a long time to recover from the effects of an unfortunate speculation in Peruvian guano and railways. The *Crédit Industriel* concentrated on transport and electricity companies. Little by little, however, the concept of short-term deposits and credits—the concept of Henri Germain—came to be accepted. Success in this respect was impressive. In 1873 there were no more than 325 million francs in deposits in the banks of Paris (about ten times less than in London) and there was far less in the provinces. Soon deposits flowed in. Security holders who had handed over their certificates to a bank for safe keeping left the ensuing interest and dividends in the bank. Sums set aside for a dowry or for a purchase or the proceeds of a sale were deposited in the bank before being put to their ultimate use. Gradually commerce and industry entrusted the great credit houses with the task of settling their accounts and of investing their available funds. The 'big four' had at their disposal in 1895 a paid-up capital of 340 millions while their deposit and credit accounts reached 1,483 millions; the corresponding figures for 1913 were respectively 725 and 5,681 millions (the latter figure representing 99 per cent of notes which the Bank of France had in circulation). The *Crédit Lyonnais*, always in the lead, easily surpassed the most powerful English banks by a wide margin. Its commercial portfolio of 2,400 millions in 1875 had risen to 17,618 in 1912. Its share of 500 francs sold in 1907 at 1,250, and the share yielded far more in income than it had cost to those who had been able to retain it since 1863.

This astonishing success was made possible by the very conditions of capitalist development and concentration of the period. The bank benefited from the various aspects of progress in industry and from the new inflow of gold which followed the opening of the Transvaal mines after 1896. The growth and acceleration of commercial transactions of all kinds, the proliferation of firms floated by share issue (3,366 in 1900 and 9,431 in 1914), Stock Exchange flotations and the growth of publicity—all these affected its activity. The great deposit banks exploited these opportunities to the full. They knew how to make customers welcome; they were very considerate and very obliging—just like their contemporaries, the great department stores. As Jules Bertaut remarked, they were 'great department stores of finance where the employees had to be very civil towards customers, where everyone was working in the public eye, where people were received without affectation and given free advice, where knowledge of finance and securities could be sought by the most humble members of society'. Their management was similar to that of the big stores with multiple branches (like the network of the *Nouvelles Galeries* or that of provincial food shops). The banks were able to dominate the whole country, to tap its smallest sources of wealth and to put an end to the suspicions which provincial inhabitants or people of modest means entertained about the manipulators of money.

The achievement of banking unity

The banking network which now covered France and whose ramifications were steadily growing was based on the Bank of France, the keystone of the whole system. This note-issuing bank supported credit houses rather than competed against them. After 1897, under Governor Pallain, it still endeavoured to reinforce its reserves of gold and to extend its activities in order to maintain its dividends. It began to accept title deeds as guarantees against advances, to make current accounts more readily available and to extend the use of the cheque and of Stock Exchange services. Yet the Bank functioned more and more as a central bank and as a deposit bank for credit houses. The accounts which the latter held at the Bank of France allowed them to control their reciprocal liabilities in turn. Their cheques could always be transformed into notes or if need be into coin, issued or held by the Bank of France; the Bank was their supreme weapon in case of difficulty. By its handling of the rediscount rate it set the example for the banking activity of the entire country. The wisdom of its management and the extent of its reserves enabled it to maintain the rate at as stable a level as possible; it varied only twelve times between 1898 and 1913 and only between 2 and 4.5 per cent, and this at a time when it underwent some sixty to seventy changes in England and Germany, changes which took it to as high a level as 7.5 per cent.

By then the network of the Bank of France operated on a national scale. There were subsidiaries and branch offices and 'linked towns' where the personnel of the local subsidiary operated on one day in five. 'Banking centres' rose in this way from a total of 115 in 1881 to 583 in 1913. The ground was prepared for the spread of credit houses. In fact, on the eve of the First World War, the *Société Générale* had 560 agencies, the *Crédit Lyonnais* 411 and the *Comptoir d'Escompte* 285. The *Crédit Industriel* had offices only in Paris but it played a part in setting up numerous subsidiaries in the provinces. The development of the banking system and that of the railway companies followed the same pattern; they used the same empirical methods and put the same emphasis on profit in the early stages, and they gradually evolved the same type of rational organisation. In 1914 one could really speak of a network of credit distribution: from sub-offices to head-offices capital circulated with flexibility. The range of banking operations had more or less reached its peak, both technically and geographically. All commercial needs could be met and essential banking services were provided for the whole country.[4]

This achievement of banking unity was of major importance. The disappearance of internal exchange arrangements—rendered useless when settlements could be made from town to town by a mere signature—was only one of its consequences. This new network also put an end to the traditional internal barriers in the economy. The *Crédit Lyonnais*, celebrating its fiftieth anniversary in 1913, hardly exaggerated when it contrasted the former backwardness of the money market with the revolution which the bank and its competitors had accomplished.

> Formerly, there was a real and unexpected shortage of capital in certain regions (after a bad harvest, for example) while in other regions money was still plentiful. This state of affairs was detrimental not only to the regions where capital was scarce. Indeed, capital available in other regions was often put into risky undertakings for want of finding better outlets. The rate of discount underwent sharp changes which occasionally unleashed violent crises. [But now] deposit banks have been established as a kind of general source of funds for industrialists, businessmen and private individuals ... Agencies have been opened all over the country to receive money wherever it is available and to use it wherever it is required.

Their role was not limited to tapping minute and dispersed sums of money in order to offer them for distant speculation: the credit houses now left that function to the industrial banks. They had found their 'true function' in adapting their activities to the requirements of particular areas, and by dividing the total capital available according to regional needs. One of their managers foresaw this necessary change when writing in 1873 : 'The *Crédit Lyonnais* has found, during recent years, an easy and lucrative way of using capital in French loans and in loans to foreign states. There might come a time when this activity would be less rewarding. It would then be convenient to have a safe outlet in the form of agencies'. In turning in this direction, the credit houses contributed more than any other institution to making ready money available and to lowering the rate of interest. They operated at the expense of the moneylender and even of the *rentier*. Yet they greatly benefited ordinary bank customers as well as the national economy.

Persistence of regional and local banks

The expansion of the great deposit banks was often achieved through merger with provincial enterprises. The *Crédit Industriel* adopted a slightly different policy. In this particular case a link was assured by regional subsidiaries like the *Société Marseillaise*, the *Crédit du Nord* or the *Société Nancéienne*. The latter had grown by amalgamation with old family banks, such as the bank directed by the Husson and Lenglet families for three generations between 1842 and 1894. By such mergers the credit houses made sure of more direct local contacts and became more acquainted with local affairs, thus reducing their own anonymity.

Yet banking concentration had its limitations. It led to a fragmentation of reserves between numerous centres of credit distribution which were not all equally profitable. It then meant that the proportion of ready cash was increasing faster than deposits and the general level of banking business, a state of affairs which tended to reduce profits. Yet it enabled local banking firms to survive; in any case, they were able to rely on their own long traditions, on their long contacts with medium-scale businessmen, industrialists and capitalists. A law thesis was published in 1913 entitled 'The rebirth of local banks'. One local bank at least is well known—that founded at Grenoble in 1863 by J. B. Charpenay, a wealthy wholesaler in sheets. His bank was a successor to the small firm of Février and Jullien and was another example of a local bank evolving from old commercial capitalism. At first it was a joint-stock firm in share ownership with a capital of 300,000 francs and it

N

practised 'discounting and collection of commercial bills'. Charpenay was for sixteen years president of the *Tribunal de Commerce* and he held a strong position in Dauphiné. His successors supplied the Bergès family in 1895 with the capital necessary to build the factory at Chedde. The paper mills, glove factories, and electro-metallurgical works of the northern Alps all received important advances or long-term credits from the Charpenay bank. In return, the regional industrialists deposited enough funds for its capital to increase to the amount of 2,500,000 francs by 1913. When it disappeared, like so many other firms in 1931, the Charpenay bank had 1,957 shareholders, 17 agencies and more than 10 milliards of annual turnover. Banks of this type played a notable role in the commercial financing and industrial expansion of their region. Their success was due to their own resources and to the medium and long-term deposits that a confident clientèle entrusted with them over a long period because the directors and the use made of customers' money were well known.

2. FRENCH WEALTH AND ITS UTILISATION

A country of small savers

The country as a whole was now no longer short of capital for its development and for the creation of a modern infrastructure. In any event, there should have been no problem, for most Frenchmen continued to be thrifty. Each year they 'put by' an important part of their earnings, though perhaps somewhat less than under the Second Empire when savings represented 13 per cent of income. Yet the downturn of the years of the 'great depression' (8 per cent savings between 1879 and 1903) was followed by a distinct upturn of 11.5 per cent between 1904 and 1910. The growth of national wealth and activity brought in its train a rapid expansion of the absolute figures. In quoting them one must make the customary warning about using them with care. Annual savings rose from 2 milliards between 1875 and 1893 to 3½ milliards for the period 1893-1911, and reached 5 milliards on the eve of the war. Moreover, all aspects of French life at the time encouraged this traditional virtue of thrift: the low birth rate together with the modest existence which people led in the country or in small towns limited immediate requirements. Monetary stability enabled people to get full value from their incomes and the purchasing power of money increased due to the slow tendency towards a fall in prices resulting from technical progress and from the development of production. Between 1815 and the end of the century, in spite of a fall in the average rate of nominal interest from 5 to 3 per cent, real income grew by 18 per cent.

The use of these savings was still very often marked by out-of-date practice. Many local studies could confirm this point. The following description applies to the Isère, a region of water power and of tourism with rapid expansion at Grenoble: 'Even about 1900, the lists of inherited wealth show a cautious society, fairly self-sufficient, whose patrimony consists mostly of rural buildings and mortgage credits rather than industrial shares and foreign bonds'.[5] Even so, bonds with fixed income and especially state funds gained fairly general approval. Fixed income stock, which had previously been an investment for the wealthy, now attracted a crowd of small savers, partly thanks to the *Caisses d'Épargne*. The average *rentier* was in credit with the state to the extent of 170 francs in 1875 and of 130 in 1902, compared with 1,047 in 1830 and 822 in 1845. What looked like bravado in the days of old Grandet had now become the norm. Around 1896 a modest depositor in the Bank of France usually held 20 per cent of his portfolio in public funds. The yield of public funds, however, had diminished as a result of conversions and as a result of the high prices they reached. Moreover, all the securities with fixed income had ended in the same way: their average return had fallen from 5.1 per cent in 1856 to 3.73 on the eve of the Great War. That trend explained the disposition of the small saver to put money in premium bonds and of wealthier and more expert capitalists to put money in variable income and in shares.

Emphasis on external investment

The lowering of yields on investments was undoubtedly a general rule. If the average dividend remained higher than the return on state funds and securities, it fell from 5.7 per cent in 1856 to 4.01 in 1913. Yet another factor made its appearance. French securities returned appreciably less than foreign securities: 4.1 per cent compared with 5.5 for foreign investments during the eighties and 3.40 compared with 4.75 in 1912-14. The fact was that the abundance of available capital acted as a drag on the national market, especially during the last quarter of the nineteenth century, when the slackening of business restrained the demand. Therefore, external investments became more and more desirable. The banks played a leading role and naturally favoured foreign activity, since they derived very high profits from foreign operations (10 to 17 per cent return from some Bulgarian or Turkish loans). The press warmly recommended them, partly because it was bribed more than once by needy governments like that of the Tsar. When its policy could be helped by such investment, the government was ready to exercise more or less direct pressure and the financial market of Paris was a useful weapon for French diplomats. Hence it is understandable why the Russian treasury was granted by France from 1888 onwards (before the conclusion of the Alliance) 52 successive loans, amounting to 10 milliards of francs divided between 1,600,000 subscribers. France, a loyal ally, went even as far as refusing credit to Persia in order not to interfere with Russian influence there; that influence was, in fact, due to the French because they had supplied the Tsar with the capital he lent to the government of Teheran. In the same way France would not authorise Japanese loans before the reconciliation between Tokyo and St Petersburg. However the taste for foreign investment was also stimulated occasionally by more mundane reasons, notably by a concern for tax evasion. On his death President Grévy himself left a deposit of £172,106 in England.

These external investments formed a considerable and growing part of the totality of liquid French wealth. The proportion was perhaps 12 to 15 milliards out of 56 in 1880; 25 to 27 out of 100 in 1904; and 45-50 out of 105-110 when the world war exploded. However rapid the total increase of the French portfolio, therefore, the rate of growth of foreign wealth was even more spectacular. Between 1901 and 1914 the industrial banks may have directed three-quarters of their investments outside France. At length, in 1914, France with 21 per cent of the total of international investment, became the second banking nation in the world, the first being the United Kingdom (which held 50 per cent), and the third Germany (which held 15 or 16 per cent). A quarter of the money lent by France was held in Russia where it represented 80 per cent of the public debt and a third of industrial investment. 23 per cent was in western and central Europe (the Iberian Peninsula, the Dual Monarchy, Italy, Switzerland, Belgium, the Low Countries), 13 per cent in the Balkans and the Ottoman Empire, more than 6 per cent in Egypt, Suez and the Levant, 13 per cent in Latin America, almost nothing in the United States and the rest widely scattered.

These foreign investments did not always imply direct export of capital. They often arose from local reinvestment of dividends produced from previously made investment: this reinvestment between

1880 and 1913 reached some 30 milliards. Nevertheless, the export of capital and the non-repatriation of income meant a substantial loss for the national economy at a moment when agriculture and certain sectors of industry were suffering from more or less acute underdevelopment. Neither the great credit houses nor the industrial banks seem to have worried about the situation. Although occasionally better advised, even the provincial banks joined the movement: their *Société Centrale*, created in 1905, invested like everyone else in South American loans. If French enterprises suffered from foreign investment, capitalists did not always gain, at least not the obscure and humble security holders. Banking syndicates reaped considerable profits while some of the stocks placed under their aegis depreciated rapidly, and major downfall was awaiting the numerous creditors of the Tsar—and what average Frenchman, moderately well-off, did not at that time have his few Russian securities?

The policies followed by the key men of French finance were also questionable in other respects. Their loans occasionally helped dubious competitors. They contributed to financing German expansion by rediscount of bills and by credits opened with houses like the Dresdner Bank. They encouraged the rise of Danish agricultural exports which outstripped French exports in the British market. Conversely they did not always assure new markets for French commerce and production. Western Europe accepted French money but it ordered manufactured products from German industry. Germany was then able to buy its raw material in France to the detriment of French industry. France sent into Austria two or three times more money than the amount of goods which she could sell there, and for 10 milliard francs lent to Russia only one milliard of French products were sold. Nevertheless, the responsibilities of the great French banks were not the only ones in question, for French industry could not satisfy all the needs of the countries which France had helped to develop. That development was in direct contrast to English development since England supplied her creditors with the products which she had put them in a position to demand. French production was organised to meet the needs of a quality, if not a luxury, market and its products could not satisfy the requirements of developing countries. This structural defect was only made worse by the fact that the great French capitalists sacrificed the internal development of the country to their own interests. They preferred to seek immediate short-term profits without always being successful in that apparently easy quest.

A specialist in capital export: Bonnardel

No doubt the search for profit had always been the prime motivation, the very 'principle' of capitalism. The new feature was the scale on which that search was now practised, and the Bonnardel family was a good example of the progressive widening of the business horizon.[6] The Bonnardels had been 'river merchants' since the sixteenth century, first at Condrieu and then at Lyon. Railway competition between 1849 and 1855 dealt a severe blow to boat traffic on the Rhône but that same competition was the opportunity for a new effort by these tenacious and enterprising men. They reacted to the situation by technical improvement and by promoting concentration. In 1862 they were managers of the *Compagnie Générale de Navigation*, whose supporters and sleeping partners were still local people. In 1870 Jean-Marie Bonnardel —the great Bonnardel—became manager of the firm, at the age of twenty-two, and he not only endeavoured to renew its facilities and to regulate the flow of river traffic but contrived by successive take-overs to turn it into the largest firm of river navigation—H.P.L.M. (Compagnie Générale de Navigation Le Havre–Paris–Lyon–Marseille); it was formed in 1894 and enlarged later. Nevertheless, the Bonnardel family had made their fortune long before that: in 1882 Bonnardel and his brother-in-law inherited more than 22 million francs in securities and possessions.

Yet during that phase of capitalist evolution the management of such a powerful transport undertaking was bound to be attracted towards industry, and both transport and industry involved finance. Bonnardel took over the Gas Company of Lyon which, under his direction, absorbed a rival company and extended its activities. Soon with the help of the banker Aynard he secured an entry into the Lyon subsidiary of the *Crédit Industriel*; he was already a director of the *Chemins de fer de l'Ouest* and was later to be chairman of the *Société Française de Constructions Mécaniques*—the successor to the Cail enterprise. The *Crédit Industriel* gave him a directorship in 1902.

The financiers of Lyon were looking for a wider and newer field of action, however, in the hope of easier profits. They turned resolutely towards 'that international involvement which is the hallmark of big business'. The President of the Chamber of Commerce was to draw attention to their internationalism in 1902. For his part, Bonnardel— who had already entered steelmaking as one of the principal shareholders of the *Fonderies et Forges de l'Horme*—built up strong holdings in Russia. In 1878 he became a director and in 1880 chairman of the iron and steelworks of Huta-Bankowa, and in 1883 chairman of those of Kama which he reorganised after the crisis resulting from the crash of the *Union Générale*. Again in Russia he was later connected with the industrial platinum company, the coalmines of Berestow and Krinka, the textile industry in Poland, and the Industrial and Metallurgical Society of the Caucasus.

Once he had become a great businessman Bonnardel left his original environment. He installed himself in Paris on the Champs-Élysées in 1894—the year when he founded the New Panama Company and resumed the work abandoned by de Lesseps. Investment in Russian industry was no longer a sufficient interest for him, just as previously river transport at Lyon was not enough. The great credit houses underwrote the operation at Panama rather reluctantly. Bonnardel squeezed 10 million francs from them out of the 60 millions he was aiming at. He did it by asking the credit houses for an account of the profits realised by them on the loans of the first Panama Company, obtaining, in exchange, a renunciation of their claims from the bond-holders of the old company. Even the former directors and managers (Eiffel among them) had to subscribe 'in order to buy off their prosecutors'. Yet this time Bonnardel failed in spite of his cunning, for he was dealing with very powerful opponents. If he had managed to impose his conditions on credit houses they were soon able to retaliate. The shareholders threw Bonnardel out in 1899, following the advice of old Henri Germain, the oracle of the business world: the implication was that Bonnardel's negotiations with the Americans was tantamount to surrendering the enterprise. They were not acting in good faith for the new board sold the business to the United States in 1904 without obtaining the partnership or the firm of mixed ownership which Bonnardel had prepared. It seems likely that the government of Waldeck-Rousseau—whose leader was a great business personality, an adviser of Eiffel and other managers of the old company—encouraged the boardroom revolution of 1899. The government had chosen to leave the field entirely open to yankee imperialism in central America, doubtless in the hope that the United States would uphold French interests against Germany in Africa and the Middle East. As Bouvier suggests: 'There might have been a connection between the American attitude towards Morocco at the Algéciras conference and the fact that France relinquished her interests in Panama in favour of Wall Street'. One may add that high French finance not only had the satisfaction of teaching Bon-

nardel a lesson but that it also benefited from the operation. Thanks to
the compromise of 1894, instead of having to refund the former
'unjustified' profits it merely had to buy the shares of the new company
which it was to sell at a profit in 1904. The *Crédit Lyonnais*, for example, gained 3½ million francs from placing the shares of 1880 and
the bonds of 1881-6; it subscribed for 4 million francs' worth in 1894
and resold them for 5 million francs ten years later. Bonnardel certainly
had something to learn from Monsieur Germain, his illustrious com-
patriot.

3. THE BUSINESS OF INDUSTRY

There was a marked growth in French industry at the end of the nineteenth and the beginning of the twentieth century. Growth was achieved
in spite of the fact that foreign investments were depriving industry of
part of the capital it needed without providing it with new outlets.
Industrial capitalism was certainly making headway at a time when
financial capitalism seemed to be attracting all the attention.

One might even speak of 'a second industrial revolution'—the revolution of electricity and of internal combustion and heavy oil engines
in succession to the revolution of steam, its leaders being—instead of
Watt and Stephenson—Gramme, Bergès, Beau de Rochas, Diesel. The
idea has gained currency especially because of Friedmann and his well-
received book of 1936, the *Crisis of Progress*. But this renewal of technological leadership, however important it was, hardly seemed to affect
our capitalists of the nineteenth century. The results were slow to
appear and just as slow to become widespread. Their effect was seen
above all on the post-1918 industrialists. In this respect the eighties
were the starting point of the new inventions, which were applied more
widely after 1900 but not widely enough to bring a radical change to
industry. The full influence of the economic and social changes induced
by the second industrial revolution were to appear later. Up to 1914
capitalism lived on the first industrial revolution: the great factory
topped by smoking chimneys, the joint-stock company, liberalism
(opposed to state intervention without altogether condemning all forms
of monopoly)—all these were, in their way, characteristic features of
the nineteenth century. During the later part of the nineteenth century,
old structures still prevailed in French industry. It was true that they
underwent changes during the period—concentration, use of banking

capital, 'depersonalisation' of management—but the need for those changes had been felt for a long time. Not all the men involved were new men and attitudes had not significantly changed.

The great steel plants

Steelmaking, for example, was developed and modernised: steel tended to take the place of iron. The location and geographical distribution of the industry changed. After 1878 the Thomas process enabling phosphoric ore to be used gave a new importance to metalmaking in Lorraine. Schneider and de Wendel, the 'iron kings' of the preceding age, modernised their own steelworks by utilising the Thomas process. The old dynasties continued in spite of technical innovations and new regional balances.

There was continuity in the de Wendel family, for example, in spite of the difficult situation created for them by the annexation of 1871. Moyeuvre and Hayange were now in Germany; 'Les Petit-Fils de François de Wendel et Cie'—a simple joint-stock partnership founded immediately after the war whose direct descendants alone could participate in the enterprise—continued operations. The family was about to find a new lease of life in France. In 1880 it formed la Société de Wendel et Cie in which les Petit-Fils de F. de Wendel were joint partners with the Schneiders, who were licensees in France for the Thomas process. There was no other alternative for them. It was at Joeuf, a stone's throw from Moyeuvre but on the French side of the frontier, that the Société was installed. The de Wendels proceeded to reach an unprecedented height of activity in spite of their archaic company constitution and in spite of the fact that they rarely borrowed from the money market. They participated in the steelworks at Longwy and they bought concessions of coking coal in the north, in the Ruhr and in the Low Countries. They joined the confederation of employers representing heavy industry and held a place of first importance among them. Robert de Wendel (of the sixth generation) was president of the Comité des Forges in 1898 and he became vice-president of the Union des Industries Métallurgiques et Minières which was founded in 1900. In 1913 the two de Wendel firms produced 3,700,000 tons of iron ore (which they used entirely for their own purposes), 1,250,000 tons of cast iron, 1,100,000 tons of crude steel and they employed 30,000 workers. Members of the de Wendel family sat as 'opposition' deputies in the Reichstag while other members sat in the French Parliament.

It was a paradoxical situation but certainly a rewarding one—if their critics are to be believed. One can understand public opinion becoming indignant immediately after the Great War at the rather strange concern which the French and German armies had shown for the interests of the de Wendels. It was the 'enigma of Briey', the puzzle of the industrial sector of the frontier which had been occupied almost at once by the German army and respected by French artillery and aircraft. Controversy on the point remains wide open.[7]

'Schneider II' (Henry Schneider, who succeeded the founder in 1875) and 'Schneider III' (Eugène, whose reign lasted from 1898 to 1942) took an active part in the development of Le Creusot. They produced a giant crush-hammer, one of the outstanding items of the Exhibition of 1878. They also made armour-plated sheeting which, thanks to the use of special steels, defied the most powerful artillery and outclassed the products of foreign competitors in spectacular trials. They installed works at Le Havre in 1897 where they made their own cannon. They started constructing warships at Châlons which they sent by waterway to Toulon, and then fitted out in their own dockyards at Bordeaux. All these activities were to add to their long-established reputation in railway equipment and bridge structures. Later on, they made a name in electrical and optical equipment, machine tools, motors and turbines. The firm did considerable work abroad, building bridges and equipping harbours in South America, in Morocco and at Alexandria. In Russia the Schneiders cooperated with the *Union Parisienne* —since industrial and banking capital were more and more closely involved with each other— and installed steelworks at St Petersburg, in the Urals, in the Donetz basin and dockyards at Reval. Both technically and economically their management was quite outstanding and they remained great business leaders.

Many other steelmasters also came from families of long standing. The first board of the *Aciéries de Longwy*, founded in 1880—like *de Wendel et Cie*, in order to exploit the Thomas process—brought together the traditional ironmasters of the region, many of noble rank: there were two barons of Adelsward (one of whom was chairman), the Labbé family, Gustave Raty, the two barons of Huart and a de Wendel. Yet their entrepreneurship was as far-sighted as that of the Schneiders. The creators of Longwy started operating on a large scale immediately: they employed considerable capital, equipped the works without stint and adopted all the latest improvements like the Martin oven without delay. They were soon on the way to vertical integration, for their activities included mines, blast furnaces, steelworks and rolling mills and they established a sales organisation.

Concentration in various forms, whether by amalgamation, joint partnerships, creation of subsidiaries and holding companies, grew appreciably. Many ties were created between the east—which was to become the main location for the production of pig iron—and the centre or the north which tended to concentrate on finished or specialised products. Schneider joined *de Wendel et Cie* and other firms in Lorraine. Châtillon-Commentry commenced operations in the east in 1897 and the *Forges et Aciéries de la Marine* (Saint-Chamond) in 1903. The steelmasters of Lorraine obtained interests in French, German and Belgian collieries. Banks supported their operations. Boards of metalmakers and of banking firms co-operated with each other more and more closely. After 1864 the *Comité des Forges* was at the apex of the structure. It started as a society for the dissemination of information but was reorganised in 1887-8 and assumed more importance under Baron Reille, an influential parliamentarian who was its president from 1890 to 1898. After 1900, it flourished and collaborated closely with different commercial secretariats under the initiative of the secretary-general, Roger Pinot, a man typical of capitalist 'high officials'. There was now a real cartelisation which had the effect of safeguarding profits by stabilisation of prices, by curtailing production and by dividing markets at the risk of slowing down the growth of producer industries like the new automobile industry which was forced to work with its overall prices artificially inflated.

Thus the identity of the modern 'ironmaster' as an individual human being disappeared behind the company title. Ownership was expressed by the board of directors—anonymous and faceless. Certainly there were exceptions like the Schneiders, and there usually remained at the head of a firm a man whose personal qualities were of the first importance—the 'director-general' who had to possess technical skill, commercial ability and a flair for human relationships. He was often the true owner. Thus when Petin and Gaudet left the *Forges et Aciéries de la Marine* in 1874 (the firm having been turned into a limited company), it was Adrien de Montgolfier, chief engineer of roads and bridges, who became manager of the firm for thirty-five years. In 1880 he installed the blast furnaces and steel mills of Boucau with a view to utilising the ores of Spain and the Pyrenees and he made Saint-Chamond one of the most famous armament manufacturers in the world. In 1903 he brought about the amalgamation which gave birth to *Marine-Homécourt*. In general, however, there was a widening gulf between the workman and this conglomerate management which replaced the 'master' of former days. As Duveau has rightly pointed out, management now looked like some mysterious machine whereas formerly the owner 'was a man of flesh and blood, a concrete reality. Today, he is rarely seen or heard; he is part of an abstract organisation and has no direct contact with his workers'.

New industries

In certain sectors, however, technical innovations led to a renewal of personal ownership. The colourful 'pioneer', if not the adventurer, reappeared. Schnerb correctly notes that if 'the self-made men of previous generations were the founders of dynasties, in every period the exploitation of a process, of an idea or of a given situation calls forth the appearance of new founders'.

New men were about to make their fortune on new ventures, like the motor car for instance. The majority of them were technical men who succeeded to the extent that they were also capable of organising and managing. Thus Louis Renault, coming from a family of merchant clothiers and buttonmakers, took a prominent interest in mechanics at a very early age and in 1898, at twenty-one, became a manufacturer. In the following year he made a new start at Billancourt with a capital of 60,000 francs. He was already employing 8,000 workmen when the war broke out in 1914, and from the taxis of the Marne to the tanks of 1918 it brought him nothing but fame and profits. Another pioneer was André Citroën—a different type of man altogether. He was one year younger than Renault, the son of a Jewish diamond merchant and a brilliant student at the *Polytechnique*. He was no jack-of-all-trades, but possessed technical knowledge, an astonishing commercial genius and an extraordinary sense of publicity. Nevertheless, before the war he was merely a small manufacturer of gear wheels and the director of a motor car firm which only truly started production in 1919 since its 13,000 workmen had been employed during the war in making shells. And again, there was Marius Berliet, a silkweaver of the Croix-Rousse district at Lyon, more interested in machinery than in fabrics; he built his first car in 1895 and was to achieve great success with his mass-produced lorry in 1906.

Yet there was also a place for the old dynasties in the new sectors. Peugeot himself became interested in the motor car at the same time as he was manufacturing the pince-nez. Armand Peugeot and two former students of the *École Centrale*—René Panhard and Émile Levassor—together assembled their first car in 1889. Soon they went their separate ways but the first two French car models had appeared. The factory at Beaulieu produced 5 cars in 1891, 29 in 1892 and 40 in 1894. After 1897 the Peugeot family (in accordance with their general policy) had two automobile firms: one at Beaulieu and the other divided between Audincourt and Fives-Lille. They were reunited in 1910 and the works at Sochaux were founded in 1912. In 1913 the firm constructed more than 9,300 motor cars and 80,000 bicycles as well as small motor cycles, but the Peugeot family also went on producing busks for corsets, springs for pince-nez and for phonographs, umbrella frames and all the articles associated with their name.[8]

Another new sphere—that of man-made fibres—was opened up in 1891 with 'the silk of Chardonnet' (otherwise rayon) and was quickly monopolised by two groups of long standing and ample means. One group was the Gillet family from Lyon, well established in the manufacture of dye products derived from imported woods, and the other was the Carnot family, numbering as many businessmen as politicians and men of learning, who managed the *Société de la Viscose*. From 1911 the two groups came to an agreement to set up a sales organisation which fixed prices and rationalised production. It was a type of agreement similar to that which the controllers of the cotton industry had reached in 1901—and one knows how influential the old family dynasties were in the textile industry! They had formed a trade association which was concerned not so much with cartelisation as with technical and fiscal problems.

Furthermore, new concerns representing considerable technical and financial resources were founded by old family businesses. Flour milling, for example, was affected by the general tendency to concentration yet the great mills of Corbeil remained under the control of the Darblay family, descendants of the postmaster under the old régime. They had made their fortune in the grain trade, in milling and in papermaking. According to the Viscount d'Avenel: 'The powerful Darblay family were associated with two new developments of the nineteenth century—white bread and flour for all'. Three of them succeeded each other in the office of 'censeur' of the Bank of France. Similarly the huge mills at Nancy remained under the traditional control of the Bouchotte and Vilgrain families. It was only after the Great War that new large-scale mills were to appear, created as entirely new firms in the most important centres of consumption like Paris at a time when electricity was making greater choice of location possible. Here again, the effects of 'the second industrial revolution' were slow in making themselves felt.

Limits of industrial capitalism

Outside large-scale industry and on the periphery of capitalist society there remained a multitude of small firms and small owners. The impact of concentration was far from complete in 1914—and it has not been achieved even today in building construction or in clothing industry. In certain sectors technical progress even tended to favour handworkers, notably in finishing, in servicing or in repair work. The clothing and automobile industries provided employment at home or in small workshops. In the France of 1911 there were still two employers for every five workers. A wide proportion of the French population—quite apart from rural workers or those employed in commerce—were little affected by capitalism or were not involved directly in its operations, still less in its way of life.

4. EXHAUSTION OF FRENCH CAPITALISM

The resistance of the small craftsman to the concentration movement and the resurgence of small-scale enterprise—encouraged paradoxically by certain aspects of capitalism—were not unique to France. In Germany, for example, the 'revisionist' Bernstein had noticed the same tendencies and used them as an argument against Marxist prophecies. Yet there were other signs of a slackening of French capitalism at the beginning of the twentieth century, disquieting even though they were limited. French capitalists continued to strive and to make progress, yet they were more and more outstripped by capitalists elsewhere. They carried less influence in the world at large even if they carried more weight in their own country.

The industrialisation of France, which was the basis of capitalist growth, was achieved at a slow pace overall. Referring to the Second Empire, which was certainly a decisive period in the history of national development, Marcel Blanchard states that 'France did not go forward by dynamic strides'. She never had superabundant quantities of coal available—an essential factor in British and German growth—nor masses of labour comparable with those that were transferred from rural areas to manufacturing districts by the change in the social and demographic structure of the United Kingdom. France did not have 'those mobile legions of countrymen who were going to rush to German towns a quarter of a century later because of the changes imposed on agriculture and because of the increase in the birth rate'. We also know that France did not always have sufficient financial resources. In any case, she did not achieve spectacular results. According to some estimates, France supplied 9 per cent of world production in 1880 and only 6 in 1913.

Certain defects were particularly serious and emphasised more clearly the general weaknesses of French capitalism. This was the case in the chemical industries. They continued, for example, to use the Leblanc process, though it was in fact no more than a temporary device invented during the revolutionary period to minimise the effects of the blockade. As an expedient it had been quite ingenious, since the basic material required was salt—which was plentiful in France—and a whole range of chemicals could be made from the process. There was one French achievement in the chemical industry and this was the Sainte-Clare Deville process which ensured a monopoly of aluminium production between 1860 and 1890, but this was an isolated case. But already the Solvay process had outstripped the Leblanc soda process and put French industrialists in a state of alarm. The revolution in dyestuffs which came suddenly at the end of the century was to have even more disastrous effects: it was based on coal and had applications in the manufacture of other products such as explosives, pharmaceuticals and plastics.

France had succeeded in adapting to the electro-chemistry of aluminium but she did not make the necessary change at the right time in other sectors of the chemical industry. Although well below Germany in the scale of coal production she was still an important producer and consumer of coal yet she made practically no use of its by-products. Nevertheless, she made some new discoveries. In 1859 Verguin discovered fuchsine or 'red solferino' extracted from aniline; and in 1862 Girard discovered 'bleu de Lyon'. Yet these discoveries were not exploited properly. The firm created at Lyon to develop fuchsine brought several lawsuits for infringement in the hope of obtaining a monopoly but went bankrupt as a result. The *Société de St Denis* was practically the only firm not discouraged by the dumping of dyes practised by the great German companies and attempted to compete with them. Having invented the fuchsine process which was immediately discovered again or improved upon by scientists on the other side of the Rhine, French technologists did not even put up a fight for the market. One must not be misled by a list of the great names of French chemistry from Lavoisier to Berthelot. Whether it was that scientists were too obsessed by theories or that technologists did not pay enough attention to their research work, scientific discoveries were seldom put into practice. The famous work of Pasteur in the field of applied science was certainly useful in silk culture, in breeding and in the production of beer and alcoholic drinks but it did not affect essential sectors of the chemical industry. It was public authorities or highly specialised producers who made use of his research. In the key sectors of the industry no one seemed to favour a close collaboration with the pure scientist or an intimate liaison between laboratory and factory. In this period cartelisation seemed to put a brake on research and development in France. The 'great' firms of Saint-Gobain, Kuhlmann and Péchiney, who believed in 'proved' processes and had little desire for innovation were content, therefore, to share the market between them and to avoid competition. The call of adventure, even in technical matters, held no attraction for them.

Furthermore, French financial institutions gave them no encouragement, and the great banks provided no support for the chemical industry. The joint capital of the forty principal firms represented only 500 or 600 million francs. Saint-Gobain with a share capital of 60 millions looked like a giant while Péchiney's capital was a mere 17 millions and Kuhlmann's was less than 7 millions. Their shares held little attraction for the average Frenchman since no one had drawn his attention to them. Meanwhile, in Germany all the resources of the great capitalists (as well as of scientific research) were put at the service of powerful chemical trusts on the way to international expansion. As a result, France was reduced to the position of a dependent country, if not a colonised one. In 1914, out of nine factories producing artificial dyestuffs operating in France, five were German and the sixth was Swiss; 87 per cent of dyestuffs used in France came from Germany. The French metal industry was to do its best to meet the considerable needs for powders, explosives and gas resulting from the war. France's 2,000 chemists—in Germany there were 30,000 chemists—had to be hurriedly recalled from the army. Improvisation was necessary in the face of many difficulties.

Certainly, the chemical industries were a specially weak feature of French capitalism. Difficulties in such a new and dynamic sector of industry were quite significant, revealing a tendency to cling to traditional practices and to show intolerance towards new ideas. It was true that other industries reacted better. During the decade before the war a veritable boom occurred in the steel industry and production of steel increased at a faster rate than in Germany or in the United States. Yet on closer inspection the picture was not quite so favourable. The long depression which preceded this period of prosperity had postponed investment; now the prospect of satisfactory profits released idle capital or brought capital investment back to the internal market which was once again yielding satisfactory dividends. It was, then, a phase of reinvestment after a crisis. The rapid acceleration of production was all the more noticeable because it had been deliberately limited by cartels in order to maintain prices and profits during difficult years. It was, then a relative boom. France regained part of her lost ground—in a sector which was no longer a new one in the early twentieth century. This upsurge of steelmaking in the years around 1910 did not seem to be a very healthy sign.

It was part of a general economic situation which contained other disquieting features. No doubt the chemical industries provided an extreme example, but not an isolated one. Another dangerous feature of expansion at this time was export of raw material. For example, iron ore exports constituted 8 per cent of iron ore production in 1902, 23 per cent in 1908, and 45 per cent in 1913. French industry was unable to use part of an excess production of her own resources and supplied it to foreign competitors. Deposits of bauxite were controlled by great aluminium trusts which were either English or Swiss-German such as Aluminium Ltd, British Aluminium Company or Aluminium Industries A.G. Not only was more than half of the extracted bauxite exported, but some French works, like those at Marseille, belonged to these foreign trusts or to their subsidiaries. It was a Belgian group which built the underground tube-railway system of Paris and then on the eve of the war constructed the great electrical workshops at Jeumont. The de Wendels of annexed Lorraine were not alone in investing in the basin of Briey: the Thyssen family and the firm of *Gelsenkirchen* acquired iron mines there and in Normandy, where they founded the steel works at Caen. The Roechlings of Saarbrücken had interests in the steel works of Longwy. It would be an exaggeration to speak of an economic colonisation of France by a more powerful

P

capitalism but no exaggeration to point to the latent danger.

It is difficult not to connect this danger with the over-emphasis on foreign investment. The paradox was that French capital helped Russia with her development at a time when Belgian capital was contributing to the development of Paris. The weakness of the policy pursued by French capitalists was that national industry was still short of capital in some sectors even if entrepreneurs were not aware of the shortage. France, then, seemed to be a nation remarkable for the amount of her gold reserves; the Bank of France could afford generous aid to the Bank of England by sending 75 million gold coins at the time of the Baring crash of 1890, and 120 millions in coin during the crash of 1906-07 as well as helping with a policy of liberal discount for English paper money. Certainly, the reserves held by Governor Pallain helped to maintain a reassuring stability on the Paris money market. Yet this gold was sterile; soon it would be dissipated and the franc would enter a long and interminable period of weakness and gradual devaluation when the pound was affected much less seriously. Undoubtedly Minister Klotz could present a flattering picture of France's international financial position in the tribunal on 17 February 1913: 'We can say with some emotion and some pride in our greatness that France is a universal creditor and nowhere a debtor'. This creditor country had world-wide investments but so many of her loans were never to be repaid, so many of them were not to be honoured and so many other sources of income were to disappear. Already France was not obtaining sufficient income from these distant investments to develop commercial exports to a proportionate extent. There was no doubt that internally there was a certain amount of under-investment and under-development in some regions and some activities. French capitalism in the nineteenth century was too diverse, too complex and too difficult to define within strict limits, for one to be able to blame it for all the evils which were to beset the French economy in the twentieth century —that is, after 1914 and especially after 1930. Nevertheless, the defects were serious enough: their widespread extent and their long duration showed that historic catastrophes like the Great War or the Great Slump only threw a harsher light on old weaknesses and mistakes and made the consequences of those errors worse. The easy confident world of our capitalists during the opening years of the twentieth century had its dark corners. The machine had begun to run down.

5
Conclusions

Our account of the history of French capitalists in the nineteenth century has shown a complex evolution. The uneven development of capitalism was continually influenced by the rise of new problems and by the responses to those problems. The picture we have given of the men and their fortunes tends to be lacking in clarity and sharpness and contains too many diverse features. Yet if one were to present the material differently and treat the men in detail in order to make a definitive general judgement, it would require as much space again as in the present simple account of important facts, dates and essential names. Another book would be necessary—all one can do here is to outline the major trends.

Diversity of capitalist society

Firstly, it is essential to show the extreme diversity of the men and the organisation to which the label 'capitalist' was applied. We have emphasised sufficiently the differences existing between differing periods of time. It is evident that there was also a diversity of functions—financiers, bankers, handlers of money, industrial owners and merchants of every kind: all need to be mentioned. We have tried to give a fair treatment, according to their importance, which varied between periods: 'King' Rothschild was replaced by 'King' Schneider. There has also been an emphasis on the interlocking of activities and interests which tended increasingly to put the many aspects of capitalism entirely in the hands of the great business magnates who sat on the boards of the various enterprises. They could be said to be the nineteenth-century equivalent of the non-specialist merchant of the eighteenth century. In this respect Bonnardel, although he was operating on a different scale and in different circumstances, had some resemblance to Périer-Milord. Yet there was also a diversity in the scale of operation. There existed large businesses which were clearly capitalist by their size, by their structure and by their financing. There could be no argument about the status of the de Wendels or of the Boucicaut family or of Henri Germain. But the workshops and small stores were capitalist both by the nature of their legal organisation—since the man running the enterprise was distinct from his salaried employees—and by their economic policy of an unrestrained search for profit. Above all, we have been concerned by the extent to which large-scale industry and business grew from this workshop type and progressively freed themselves from it by successive stages of concentration. As for the mass of small savers—who could not be considered as capitalists from the point of view of their wealth, their style of living or their professional occupations—they should be mentioned here since, after all, 'business consists of other people's money'. Indeed, it was precisely from small savers that industrial firms and credit houses received the capital they needed for their activity and their development. To become a shareholder was to be admitted into capitalist society. The subject of capitalism is not exhausted simply by a mention of the great names. To assess it more accurately one must also appreciate how deeply national life had been influenced by its outlook and its activities.

In the circumstances, it would be wrong to say that capitalists constituted a homogeneous class. In this context, 'class' signifies a group of people who are in similar positions in society and who have identical attitudes concerning the relations between capital and labour. The capitalists were those who possessed the means of production (especially money) which they used themselves or which they entrusted to men who could turn them to account. They were entrepreneurs and moneylenders. That was the simple fact but it was not the whole story, for the capitalists also belonged to very different social categories. Their place in society was expressed more easily by their relations with other classes than by a direct definition of their own outlook and activity.

Nobility, bourgeoisie and capitalism

The status of the capitalists changed considerably during the course of the nineteenth century. At the beginning, they were still in the category in which they had been at the end of the previous century—one of the principal elements of the revolutionary bourgeoisie. As we have seen, the old aristocracy certainly played a part in the business world before the Revolution, but it was a secondary part and a temporary one. The capitalism of 1789 was essentially bourgeois and was to become more bourgeois, an emphasis which was an essential element in the Revolution. Hence the principal conflict of class warfare was waged between the bourgeoisie (synonymous with liberalism and individualism) on the one hand and the aristocracy of the old régime on the other. The conflict was gradually resolved during the first half of the nineteenth century. The Napoleonic episode confirmed the revolutionary victory of the bourgeoisie but the Restoration again seemed to question its position. 1830 dealt a final blow to the old nobility and to absolutism. In this conflict the capitalists clearly showed their allegiance. Delessert and Fulchiron were among the demonstrators of July 1789: at a moment of need the bankers came down into the street leading their customers. The episode of the *Trois Glorieuses* confirmed the point very forcibly. On the news of the Decrees some Parisian merchants and manufacturers, gathered together at the Hôtel de Ville to elect the members of the Tribunal of Commerce, decided to close shop and allowed their workmen to take part in the rising. Fighting took place around the Stock Exchange. Laffitte and Périer—rather cautious and circumspect until the fighting was over—were among the organisers of resistance to the royal coup d'état. High finance was soon to be rewarded for its concern. From 1831 the new régime allowed principal bankers access to the peerage; Davillier and others were to have a seat in the Luxembourg. The Dalloz reference book thoroughly approved the new development: 'We have come a long way since the days when the barbarous law inspired by religious feeling placed the business of banking among the lowest activities of society'.

Socially and politically supreme, the bourgeoisie naturally retained control over the economy. Almost all the creators of new enterprises, and almost all the great initiators and the majority of the founders of dynasties mentioned in this book were bourgeois. Most of them were of humble origins, if one goes back far enough, and their promotion to large-scale business was achieved—in spite of exceptions like Laffitte —by successive stages in small and then in medium-sized commerce. They rose from artisan ownership to small manufacturing. There were some who went into the civil service or the legal profession. Thus Decazes, the creator of the ironworks named Decazeville, was a barrister (and the son of a solicitor) before becoming President of the

Conseil and a duke; and the Talabots were sons of magistrates. The old aristocracy experienced a marked decline in spite of such regional survivals as the ironmasters in the east and dynasties in Champagne where the Moët family of Dutch origin had been raised to the nobility by Charles VII. Nevertheless, some aristocrats made a name for themselves in scientific or technological fields. The count de Chardonnet, for example, was the father of the artificial silk industry; and he managed to persuade one Baudry d'Asson—from an old Vendée family—to join him in setting up a factory. It must be said, however, that the profits were promptly invested in landed property. The Marquis de Dion—with his associate, the former locksmith-mechanic, Bouton—was to be one of the pioneers of the motor vehicle industry but not the founder of a lasting firm. The 'great names' of France had not lost all their prestige—far from it. Their reputation still had a market value and the capitalist bourgeoisie was quite ready to join them in mutually beneficial partnerships and to accept them on boards of directors.

Marriages between the business world and the nobility multiplied in the course of the century, especially in the last third. The wine producers of Champagne—some of whom were already noblemen—reinforced their links with the aristocracy by marriage: in 1816 Adelaide Moët married a Chandon de Briailles from a family of magistrates; a Chandon married one of the Clermont-Tonnerre family; and in 1817 Madame Clicquot-Ponsardin—the widow Clicquot—married her daughter to the Count de Chevigné, with the result that her granddaughter became Countess de Mortemart and her great granddaughter the famous Duchess of Uzès. Werlé—a partner in the firm of Clicquot —married a Lannes de Montebello, who was doubtless of recently created nobility, but their daughter married the son of Albert de Mun. The board of the Clicquot firm in 1851 comprised a Count de Mun, a prince Caraman-Chimay, a princess Poniatowska, the countesses d'Harcourt and de Vogüé—all connected by marriage. The Polignac family directed the firm of Pommery and there were very many similar links. In the sugar industry marriages took place between a Say and a prince de Broglie, between his sister and the Marquis de Brissac, and between the Sommier and Barante families. In steelmaking, marriages occurred between the Talabot and Nervo families, and in 1903 the Baron de Nervo became chairman of the *Comité des Forges*. Even in banking there was one example of an aristocratic founder—the Marquis d'Audiffret, father of the *Crédit Industriel*—as well as men who had recently been granted a title, like Davillier or Neuflize. In spite of the occurrence of antisemitic feeling, a Duke de Grammont married a Rothschild, a Marquis de Breteuil married a Fould, and there were many other instances of such marriages. A board of directors composed of titled members was bound to look impressive and to inspire confidence, especially in the insurance world; whether those titles had been acquired through marriage or not was irrelevant. From 1819 a Count de Montesquiou was on the board of the *Phénix*, and in 1930 the board of the *Paternelle* included the Duke de Lévis-Mirepoix, the counts de Chabrol, de Lasteyrie, de Miribel, and de Vogüé, the barons de Barante and de la Bouillerie, the Viscount Decazes and Monsieur Maurice de Wendel.

The new social problem

The integration of aristocratic elements into the bourgeoisie was greatly facilitated by the fact that the participants in the social class struggle had changed sides since 1848. There was no longer an aristocratic 'counter-revolutionary' danger; the enemy for capitalism was now on the left. Of course one must not oversimplify, for the violent political struggles of the Third Republic show only too well that the ruling class were, in fact, divided. Dubochet, ex-follower of Saint-Simon, an important owner of Parisian gasworks, financed the republican campaign after 16 May; as a friend of Gambetta he was among those who foresaw and welcomed the arrival of 'new foundations to society'. One cannot take for granted the theories of Beau de Loménie according to which bourgeois dynasties who held opposite views in politics would always be reconciled when it came to a business deal or to taking advantage of the state. This unity was achieved, he thinks, by the clever manipulators of finance (Brumairian, Orleanist, or Left-Centre). Nevertheless, it is true to say that the leading capitalist personalities were almost unanimous, as might be expected, in refusing to consider the social problem of their time which involved the working-class question, socialism and even social intervention. There was something deeply significant about the two 'opposed' leaders: the Duke of Audiffret-Pasquier, head of the monarchist right centre, and Laurent Casimir-Périer, associated with the conservative republicanism of Thiers. They both became the sons-in-law of a rich naval supplier; both were administrators of *Anzin* (the former being chairman of the board) and they both lived on the Champs-Élysées in two nearby mansions.

Existing capitalists had no intention of closing their ranks to new-comers. They rewarded politicians who served their interests by admitting them to their circle. The new and growing importance of techniques—industrial, commercial and financial—favoured the promotion of those who had become masters of their own specialism. First, under the Second Empire, there were simple workmen like Cail or men employed in shops like Boucicaut, Chauchard and Jaluzot. Then there were inventors or 'constructors' like Renault and Berliet. To these must be added the superior technologists reared in the *grandes écoles*—upstarts of the education system, one may call them, like the men from the *Polytechnique* or the finance inspectors—whose influence grew continually greater. Henri de Peyerimhoff, for example, who was a member of the *Conseil d'État* and involved in administering agricultural affairs in Algeria, became secretary and then president of the *Comité des Houillères*.

Yet these new elements did not really alter the capitalists' social outlook but were simply absorbed by it. At the beginning of the twentieth century the majority of the great leaders of the French economy still clung to their traditional social views. Undoubtedly they became more philanthropic, in the manner of American millionaires. Yet their philanthropy did not consist so much of charity or almsgiving, which were aristocratic practices. It manifested itself in their paternal attitudes towards their workers: they provided workers with houses, medical dispensaries and children's nurseries. It was also reflected in gifts and spectacular legacies, like those of Boucicaut, Cognacq-Jay or Baron Alphonse de Rothschild who set aside 10 million francs for the construction of cheap housing.

On the other hand, workers' demands and state intervention were opposed in the name of liberalism, still regarded as a sacrosanct principle even though it was beginning to be eroded by the tendency to cartelisation and monopoly. The reply of Henry Schneider in 1897 to a question by the journalist Huret was significant; it came at a time when Parliament had just voted two laws permitting discretionary arbitration between employers and employees and limiting the working day of women and young people to eleven hours:

> State intervention in the workers' problems? Very very bad...I do not think it is fit for a Prefect to meddle in strikes...The new work regulations for women and children are nothing but obstacles; they are too narrow and really useless...As for the eight-hour day, it is still a hobby-horse, an idea of the Boulangistes. In five or six years' time it will be forgotten and it will have been replaced by something

else ... To my mind a workman doing his job properly can very well do ten hours and he should be allowed to do more if he feels like it.

In fact, Schneider was expressing one of the deepest convictions of the capitalist; his outlook arose from his particular place in the economic structure and the structure itself was the main unifying element of the heterogeneous group of capitalists. It was natural enough, therefore, to find an employer like Schneider holding such views. The journalist Huret also questioned Alphonse de Rothschild. This was the Baron's reply:

> I am sure that workers—I speak in general terms—are well content with their lot, that they have few complaints and are not concerned with what is called socialism. Certainly there are leaders of the workers [but] one has to distinguish between good and bad workers. Those who demand the eight-hour day are the lazy incapable ones. The others, the steady serious fathers of families, want to be able to work long enough to provide for themselves and their family. But if they were all compelled to work only eight hours a day do you know what the majority of them would do? Well, they would drink! They would spend more time in the bars and that is all. What else would you expect them to do?[1]

The banker and the industrialist had the same reaction and expressed similar views on the subject; and their viewpoint may well have been held by the small shareholder. It was the typical reaction of the capitalist but it often spread into middle management, among the engineers, for example, who were an integral part of the whole system.

Standards of living and styles of living

There is no doubt that the style and standard of living of the capitalists varied a great deal. Unequal distribution of wealth was very marked, though difficult to measure. Around 1880 some 700 or 800 persons gained at least 250,000 francs in income (naturally in gold francs), great landed proprietors among them. In the nineties 3,000 incomes exceeded 10,000 francs, 185,000 ranged between 10,000 and 100,000 francs, and 1,300,000 incomes were between 2,500 and 10,000 francs compared with 9,512,000 lower than 2,500 francs. The life of a great banker, or the owner of a large factory or of a department store had obviously nothing in common with that of a small *rentier*. But those are only general considerations. Moreover, it would be difficult to distinguish among these privileged men of wealth those whose activities and income were strictly capitalist. Each section of the capitalist class had, in fact, the same standard of living as the bourgeois class to which it belonged. There was no intrinsically capitalist way of life.

The social contacts of the very rich capitalists were not confined to their business connections; they were acquainted with all the fashionable people, with what was known as *le tout-Paris*. Yet they were not the leaders of fashion. In this respect the aristocracy continued to play its former role, even during the Third Republic when the men who reigned over Parisian salons were men like the prince of Sagan, Boni de Castellane and Robert de Montesquiou. The faubourg Saint-Germain and the Sainte-Clotilde district did not always accept the newly-rich without reservation. The Marquis de Brissac, née Say, on several occasions had to endure affronts from the nobility who frequented her residence in the Place Vendôme.

Yet the social barriers finally crumbled. The first Parisian 'Social Circle', founded in 1828 during a period of anglophil sentiment, was the *Cercle de l'Union* and even though it was highly aristocratic it immediately admitted the great bankers Rothschild, Hottinguer, Mallet, Casimir-Périer, Rougemont de Löwemberg, William Hope and Aguado. The Jockey-Club was even less exclusive; a Parisian notary gave a curious but realistic assessment of a Jockey-Club membership: 'For a bridegroom being in the Jockey is like receiving an extra 200,000 francs' worth of wedding presents'. Besides, the club experienced financial difficulties and it was naturally the Fould, Rothschild and Laffitte circles who helped it to overcome them. It reached its high point during the Second Empire.[2] Men could join just as easily the circle of the rue Royale. Businessmen, however, felt more at home in the *Cercle des Chemins de Fer* founded under the patronage of Morny in 1854—the name, the date and the patronage were significant—or in the *Union artistique*. The receptions and balls of the wealthiest of the great capitalists attracted high nobility as much as high financiers. The Rothschilds in their mansion at Paris with its overpowering display of luxury and in their châteaux at Suresnes and Ferrières offered their guests the best fare of the time under the supervision of Carême, ex-chef de cuisine of the Tsar and of the English Court. The Rothschilds had racing stables that were numbered among the most famous in existence. They launched Aix-les-Bains (a good business proposition just as much as a sign of their worldly status) in the same way that Aguado, Marquis of Las Marismas, launched Dieppe, or in the same way that Morny launched Trouville and Deauville, or the whole business circle of Napoleon III launched Vichy. Equally brilliant were the festive occasions given by William Hope in the rue Saint-Dominique: around 1840 chroniclers wrote that 'people talked of nothing else but Croesus taking up residence in the venerable fauborg St Germain'. Later there were similar social gatherings at the home of the Péreires in the faubourg St Honoré; but they at least sometimes felt that the festivities were too ostentatious. 'I know that there is too much show,' said Émile Péreire, 'but the situation will gradually improve'. Besides, the splendid evenings cut into their normal life which was simple and hardworking and very much a family affair.

Others displayed their wealth in a more flashy and uninhibited way, a feature that was true of Mirès or of Millaud and even more often of the parvenus of the Third Republic. Dufayel, ex-groom and creator of the ready-to-wear shops in the rue de Clignancourt, had the hotel d'Uzès in the Champs Élysées pulled down. 'I am too wealthy to live in other people's filth', he said, and he replaced it by a 'palace' designed according to his own plans and filled with extravagant horrors. Chauchard decorated his mansion in the avenue Velasquez and his château at Longchamp with 'artistic' bronzes straight out of the Louvre department store. Sometimes the inheritors of great business dynasties found in Parisian life a way of spending their fortune which they had no intention of increasing or even of preserving. That was the sorry story of 'Le Petit Sucrier'—Max Lebaudy—who received, like each of his three brothers and sisters, an inheritance of 27 million francs, and who died young after having led a brief life of pleasure. He launched Maxim's and put his money in the hands of a group of adventurers. Jaurès commented that what Lebaudy had achieved was to enable suspect foreign adventurers to acquire the wealth produced by the work of the founders of capitalism.

Nevertheless, some of the great capitalists did not have the time or the inclination to indulge in constant festivities or to be involved in the social whirlpool. That type of existence, in spite of the increasingly mixed character of 'high society', remained essentially the sphere of the aristocracy. Many businessmen lived very spaciously in their rich mansions in the chaussée d'Antin or in the rue St Honoré or later in the new western district: Parc Monceau, Ternes, Étoile, Champs-Élysées, Chaillot and Passy attracted them in turn. Yet they lived a quiet and often a simple kind of life. We know that the salon of Henri Germain was serious and even solemn, concerned above all with literature and politics. The Boucicaut and Cognacq families continued to lead a simple life which bordered on parsimony. Especially in the provinces, if the capitalists' way of life tended to overshadow that of an impoverished nobility and they sometimes took over the residences of the nobility, the great business or industrial bourgeois led an existence which was comfortable rather than showy. In general, their way of life was at least outwardly highly respectable, if not stern. Nevertheless, because of their wealth and their class solidarity, the fine districts where they lived became sharply separate from other districts. The Chartrons at Bordeaux; the neighbourhood of the place Bellecour, of the rue Sala or of the parc de la Tête d'Or at Lyon; the cours Pierre-Puget, the Paradise quarter or the cours du Chapitre at Marseille; the rue de la Liberté at Lille; the rue Jeanne d'Arc at Orléans—all contained groups which were more and more inward-looking and exclusive.

The brilliant life of the great capitalists tended to conceal the less spectacular life led at a lower level. No special feature here attracted attention. On the whole, all bourgeoisie lived in much the same way, whether their resources came from land, commerce, industry or banking. For a long time this remained exactly as it had been described by Balzac—traditional, dull and modest, though of course, there were the exceptions who dissipated their fortunes. The situation altered slightly at the end of the century through a widening of contacts and a broadening of horizons. In any case, participation in capitalism either directly or as a shareholder was not enough to cause men to change their way of life. The distinctive features of the capitalist 'class' were not to be found in social behaviour.

Cosmopolitans, dissidents or conformists?

The capitalists did not have particularly original tastes or cultural attitudes. Undoubtedly, some capitalist circles were distinct from the rest of the country by religion if not by race. We know the part played by foreigners in major French banking. It is significant that men coming from countries more advanced in this sphere succeeded in arousing in France an inclination towards capitalist activity, and this in spite of the reluctance and indecision they encountered. It explains also why great protestant and Jewish bankers were still regarded with suspicion by the public and subjected to accusations of 'cosmopolitanism' that were aroused by xenophobe or anti-semitic passions. Long before Toussenel or Drumont, the author of a supposed 'letter from Monsieur Turgot to Monsieur Necker' stated in 1779 that 'the bankers have two fatherlands, one where they obtain money cheaply and the other where they sell it very dearly' and it pointed an accusation at Necker which came to be used frequently afterwards: 'Through the banking game you are the most dangerous cosmopolitan'. This was an essential theme in the image of the financier as a 'lynx', enriching himself at the expense of the country that offered him its hospitality. When the crisis of 1914 aroused nationalism in Paris, people blamed German business houses especially—or those thought to be German.

We know also, though the links between protestantism and industrialism have been exaggerated, that some important industrial circles were exclusively protestant. There were examples of these at Mulhouse and among the hosiers of the Gard, among the weavers of Castres and of Mazamet, besides others. It may seem strange—and yet it is easy to see the reason why—that the business circle of Cette during the time of Louis Philippe approved of two bizarre deviations—one calvinist (the evangelical church of Marguerite Coraly Hinsch) and the other catholic (the teachings of Vintras)—both in some respects quite close to each other.[3] Yet it is doubtful whether one could say that capitalism had somehow evolved from a religious movement. It would be more interesting to determine to what extent the behaviour of French protestants was affected by the confiscation of property belonging to the devotees of the R.P.R. in the eighteenth century; small fortunes and landed property possibly suffered more than great fortunes and moveable possessions. Confiscations certainly contributed to promoting a bourgeois outlook among protestants and to steering them towards commerce and banking. 'It is a long story and it has not all been told yet.'[4] But whether they were catholic (like employers in the north) or protestant (like employers in Alsace), capitalists had features in common. Industrial genius and enthusiasm for business was not confined to protestants, as is often thought: it was found also among that section of French capitalists reputed to be catholic and lazy. According to Audiganne's evidence it was quite usual for the manufacturers of Nîmes to retire with their nest-egg once they had accumulated a modest fortune, but too much must not be made of special examples.

No particular moral or spiritual outlook seemed to distinguish the generality of French capitalists from the majority of the bourgeoisie (with the exception of the lesser bourgeoisie who numbered many unbelievers vigorously promoting the anticlerical struggle). Capitalists were, in general, going through the same process as the bourgeois, abandoning their Voltairian ideas inherited from the eighteenth century and gradually returning to religious faith. At first the movement was rather superficial and largely inspired by the reaction of social conservatism which followed the great fear of 1848. Gradually it assumed more significance and dynamism. The change took place as young people educated in religious institutions reached adult age and when, at the end of the nineteenth century and the beginning of the twentieth, general currents of thought and feeling began to alter. It was rather similar to the changes in outlook experienced by Thiers. In fact, besides being head of the government he was himself a great capitalist since he was president of the *Compagnie d'Anzin*. He had been a free-thinker, but in 1848 he became the faithful champion of a 'religion for the people' and one of the authors of the *loi Falloux*. It was as if Thiers had had grandchildren—brought up by the Fathers but later enticed by Bergson or the masters of neo-spiritualism, or even becoming members of the Catholic Association of French Youth founded in 1906. Of course, in the capitalist world there was always a whole range of attitudes in evidence, from religious ardour to scepticism and from free-thinking to religious observance. Some silkmakers of Lyon, for example, still remained strongly religious although in the Périer family the 'great religious fervour of the women' was only matched by the 'respectful indifference of the men'.[5] On the other hand, even at the end of the century the *Compagnie d'Anzin* engaged its young workers only after their first communion.[6]

Cultural attitudes

The intellectual standards and interests of capitalists naturally varied with their upbringing and with their family environment. The inheritor of a dynasty had more cultural opportunities than the self-made man, while the knowledge and outlook of a technocrat who had risen in the world through his own ability were not at all those of the son of an established familily. Yet even old families of the high industrial bourgeoisie sometimes showed a marked utilitarianism. The men of Mulhouse, as seen by a sub-prefect in 1821, 'showed no interest in the literary world, in legal principles or in human knowledge which had no immediate relevance to other industry', but his judgement was not applicable to all capitalists. Nevertheless, this attitude towards the relevance of knowledge explains the frequent connections between business circles and geographical societies, as at Lyon or at Marseille. Literary circles, when they existed, generally remained classical in outlook, and the new ideas of recently formed movements were either misunderstood or not well publicised. Of course, distinctions must be drawn: Paris was not like the provinces and the great bourgeois, especially if he were a man of the world, had more cultural contacts and opportunities for refining his taste than the small 'rentier'. Overall however, the gulf widened between the tastes of the great public and those of lively artistic circles. Already the romantics were denouncing the philistines, but it was later in the century that all contact was lost. It was a far-reaching problem, this divorce between the intellectuals and the rest, this coming of a time when, as Malraux has written, 'artists no longer addressed themselves to everyone nor even to a class but to a group exclusively defined by their own values'. The problem goes far beyond the particular outlook of the capitalists.

One could hardly expect capitalists to be artists or authors or even connoisseurs. Yet by tradition the possessors of great fortunes were collectors and patrons of art, and it was a role which continued to flatter or to appeal to many of them. A multitude of pictures, marble, bronzes, porcelain, works of art of every kind, adorned their mansions. From an artistic point of view the result was not always a success and for every Guimet or Cernuschi there were many like Cognacq or Chauchard. In contemporary art, discrimination became even more difficult. Isaac de Camondo and Alphonse de Rothschild passed for enlightened amateurs but the majority continued in a stilted traditional outlook. With his usual acuteness André Siegfried noticed the source and inspiration of the tastes of the high business bourgeoisie in which he was born and brought up: Bouguereau was its god, Monet caused a scandal and Cézanne was unknown. Meyerbeer, a protégé of Baron James, met the needs of the July bourgeoisie but Wagner shocked the Second Empire. It was true that fifty years later Wagnerism was in good repute and the French version of Parsifal in 1914 was one of the last performances at the Opéra before the war. Debussy, however, caused an uproar. A certain group of the Parisian élite occasionally found the means, thanks to its snobbery, of not being left too far behind the advanced ideas of the age. Nevertheless, if the salon of the Countess Greffulhe made the reputation of 'Claude de France' it failed to recognise any merit in 'The Rite of Spring'. One can only repeat that capitalists of every dimension generally followed the tastes and prejudices of the social categories to which they belonged. Their particular kind of activities and experiences did not engender any original thought or feeling. There was nothing comparable here with the Florentine or Venetian painting of the quattrocentro; that period had been influenced by the social conflicts and widening economic outlook of the bourgeois of the great Italian cities. Medieval capitalism—in this context it matters little whether or not it was true capitalism—had a cultural usefulness: it was the buttress of a civilisation. French capitalism in the nineteenth century was an inherent part of social and economic arrangements; but superior forms of life, especially cultural expression, bore less the imprint of capitalism than that of the bourgeoisie in general from which it was indistinguishable.

The politics of the capitalists

The question arises whether or not capitalism was a political force, whether or not capitalist politics were a substitute for capitalist art or thought. It was obvious that capitalists exercised more influence in politics than had formerly been the case. In 1857 Jules Vallès wrote to Mirès: 'The future of France is no longer debated in the classic places of uprising—the rue Saint-Denis or the place de Grève—but in the rue Vivienne, the place Vendôme, at Péreire's residence and in your own circle'. In 1878 the German ambassador declared: 'In Paris the world of finance is in command'. As we have seen, the business world was widely represented in politics from the time of Périer and Laffitte down to Rouvier and another Casimir-Périer. A long list of names could be quoted as evidence. Beau de Loménie has mentioned scores of them without exhausting the list. He has also pointed out that if capitalists gained access to public life, parliamentarians or more often ministers—intent on safeguarding the interests of influential people—could secure entry to business circles. For example, around 1910 Étienne, Doumer, André Lebon, Jonnart, Jules Siegfried, Charles Roux and many others were on the boards of numerous companies. There were also more modest collaborators: Bénac was head of Raynal's cabinet during the vote on the agreements of 1883; and Laurent-Atthalin, attaché in Thomson's cabinet and Minister of Marine, became in 1911 at a still youthful age secretary-general of the *Banque de Paris et des Pays-Bas*. If these examples were not enough, one has only to think of the scandals which erupted from time to time in the political and business world, from Teste and Cubières to Panama (which was not the last), to appreciate that money and power were interlinked.

Yet over-simplifications must be avoided. At times capitalists, far from imposing their own views on governments, were used as pawns in political manoeuvre. French diplomats used the Parisian financial market as a weapon first to persuade Russia to conclude the alliance and then to make it work—notably at Algeçiras. Moreover, some capitalists were unable to see where their own true interests lay, or were unable to make them prevail, however strange it may seem. The foreign investments of the great French banks and the connections of French banks with foreign business circles made a world war rather undesirable for them in 1914. There is no evidence that they either wished it or provoked it, yet it does not look as if they tried to avert it. It is true that 'the cannon merchants' knew how to exploit the demand created by hostilities to the best of their interest, but it does not mean that they can be held responsible for the conflict. They seem rather to have been waiting for the event, ready to take advantage of the opportunity once it was offered, just as high finance did in the coup d'état of 2 December 1852. Besides, the capitalists were not all-powerful. Even in the period of the elected monarchy when money was the criterion of political power, other forces existed—royalty, landed aristocracy, the Church, public officials, public opinion—over which capitalists certainly had some influence but which they could not hope to dominate continually, even had they wished by common agreement so to do. Account must also be taken of independent new and sometimes hostile forces like universal suffrage and the trade unions. No doubt, their influence over the press, which was to a considerable extent controlled by them, allowed them some voice in events, yet here again the press was, like them, often divided. They had no monopoly of power. However great their influence may have been, the whole of French political life cannot be written in terms of their activities. To do so would be to create a myth, rather similar to that of the Jew and the Freemason who are sometimes made responsible for everything.[7]

Capitalists and the state

Greater justice would be done to capitalists and to the subject of their political power if one tried to define their exact role in each particular political episode. It cannot be done here. In general, capitalists were in favour of arrangements and of institutions which served their economic activities and maintained their social power.[8] Yet undoubtedly they became more involved and tenacious in defending their interests over the issues of taxes and tariffs, which were the principal spheres of state intervention and where new policies could directly injure their interests. They were active in the struggles for protection—during the Restoration, under Guizot, in 1860, in the National Assembly of 1871 and in the Méline period. With some few exceptions, they fought with

P

acrimony and perseverance against income tax and against the man who symbolised it—Joseph Caillaux. The latter was very close to them in some respects but perhaps more clear-minded, and one may believe the statement of the great financier Octave Homberg in 1926 that their resistance to direct taxation—successful up to the war—was 'not very far-sighted'. With regard to the different economic functions of the state, they readily accepted the levying of customs duties, and even asked for them provided the duties were to be applied fairly. They agreed with the collection of the *quatre vieilles* (the four direct taxes dating from the Revolution) and of taxes on consumption, especially if there were no searching enquiries. They accepted the role of the state as banker on certain occasions—when they had to obtain the services of an issuing house for difficult operations, when it was necessary to provide capital for a low income-producing sector, or when it was necessary to guarantee dividends of railway stock. Yet it was axiomatic that support for the state as producer or manager in the economic sphere was anathema. The arrangement over the Freycinet Plan in 1883 put an end to the state's pretensions for a long time. At the most the state was asked to take over loss-making enterprises like the railways of Charentes in 1878, which was how the 'state network' started. In social policy the state fulfilled two very different functions: in acting as a policeman it was considered beneficial since it protected the established order; but in attempting to act as a supreme provider it would have been very unpopular had its role not been an illusory one (for the reason that projects of state intervention in work legislation or working-class problems were extremely timid). Such were the broad lines of the attitude of the capitalists to the liberal state.

Colonial horizons

We should also appreciate the role of the great capitalist interests in international relations, especially during the epoch of imperialism. Peyerimhoff, a witness free from bias, declared in June 1914 that 'business politics had gained a place beyond the national frontiers along with other politics'. The capitalist attitude in the sphere of colonial expansion needs special definition.[9] The principal episodes were as follows: the profit obtained from Algeria and the exploitation of mineral resources by concessionary firms; the interests behind the occupation of Tunisia and the various Indo-Chinese territories and the exploitation of these new protectorates; the beginnings of French rule in black

Africa which was a more extensive continuation of the African operations already undertaken by merchants of Bordeaux or of Marseille; the Malagasy loan placed by the *Comptoir d'Escompte* and the conquest and colonisation of Madagascar; and the interconnection between politics and diplomacy in the Moroccan question which, more than any other event, was a product of grand diplomacy and which twice led to the brink of European war. A study of these episodes promotes better understanding of the choice which was made in each instance between the liberal concept of commerce independent of politics and that of the imperialists for whom commerce followed the flag. Detailed study no doubt explains the relative sacrifice of the colonial market—which in 1914 did not absorb a tenth of French external investments—for the benefit of other markets like Russia.

In a number of these cases some capitalists were probably more hesitant, more fearful and more inclined to peaceful policies than their reputation suggests. Yet in the motives which historians often impute to them, individual responsibility was less significant and individual actions less effective than the operation of the system as a whole. When one analyses the conditions of working-class life in the forties one discovers that they were not caused so much by the inhumanity of the employer as by the play of free competition and its overall consequences. Many business circles can doubtless be cleared of charges of 'war-mongering' when their attitudes are closely studied. Yet when one considers Europe at the beginning of the twentieth century, one cannot altogether dismiss the striking phrase of Jaurès: 'Capitalism brings war as the great cloud brings a storm'.

Capitalist France

To conclude, we must return to the capitalists' own sphere of activity, the only sphere in which final judgement can be passed on them, if there are final judgements in history. Their world was not that of the salons, of the churches or of the picture galleries, it was not the factory as a place of social contact, and not even the parliamentary platform or the ministerial office. It was the province of economic management: production, capital equipment and the circulation of money. In this respect they were the agents of a very important change. In the course of the century the growing wealth and the material progress of France were attributable to them. In this respect France changed more in a century than she had done during all her previous history and, once more, it was the capitalists who controlled the course of economic change. They had been the first to show some interest in expansion in a slow-moving economy and made it a subject for debate: 'At a time when Frédéric Bastiat preached peace and harmony and when the latter-day disciples of J. B. Say elaborated their theories concerning supply and demand and the money market, devising means to preserve the existing equilibrium, the masters of the great business combines were without illusions. As far as they were concerned, conflict was inherent in economic growth and they were prepared to engage in conflict in order to achieve their aims'.[10]

If France was modernised as a result of capitalist activity, the question arises whether her modernisation was as rapid and complete as that of other great contemporary powers. We already know the answer: her relative backwardness was to be judged by the limited nature and incompleteness of her economic change by 1914. It was partly due to a lack of raw material, but the deficiency in coal did not explain everything. The capitalists themselves could be overcautious and some of them were unable to make the most of their historical opportunity. In passing judgement on their attitude in regard to the market, André Siegfried seemed to sympathise with them rather regretfully:

> Before 1914 and even before 1939 France held the enviable position of having little need of the outside world (whether as supplier or as customer). We more than made up the deficit in our balance of trade by the income derived from capital invested abroad or by various invisible exports. In contrast to the military insecurity engendered by an ever-threatened frontier, a gratifying feeling of economic security was produced by the traditional affluence and financial autonomy, to a degree unknown, for example, by England. It was rather like a domestic blessing, openly shown off and offensive to neighbours. Méline's policy, born of an alliance between industry and agriculture, had increased this feeling of security and rather encouraged the sluggishness of industrialists in respect of exports. The French producer was set not so much on conquering new markets as on defending his own by privilege.[11]

And, at home, French capitalists used compromise as much as combat. Quite early on, when the concentration process had already claimed victims, it was as if they were moved by the protests of threatened producers and they came to a typically French agreement. They joined up with the 'small men' instead of destroying them and even acted as their spokesmen in order to defend a policy of high prices. Economically, it meant a higher profit differential for the better firms through their increased productivity, but it retarded modernisation: it led to a Malthusian outlook, limited advance both quantitatively and qualitatively, and socially it only postponed the day of reckoning and paved the way for more painful economic crises. Doubtless the social structure which had emerged from the Revolution—with the rural sector 'sheltered' and stabilised where a firmly embedded peasantry survived in economic stagnation—was rather unfavourable to the capitalists. Its individualist and egalitarian tradition diminished the influence of 'famous men' and gave full meaning to the phrase 'universal suffrage'. Undoubtedly, if capitalism was prepared to compromise rather than to engage in cut-throat competition the reason was that capitalists did not find themselves in a strong enough position.

Capitalism was also hindered in its development by the traditional attitudes of landowners and artisans in France. A great deal of time and painful experience were needed to overcome their objections to the new use of credit, which were expressed in the disparaging and haughty phrase: 'being reduced to borrowing'. It was no easy task either to overcome the fixed-income mentality which was inimical to the capitalist outlook, even though the savings amassed may have been necessary for launching other men's enterprises.[12] Today it is difficult to imagine the idle *rentier* of nineteenth-century France—with his modest needs—who frittered away human resources and dissipated his capital in an unspectacular way. His whole existence was supported by fixed income and if that income was absent life was disastrous. It was a way of life while it lasted. A picture of the *rentier* is provided by the poor hero of *A Sentimental Education*—Frédéric Moreau; no doubt Moreau was a mediocre example, but there were few living on fixed income who were exceptional people. Flaubert tells of Moreau's beginnings in Paris which were reasonably happy ones. Then the true state of his fortune became known: 3,000 francs in fixed income, a mere nothing—there he was 'ruined, laid bare, lost'. He was allowing himself to be maintained by his mother at Nogent, living a life of dull routine, all his vitality gone. 'She dreamed of buying him a registrar's office in the tribunal: Frédéric did not altogether reject the idea. Now he accompanied her to Mass, had his game of cards in the evening, settled down to leading a provincial life and became fixed in his ways.' Then his uncle died, leaving him his fortune. It was a resurrection and he went back to Paris. He even became ambitious. 'Madame Moreau asked him what he wanted to become. A Minister, replied Frédéric.' Of course, he did not become one. He would not become anything. He was a *rentier*.

Thus, French capitalism came up against various obstacles which prevented its full development. It certainly included enterprising individuals as well as whole dynasties who stood comparison with the great names among foreign businessmen. Yet a balance sheet is not a prize list. The moderate success achieved was not sufficient for France to retain the place in the world which she held before capitalism influenced her destinies. There were many reasons for this state of affairs and the main ones were in general external to France and to the way in which her policies were managed: those reasons are summed up in the experience of better favoured competitors. Yet if in the balance sheet the modernisation of France is put to the credit of capitalism— even though that modernisation was not due solely to capitalist activity —one cannot in return discharge capitalism from all responsibility for the nation's relative decline. In the course of the nineteenth century the history of capitalism was that of a difficult adaptation for a country which was not fully in accord with its ethos. Hence capitalism did not wholly succeed. The Trade Union leader Griffuelhes regretted the situation in 1910: 'We ask French management to become more like American management. We want a businesslike country, a real hive of activity always on the alert'. The comparison was certainly out of proportion and the wish was not to the point. No doubt it was necessary —if there is necessity in history—for French capitalism in the nineteenth century to be what it was: a human achievement, with its light and dark sides, yet not an achievement to evoke the nostalgic complacency which too often suggests the myth of *la belle époque*. The period is remote enough to be considered as the distant past and the world of those men has little in common with ours. That can perhaps be our excuse if we have failed to understand them and to bring them fully to life.

Notes

Introduction. Capital, Capitalist, Capitalism (pages 31-38)

1 Voltaire, *Romans et Contes* (Bibl de la Pléiade), 304
2 It was concerning the word 'civilisation' that L. Febvre laid down this rule of study (*Civilisation, le mot et l'idée*, Centre International de Synthèse 1930, 1-55). However, he was himself interested in the term which we are now studying and he welcomed especially an article of E. Silberner in *Annales d'Histoire Sociale*, II 1940, 132. Also Marc Bloch: cf *Apologie pour l'Histoire ou Métier d'Historien*, 1949, 86, 88-9, 94

1. The Prelude to Capitalism (pages 39-74)

1 F. Perroux, *Le Capitalisme*, 1948, 5
2 Marx-Engels, *Manifeste du Parti Communiste*, trad Molitor, 61-2
3 Or, equally, money used to produce merchandise the sale of which will bring in a greater return of money than the cost of production. There is no difference here between the commercial and the industrial action
4 François Perroux, in his brilliant study *Le Capitalisme* previously quoted, draws our attention to the danger of making a premature choice among the 'over-numerous and over-diverse definitions which have been put forward, definitions which are also too much influenced by the preferences of each writer' (op cit, 10). It seems unwise, therefore, to depart from the analysis of Marx. But we have held only to a general formula which seems acceptable for everyone and is specially useful for the historian because it allows him to single out and to give depth to the well-known contrast between an economy of subsistence and one of profit. The 'doctrine' for Marx and the assuming of a personal position begin only with the explanation of surplus value (an indisputable and even obvious feature of capital) leading to the exploitation of the worker
5 P. Vilar, *Atti du X⁰ Congrès International des Sciences Historiques*, Rome, 518-20
6 Such was the case in economies operating before capitalism and so contrasting with capitalism; cf on this point the observations of W. Kula concerning backward sectors and regions in the formative stages of a capitalist economy, *Studi Storici* I, 3, April-June 1960, 569-85
7 A. Soboul, *La Pensée* 1946, 51; 1954, 47

8 Cf Gaston-Martin, *Nantes au XVIIIe siècle. L'ère des Négriers*, 1931; and Père D. Rinchon, *Les armements négriers au XVIII siècle*, Brussels 1956
9 P. Vilar, op cit
10 Cf the writings of D. Ligou, especially *Atti* du Xe Congrès ... quoted supra 502
11 P. Léon, *L'Information Historique* 1958, 105
12 'The struggle for agrarian individualism in eighteenth-century France', *Annales d'Histoire économique et sociale*, 1930
13 Memorial to the Provincial Assembly at Orleans, 1788; quoted by Ch. Parain, *Atti* du Xe Congrès ... quoted supra, 479
14 Quoted by J. Jaurès, *Histoire socialiste de la Révolution Française*, I, 1901, 180-1
15 E. Coornaert, *Atti* du Xe Congrès ... quoted supra, 494-5
16 Id, *Les Corporations en France avant 1789*, 1941, 139
17 Cf P. Verlet, *Annales*, 1958, 10-29
18 Cf A. Soboul, *Annales Historiques de la Révolution Française*, 1954, 256
19 Cf L. Dermigny, *Naissance et croissance d'un port. Sète de 1666 à 1880* (Montpellier 1955)
20 Here we should remind ourselves of some essential definitions. Personal firms—which obviously comprised the least developed form of enterprise—could take two forms. 'Under a group name' they brought together a few partners, often parents or friends, who all shared in the management, in the risks and in the profits of the common enterprise. 'Under investment partnership' there was a distinction between the receivers of investments, who shared directly in the business and were liable as in the previous case even to their personal belongings, and the investors who participated only by their provision of capital and who were rewarded in proportion, being liable only to the limit of the sum invested; hence they occupied an intermediate position between a full partner and a simple moneylender. Later on it would be a question of organising finance companies, alone capable of collecting the considerable sums which large-scale business was going to require more and more in the nineteenth century. The law under the old régime was in any case not very concerned with business firms. It did not distinguish clearly either between kinds of participant—whether creditors or joint owners—or between the kind of property held—whether fixed or movable. On the latter point Napoleonic lawyers themselves hesitated, but in present law all transferable wealth is movable. The only clear requirement was that of royal authorisation, needed even for firms not provided with a royal privilege (that clause would recur for limited companies). The rest was left to the statutes covering each firm and to commercial custom. It was a delay in the change of law reflecting the delay in change of historical facts
21 Cf J. Meyer, *Annales*, 1949, 120-9
22 Cf F. Spannel, *Provence historique*, April-June 1957, 95-130
23 Cf P. Goubert, *Les Danse et les Motte de Beauvais*, 1959, and summary by the author, *l'Information historique*, 1958, 210
24 Even in the largest enterprises which employed several dozen journeymen the owner 'retained his trade qualification'. Such was the 'carpenter' Duplay, host of Robespierre, whom we should call today a self-employed carpenter. He kept a distance between himself and his wage-earners. He was already a capitalist by virtue of the importance of his funds and of the amount of labour which he employed. Yet he was not bourgeois in the old meaning of the term, since he was more or less working with his hands or

had so worked. Cf A. Soboul, *La Pensée*, January 1954, 39-62
25 P. Léon, *La Naissance de la grande industrie en Dauphiné*, 1954
26 B. Gille, 'Les forges françaises en 1772' (1960) gives a list of forge-owners, comprised of nobility for the most part—with 21 abbeys, 2 *commanderies*, 2 priories, 4 bishops. There were also examples of gentlemen-glassmakers
27 For the peasants it was an auxiliary seasonal activity which they undertook when work in the fields allowed them to be free
28 Cf P. Verlet, *L'Art du meuble à Paris au XVIIIe siècle*, 1958, 63
29 Cf L. Trénard, *Lyon de l'Encyclopédie au Préromantisme I*, 1958, 23, 39, 45, 51, 58-9
30 Cf J. Lambert-Dansette, *Essai sur les origines et l'évolution d'une bourgeoisie. Quelques familles du patronat textile de Lille-Armentières (1789-1914)* (Lille 1954)
31 P. Léon, *l'Information Historique*, 1958, 104; F. Spannel, op cit
32 On the other hand, discounting of promissory notes was at least tolerated. But the promissory note, even if it resembled a bill of exchange, was not one. It was a simple undertaking from Paul to pay a certain sum, on a fixed date, to Peter; and it was a business transaction only if it was undertaken by a merchant. By contrast, the bill of exchange, besides specifically containing the latter feature, implied the participation of three people (from the time when it no longer involved the moneylender—of whom there was hardly any more mention in the eighteenth century) : they were the drawer, who had received the value of the bill and who had underwritten it; the beneficiary or payee, who would receive the total sum in another place and in another currency on a fixed date; and the paying agent or drawee who would pay out the sum to the payee. In the case of a promissory note, drawer and paying agent were one and the same person
33 In reality, as the interest required by the banker buying a bill of exchange was included in the rate at which he bought it, he had the greatest opportunities of reaping a profit in the end. Yet that profit was not exactly known in advance, for it depended on the rate at which he could gain a return on it. The rate could be favourable to him and in that case a supplementary profit was added to his interest. Yet conversely he suffered a loss on the exchange so that he lost some of the interest, and in theory the overall loss could even be greater than the interest. It was a slight risk but it distinguished this kind of speculation fundamentally from discounting, where profit was certain and fixed in advance. Cf R. de Roover, *L'Evolution de la Lettre de Change*, 1953, 119-46
34 The stock of precious metal existing in France on the eve of the Revolution has been variously estimated. Out of a minting of 2,446 millions between 1720 and 1780, Necker believed that about 2,200 of it remained in 1784; a document of 1786 fixed it, by contrast, at 1,200 millions to which 300 approximately could have been added by 1789 (cf L. Dermigny, *Annales*, 1955, 489); yet in 1792 it was a matter of 2,674 millions, plus 22 of copper and base coin (cf G. Thuillier, ibid, 1959, 66). Georges Lefebvre stated cautiously 2 to 3 milliards
35 P. de Saint-Jacob, *Bulletin de la Société d'Histoire Moderne*, 1958, xii, 4, 8—and the ensuing discussion
36 Quoted by R. Bigo, *Les banques françaises au cours du XIXe siècle*, 1947. The transfer of effects (which meant debts) was an operation of compensation. The debtor transferred to his creditor in settlement of his debt a credit of the same value as that to which he had title
37 The bill of exchange, in fact, if it was hardly yet discountable, had become

perfectly negotiable thanks to the order clause and to endorsement (which seems to have been introduced in France in the first half of the seventeenth century). It tended to become therefore like a fiduciary currency, that 'currency with a universal rate of exchange', 'without inflow or outflow of specie', referred to by the members of the Miromesnil commission under Louis XVI, when they were considering the revision of the grand ordinance of 1673 concerning commerce. Trade in bills of exchange from one place to another in the interior of France, in spite of a common currency, was explained by the physical difficulties of transporting specie. Besides, it was known that the existence of 'a varied number of places' was an essential condition for the bill of exchange: a number of places made it appear as a pure and simple act of exchange and camouflaged its character as an instrument of credit. The Code of Commerce of 1807 held that 'the bill of exchange is drawn from one place on another'. It was only in 1894 that the law added: 'or from one place on the same place'. Yet internal exchange disappeared little by little in the course of the nineteenth century, thanks to the widespread use of the bank-note and to the setting up of the banking network

38 Besides, Paris always knew a relative abundance of currency—brought in especially by taxation—which was unknown in the provinces. It had also a special banking activity: the Royal Almanack already counted 66 bankers there 'for bills and settlements from place to place', which meant trade in bills of exchange with the provinces and abroad; they dealt also in 'all negotiable effects', company shares, 'royal property' ('orders' or undertakings of payments from the receivers-general, 'transfers' on the Treasury, 'notes' of tax-farming), notes of the royal lottery—and naturally also exchange of currency, especially trade in Spanish piastres

39 Their astonishingly complex history has only recently been unravelled by the work of Herbert Lüthy. Cf especially *Bulletin du Centre de Recherches sur l'Histoire des Entreprises* (roneotyped) no 1, January 1953, 1-35; *La Banque protestante en France de la Révocation de l'Edit de Nantes à la Révolution* (vol 1, 1960; vol 2 in preparation); and on Necker, *Annales*, 1960, 852-81

40 Others set up in the provinces before installing themselves in Paris, for example the Delessert at Lyon who were from the Vaud; Panchaud seems to have passed by Berne and not by way of Geneva. Among the latecomers were the Perrégaux of Neuchâtel and the Hottinguer of Zürich known in Paris under Louis XVI. Others again joined them during the Revolution. The André family, originating from Nîmes, established as merchants, shipowners and bankers at Genoa, were themselves closely linked with Genevese circles, and their firm in Paris was later to become that of the Neuflize family. Such was the origin of high protestant banking

41 Not of the Périer family of Grenoble

42 A type of finance company (of a form comparable with simple investment, but where the investors, instead of being a few capitalists, constituted a vast public bearing transferable shares) allowing an indefinite extension of capital

43 The judgement of 1724, a real constitutional charter of the Paris Stock Exchange (already set up in the rue Vivienne), required the handing over of titles in twenty-four hours. This prohibition of dealing forward was renewed in 1785; the Penal Code lifted it by implication but the law followed suit only in 1885

44 Quoted by H. Lüthy, *Bulletin* . . . listed supra, 4

NOTES 235

45 P. Léon, in *Contributions-Communications* of the 1st International Conference of Economic History (Stockholm 1960), 163-204
46 L. Trénard, *Lyon de l'Encyclopédie au Préromantisme, I,* 1958, 34-5
47 Cf A. Soboul, *La Pensée,* January 1954, 43
48 Cf L. Dermigny, *Cargaisons indiennes* : Solier et Compagnie, 1960
49 Cf R. Sédillot, *La maison de Wendel de 1704 à nos jours,* 1958, 34-94
50 Even in new firms like Anzin or Aniche the capital was not divided into shares exactly comparable with those of present-day firms but in 'sous' and 'deniers', which were not easily transferable titles with a fixed value but proportions of total assets whose transfer was subject to the agreement of the firm's board of directors. Anzin was to keep that form of organisation during the first half of the nineteenth century. Cf B. Gille, *Recherches sur la formation de la grande entreprise capitaliste,* 1959, 33-4
51 During the eighteenth century world production of gold declined while the mines of Potosi and especially of Mexico yielded more and more silver. Hence there was a depreciation of silver and a rise in the value of gold: the weight of precious metal contained in a louis d'or was eventually worth more than the legal value of the louis. The reform of 1785 rectified this anomaly (which led to the flight of the louis abroad) by diminishing the weight of the louis without fixing its legal value at a nominal amount
52 L. Dermigny, *Annales,* 1955, article quoted. There was an Anglo-French treaty of commerce with free-trade tendencies in 1786
53 Cf R. Mauzi, *L'Idée de Bonheur dans la littérature et la pensée françaises au XVIIIᵉ siècle,* 1960, 277, 284-8 — the 'patriotic merchant' was called Bedos
54 M. Reinhard, *Revue d'Histoire moderne et contemporaine,* 1956, 5-37
55 Cf G. Richard, *L'Information Historique,* 1957, 185-9; 1958, 185-90, 201; 1956, 156-61
56 Cf J. Choffel, *Saint-Gobain, Du miroir à l'atome,* 1960
57 Quoted by R. Mauzi, op cit, 273
58 The outline of a planned economy to which the great Committee of Public Safety had recourse, though it may have been lacking in detail and in coherence, is hardly a problem in this connection; at most it tended to limit profits, yet to what extent remains very uncertain
59 Under the Empire Saint-Gobain added to glassmaking, which was its initial activity, the production of soda (the Leblanc process dated from 1791)
60 Cf P. Léon, op cit, 177-8
61 Cf J-J. Hémardinquer, *Annales,* 1958, 564-72
62 This in spite of the efforts of men like Albert 'the industrial spy' in Manchester at the beginning of the Revolution, who was subsequently, after six years spent in English prisons, a spinner and a builder of machines; or like Douglas who manufactured machines for spinning wool; or like Philippe de Girard who perfected mechanical spinning of linen thread
63 Cf R. Sédillot, op cit, 101-48
64 J. Labasse, *Le commerce des soies à Lyon sous Napoléon et la crise de 1811,* 1957, 7-9, 17-22, 36, 57-66, 127-30
65 *Manifeste,* trad Molitor, 66
66 Cf M. Reinhard, *Annales,* 1959, 553-70
67 Or, when an order was imposed it was as a rule favourable to large-scale capitalist undertaking rather than to artisan enterprise: thus the law of 1810 on mining concessions allowed the mining companies to evict surface owners. Cf P. Guillaume, *L'Information Historique,* 1959, 195-9
68 This was so for employers also. Yet the emphasis was not equal. The Code

was itself more severe for workmen and courts of law would be even more so; in their case offence was much easier to prove

69 Acceding to the demands of the *cahiers* (and even of the majority of *cahiers* of the clergy) the law of 3 October 1789 authorised lending with interest, the Civil Code and the law of 3 September 1807 fixed limits for it (5 per cent for civil transactions and 6 per cent for commercial ones), and these limits were not lifted until 1918

70 The Code of Commerce of 1807 regulated firms with investment supplied by shares and created the limited liability company. In this last type (the most supple and, overall, the ideal of capitalist society) all the partners were moneylenders without distinction between invested and investor; it was the 'real' element, the money, the capital, which was all-important

71 P. Vilar, *Atti* du Xe Congrès International des Sciences Historiques, Rome, 535

72 Cambon, the great financier of the Committee of Public Safety, and his family, who owned at Montpellier spinning mills, dyeworks, a handkerchief factory and an export organisation, bought in this way more than 1,000 hectares (paid in depreciated *assignats*) part of which they sold at a profit. In the towns, the purchase of vast buildings and lands belonging to religious orders allowed numerous manufacturers to set up workshops: this was one of the factors in the development of Paris, for example. For others it afforded the opportunity for fruitful building speculations (which happened well before Haussmann)

73 *La Caisse d'Amortissement* was created by Gaudin and managed by Mollien, the main experts of Napoleonic finance. It was fed by the collateral demanded from the tax-collectors and charged with maintaining the price of government stock on the Stock Exchange in order to lower the rate of interest and hence to allow the Treasury to borrow (in the same way as private firms) on satisfactory conditions

74 The Bank had taken over at its commencement *La Caisse des Comptes courants*. It was in this way that it could begin operations. The other issuing houses in Paris disappeared in 1803; the main one, *la Caisse Jabach* (*Caisse d'Escompte du Commerce*) invested its capital in shares of the Bank and became an intermediary between the Bank and the commercial houses of Paris

75 It was reserved according to a fixed principle designed to ensure the value and liquidity of commercial paper, itself a gauge of note-circulation, with bills carrying three signatures—this meant preliminary endorsement by a banker who consequently became responsible, and for at least 90 days

76 Formerly a merchant in colonial supplies at Nantes, a monopolist under the Revolution, a supplier and banker for the Directory. Often in prison (under the Terror, in 1800 and from 1809 to 1813), he had a genius for making a comeback. In 1823 he had to fit out the expedition to Spain, and accused of fraud once more was sent to Sainte-Pélagie for five years

77 'Napoleon scarcely liked manufacturers and merchants. The Imperial nobility was not a commercial one. The business élite was not integrated into the official élite.' (M. Reinhard, *Revue d'Histoire Moderne et Contemporaine*, 1956, 36.) Here again, however, there were some significant facts, even if isolated ones: the first baron of the Empire to set up a title of primogeniture (a necessary condition for the inheritance of a title) was a great merchant from Marseille, Anthoine, son-in-law of the Clarys; the first count was likewise the Parisian banker Perrégaux (L. Madelin, *Histoire du Consulat et de l'Empire*, VII, 47)

2. Progress and Delay: 1815-48 (pages 75-115)

1 Cf R. Rémond, *Revue d'Histoire Moderne et Contemporaine*, 1960, 193-214. The book, translated in 1776, went through 32 editions (some 50 if reprintings between 1815 and 1852 are counted) and the majority were before 1834

7 Cf le Père Droulers, *Action pastorale et problèmes sociaux sous la Mon-* 1959, 67-8, 161-2

3 Balzac clearly saw the part which railways were going to play; the money of Madame Hanska allowed him to purchase shares in the *Compagnie du Nord* himself

4 According to a valuation of 1843, perhaps 3 milliards of silver and 500 millions of gold. It would be at least a third of the total European stock. England then held only 750 millions in specie but had a much greater fiduciary issue, and the use of the cheque supported a clearly more abundant and more rapid circulation of money. In 1833 Emile Péreire saw in the cheque 'the secret of the industrial and political power of Great Britain, a power which one would seek in vain to explain by other means'

5 Cf G. Thuillier, *Annales*, 1959, 65-90

6 They received in different ways more than 1,300 millions

7 Cf le Pére Droulers, *Action pastorale et problèmes sociaux sous la Monarchie de Juillet chez Mgr d'Astros . . . ,* 1954; and *Revue d'Histoire Moderne et Contemporaine*, 1957, 289

8 Since the classical works like that of G. Lachapelle, *Le crédit public* (1931), the problem has been reopened by two fundamental books: B. Gille, *La Banque et le Crédit en France de 1815 à 1848* (1959), and J. Bouvier, *Les Rothschild* (1960)

9 It might be a matter of French or foreign capital. The first borrowings of the Restoration were placed on the markets of London, Amsterdam and Hamburg by the banks of Baring and Hope; in 1818 a panic on the Stock Exchange cunningly organised by Parisian banking (with Casimir Périer leading the operation) persuaded English bankers not to meddle in France again until about 1840. Yet Rothschild—who subscribed all the public borrowings from 1823 onwards—placed a good proportion of them abroad

10 Besides, there were its origins: it was a matter of *merchant bankers* (the expression has no exact French equivalent) 'coming from the area of merchant activity into banking' (D. S. Landes, *Revue d'Histoire Moderne et Contemporaine*, 1956, 207-8

11 From 13 January 1820 to 14 January 1847 the rate remained perfectly stable at 4 per cent

12 Cf Balzac, *Le Curé de village*: 'No one has 500 franc notes at Montignac; they are rare enough at Limoges where no one accepts them without a discount'

13 Rouen (1817), Nantes, Bordeaux (1818), Lyon, Marseille (1835), Lille (1836), Le Havre (1837), Toulouse, Orléans (1838); each one had its own issue

14 Reims, Saint-Etienne (1836), Saint-Quentin (1837), Montpellier (1838), Grenoble, Angoulême (1840); then after the law of 1840 which showed a clear preference for the *Comptoirs* (these could be created by a simple ordinance whereas a law was necessary for the creation of a departmental bank—and, in fact, no more of these were founded), there were *Comptoirs* at Caen, Châteauroux, Besançon, Clermont-Ferrand (1841), Mulhouse (1843), Le Mans, Nîmes, Valenciennes (1846). Formerly, the Bank had

merchants and manufacturers as its provincial correspondents. Local bankers and discount men had done what they could to delay this spreading of the Bank of France, adding the weight of their resistance to the hesitations of the regents. The campaign for monopoly, led by Pillet-Will, was to be terminated by the crisis of 1848

15 They misunderstood the controversy between English economists, in which one side was attached to the currency school of Ricardo (imputing the crises to excessive note issue) and the other to the banking school of Tooke (hostile to all artificial limitation of circulation), and reduced the problem to the secondary one of monopoly and of liberty of note issue. Inexperience explained it : the Bank of England itself dated from 1694

16 Society dealt at the time with the insolvent debtor with particular severity : arrest for debt was abolished only in 1867. Sainte-Pélagie, a debtors' prison from 1798 to 1834, was a familiar place in the literature of the time. The Code and the law of 1838 were very harsh for bankrupts; their severity was tempered only in 1889

17 Let us note however that the 'model' who inspired Balzac for the personality of César Birotteau—the perfumer Bully who operated at 259 rue Saint Honoré, a bankrupt in 1830—seems to have been much less honest than his fictional counterpart. Cf M. Fleury, *Bulletin de la Société d' Histoire Moderne*, XI, no 13, 1955, 11

18 Cf W. Henderson, *Britain and Industrial Europe, 1750-1850* (Liverpool 1954)

19 Cf P. Léon, in *Contributions-Communications* of the 1st International Conference of Economic History (Stockholm 1960), 184

20 G. Gille, *Recherches* ..., 39-40. Cf also Ch. H. Pouthas, *La population française pendant la première moitié du XIX* siècle*, 1955

21 Cf L. Girard, *Revue d'Histoire Moderne et Contemporaine*, 1960, 76-8

22 To this fragment of *Cousine Bette*, let us join here another from the same novel: 'If the speculations in housing in Paris are sure, they are slow and capricious. The boulevard between la rue Louis-le-Grand and la rue de la Paix will bring returns only after a long period. Business came here only in 1840 to display its splendid shop-fronts, the gold of the changers, the fairy tinsel of fashion and the crazy luxury of its small shops. Flats fetched a high price because of the change in the business centre which was then established between the Stock Exchange and the Madeleine, henceforth the seat of political power and of the finance of Paris.' Under the Restoration, Birotteau had already ruined himself in speculating on the land of the Madeleine

23 Then the building of the Ministry for Foreign Affairs—where the son-in-law of Madame Dosne, Monsieur Thiers, accordingly lived

24 Quoted by D. Halévy, *Le courrier de M. Thiers*, 1921, 49

25 Cf B. Gille, op cit, 67-8

26 Cf Henriette Vanier, *La mode et ses métiers*, 1960, 101-3

27 'Dauriat and Ladvocat were pre-eminent,' he said; but Ladvocat was a real person, one of the great publishers of novels, whereas Dauriat only existed in the *Comédie Humaine*

28 Cf R. Marquant, *Thiers et le baron Cotta*, 1959, 35-44

29 In 1834 the economist Villeneuve-Bargemont, who was certainly a traditionalist, gave this advice: 'The only way of placing capital is that which does not allow the capital invested to be swallowed up entirely. The most productive manufacture is destroyed by natural circumstances (commercial luck, death of the entrepreneur, the children not continuing the business).

The most solid wealth is land ...' (*Economie politique chrétienne*, I, 310)

30 Cf G. Lefebvre, *Bulletin de la Société d'Histoire Moderne*, XI, 16, 1955, 8-12

31 Additionally, to a lesser extent, there were financial officials, like the special tax-collectors for the arrondissements, who accepted deposits from traders, from peasants and even from workmen and put them to use

32 It was only in 1890 that a decree forbade notaries 'to receive or to keep deposits on trust to use the interest'

33 Stock was then perpetual: redeemable stock appeared only in 1878

34 As for property or landed investments, this choice was undoubtedly not an arbitrary one. 'Caution in the matter of investments ... and preference for stock issued by the state shows itself in all backward countries. It is not only the expression of a backward state of mind but it is also the only reasonable way of acting in the given circumstances.' (W. Kula, *Studi Storici*, I, 3, April-June 1960, 573-4)

35 Cf B. Gille, op cit, 37-8

36 Cf J. P. Palewski, *Histoire des chefs d'entreprise*, 1928, 157-8, 187, 210-11, 255-6

37 Cf the works quoted by B. Gille, J. Choffel; also J. Boudet (and others), *Le Monde des affaires en France de 1830 à nos jours*, 1952; A. Dunham, *La Révolution industrielle en France (1815-1848)*, 1953; C. Fohlen, *Revue d'Histoire Moderne et Contemporaine*, 1955, 46-8

38 Cf R. Sédillot, *La maison de Wendel de 1704 à nos jours*, 1958, 153-92

39 Cf R. Sédillot, *Peugeot. De la crinoline à la 404*, 1960, 1-43

40 Not all the men of Mulhouse supported free trade. Controversy raged among them on the matter in the years 1835-40, dividing even families like the Koechlin family. Cf B. Gille, *Recherches ...*, 134

41 The Rislers, for example, later joined by the Koechlins, created machine shops, which formed one section of the various factories later combining in the firm of Alsthom. Similarly for the Schlumbergers and so on ...

42 Among a large number of works the most recent and the most authentic treatment is in P. Leuilliot, *L'Alsace au debut du XIXe siècle*, 3 vols, 1959-60

43 At a time when certain great textile millowners themselves came from old privileged enterprises: at Lille the dynasty of the Cuvelier family owned a Royal Manufacture under Louis XVI

44 Cf the works quoted by J. Lambert-Dansette and by Cl. Fohlen; also by Fohlen, *L'Industrie textile au temps du Second Empire*, 1956

45 Cf B. Gille, *Recherches ...*, 46, 126-8

46 Cf G. Thuillier, Georges Dufaud et les débuts du grand capitalisme dans la métallurgie en Nivernais au XIXe siècle, 1952

47 Cf J. P. Palewski, op cit, 190-2; P. Leuilliot, *Revue de Synthèse*, 1953, tome 74, 154-5

48 Cf Adeline Daumard, *Bulletin de la Société d'Histoire Moderne* XII, 2, 1957, 3-6; and *Annales*, 1959, 686

49 Cf Cl. Fohlen, *Une affaire de famille au XIXe siècle : les Méquillet-Noblot*, 1955; and P. Léon, op cit, on Dauphiné

50 Cf B. Gille, *Recherches ...*, 34-7

51 Cf B. Gille, ibid, 131-47. The controversy grew more intense in 1845-6: the Central Association for Freedom of Trade, presided over by the Duke d'Harcourt, and inspired by the group of liberal economists, Bastiat, Adolphe Blanqui, Michel Chevalier, Léon Faucher, Horace Say, confronted the Association for the Defence of National Employment in which some

'realists' dominated, Joseph Périer, the industrialist Mimerel, and the banker Odier—but the question was never resolved

52 K. Marx, *Les luttes de classes en France* (Ed. Sociales 1948), 39
53 The two books already quoted, by B. Gille (*La Banque et le Crédit...*) and by J. Bouvier (*Les Rothschild*), virtually dispense with the need for other references on this subject
54 Of ten sons and sons-in-law of Claude Périer, eight were to be deputies (Rémusat also among them). Cf P. Barral, *L'Information Historique*, 1960, 34-5 (appraisal of a supplementary thesis in preparation)
55 Investment was *en commandite* [a share partnership] to avoid having to seek the necessary authorisation for a limited liability company, an authorisation refused in 1826 to the *société commanditaire*
56 To the extent that the law of 15 July 1845 compelled stockbrokers to require the effective deposit of half, at least, of the nominal value of the shares subscribed
57 Railways were already enough of a worry to the navigation companies on the Rhône to spur them to adopt an almost general tariff agreement—the first step in a fusion which was to be accomplished under the Second Empire. Cf B. Gille, *Recherches...*, 149-50
58 The metal firms agreed among themselves to share these orders (especially for rails), thus laying themselves open to complaints of monopolistic practice

3. The Great Upsurge: 1848-82 (pages 116-178)

1 The Périers remained hostile: was this the caution of men of the world in respect of adventurers? However, on 18 Brumaire!...
2 Cf especially, for all this section, P. Dupont-Ferrier, *Le marché financier de Paris sous le Second Empire*, 1935; L. Girard, *La politique des travaux publics du Second Empire*, 1951; J. Bouvier, *Les Rothschild*, 1960. These are fundamental works and will be referred to again
3 De Lesseps, after the floating of Suez, heard a cabman say: 'I am your shareholder'
4 In 1870 out of some 10 milliards which railway construction had cost, 1,600 millions had been supplied by the state and the remainder by small savings. Cf R. Sédillot, *La maison de Wendel...*, 185-6
5 Between 1849 and 1851 the Montagnards, reappraising their policy (if rather late in the day), stopped the propaganda they had been directing at the peasants on the necessity of creating agricultural banks and of using mortgage notes. This was a strikingly successful move
6 After the Bank of France, the greatest capital of a French bank at that date
7 The attempts of 1826 and 1837 are well known. Though they failed and though the *Caisses* of the 1840s disappeared in 1848, the Société Générale of Brussels, founded in 1822, prospered by following a similar course of industrial investment after 1835. Cf D. S. Landes, *Revue d'Histoire Moderne et Contemporaine*, 1956, 215
8 L. Girard, *Rapports* du XIe Congrès International des Sciences Historiques (Stockholm 1960), V, 105
9 The law of 1865, sanctioning the use of the cheque, a use which was borrowed from England like the operation of credit itself, gave it great flexibility in the management of current accounts. Yet the use of the cheque in France spread slowly

10 J. Bouvier, *Les Rothschild*, 176
11 L. Girard, op cit, 105
12 Cf J. Bouvier, *Annales*, 1956, 458-80
13 It was a matter initially for the capitalists of Lyon or of St Etienne, merchants or industrialists, to reinforce their finances in order to adapt themselves to the free trade situation which the treaty of 1860 had just inaugurated. The history of *Crédit Lyonnais* from 1863 to 1882 has been brought up to date in a forthcoming thesis of J. Bouvier; cf in the meantime *L'Information Historique*, 1959, 205-7. [*Translator's note*. A shorter popular version of J. Bouvier's thesis has appeared as follows: J. Bouvier, *Naissance d'une Banque : Le Crédit Lyonnais*, Flammarion, 1968]
14 The Rothschilds supervised the *Société Générale* more than any other credit establishment, admitting it alone into their group in 1871 at the time of the great borrowings after the war. Yet in 1874 the *Société Générale* joined the 'syndicate' formed by their enemies
15 J. Bouvier, *Les Rothschild*, 177
16 J. Bouvier, *Annales*, 1956, 478
17 Cf J. Labasse, *Les capitaux et la région*, 1955
18 Cf G. Thuillier, *Annales*, 1955, 494-512
19 D. S. Landes, *Revue d'Histoire Moderne et Contemporaine*, 1956, 204-22 *J* (an essential article)
20 Cf the works quoted by L. Girard and J. Bouvier, together with R. Schnerb, *Rouher et le Second Empire*, 1949
21 L. Girard, *Rapports* du XI° Congrès . . . , quoted supra, 105
22 Cf L. Girard, *Bulletin de la Societe d'Histoire Moderne*, X, 22, 1951, 8-10; and R. Schnerb, op cit
23 Cf P. Guiral, *L'Information Historique*, 1954, 15-20
24 Cf B. Gille, *Recherches* . . . , 96-113
25 The Boigues of Fourchambault equally shared in the 'refloating' of le Creusot in 1836. Cf B. Gille, *Recherches* . . . , 82
26 R. Sédillot, *La maison de Wendel* . . . , 171-200
27 Cf G. Thuillier, *Georges Dufaud* . . . , quoted supra
28 Cf R. Sédillot, *Peugot* . . . , 43-68. The firm of Japy Fréres (watchmaking, lockmaking, etc) itself employed 5,500 workmen in 1855. Cf G. Duveau, *La vie ouvrière en France sous le Second Empire*, 1946, 192-3
29 He denounced it as the most sinister event in our history since the Revocation of the Edict of Nantes, the work of 'universal cosmopolitanism', even of 'universal communism' (J. Choffel, op cit, 58)
30 Cf the works, already quoted, of J. Lambert-Dansette and, especially, Cl. Fohlen
31 Cf F. Dornic, *Revue d'Histoire Moderne et Contemporaine*, 1956, 38-66
32 Cf J. Choffel, op cit
33 C. J. Gignoux, *Histoire d'une entreprise française*, 1955
34 There were seventy employers' associations in 1871
35 Equally as much 'capital responded untiringly to the repeated appeals of the city' (L. Girard, *Revue d'Histoire Moderne et Contemporaine*, 1960, 76-8 : in connection with D. H. Pinkney, *Napoleon III and the Rebuilding of Paris*, Princeton 1958)
36 The scale of his enterprise depended, however, on the average size of firms in the building industry which, being very little mechanised, was not at all concentrated: 10 workmen for one entrepreneur in Paris in 1847, 13 in 1860. On the other hand, the production of construction materials experi-

Q

enced important development with the appearance of cement; the Vicat works at Grenoble dated from 1858. Cf A. Chatelain, *Annales*, 573-85

37 R. E. Cameron. Among his numerous works cf, in French, *Revue d' Histoire Economique et Sociale*, 1955, 347-53; and *Annales*, 1957, 243-57

38 Cf Gille, *Bulletin de la Société d'Histoire Moderne*, XII, 13, 1960, 4-7

39 Cf J. Bouvier, *Bulletin de la Société d'Histoire Moderne*, XII, 10, 1959, 10-13; and *Revue Historique*, 1960, vol CCXXIV, 75-104. On Suez: *Le Canal Maritime de Suez* (publication of the Company, 1937); and G. Edgar-Bonnet, *Ferdinand de Lesseps*, 2 vols, 1951-9

4. Maturity (pages 179-210)

1 J. Bouvier, *Les Rothschild*, 175-8

2 While altering its time period according to his usual practice

3 Cf on all the foregoing the works quoted above by J. Bouvier; and by the same author, *Le Krach de l'Union Générale*, 1960

4 Cf J. Labasse, *Les capitaux et la région*

5 P. Barral, *L'Information Historique*, 1960, 32

6 Cf J. Bouvier, *Revue d'Histoire Moderne et Contemporaine*, 1955, 185-205

7 Cf R. Sédillot, *La maison de Wendel . . .*, 209-82

8 Cf R. Sédillot, *Peugeot . . .*, 68-111

5. Conclusions (pages 211-230)

1 Jules Huret, *Enquête sur la question sociale en Europe*, 1897. The statement of Schneider is quoted by E. Beau de Loménie, *Les responsabilités des dynasties bourgeoises*, II, 1947, 235; that of Rothschild by J. Bouvier, *Les Rothschild*, 237-8

2 Cf J. A. Roy, *Histoire du Jockey-Club de Paris*, 1958

3 Cf E. Appolis, *Annales*, 1957, 231-42

4 Cf J. J. Hémardinquer, *Annales*, 1960, 1155-67

5 Cf P. Barral, op cit

6 Cf M. Gillet, *Bulletin de la Société d'Histoire Moderne*, XII, 2, 1957, 7-10

7 The problem has just been reinvestigated in the important work of J. Lhomme, *La grande bourgeoisie au pouvoir (1830-1880)*, 1960

8 Two important examples analysed by J. Bouvier: 1870-1871 (*Revue d' Histoire Moderne et Contemporaine*, 1958, 137-51) and 1873-1874 (*Revue Historique*, 1953, CCX, 271-301)

9 For colonial problems which it has not been possible to treat here one may refer to H. Brunschwig, *Mythes et réalités de l'impéralisme colonial français, 1871-1914*, appearing in 1960 in the present collection (Armand Colin)

10 P. Léon, *Contributions-Communications . . .*, 165

11 Introduction to *L'Année Politique*, 1957, XVIII

12 'Capital does not make the entrepreneur; it is the entrepreneur who uses and makes value out of idle and sleeping capital. The entrepreneur is the absolute contrast of the unearned-income receiver.' (L. Girard, *Rapports du XIᵉ Congrès . . .*, V, 97)

Select Bibliography

An attempt has been made in this necessarily limited select bibliography to bring together works which have seemed the most important, the most recent and the most accessible as well as those, naturally, to which the present sketch is especially indebted. Many classical works have not been indicated: it will be easy to come across them from the titles which have been mentioned. Likewise reference has been made only to the most characteristic among the many contributions of certain authors: the references will readily afford guidance to their other publications. The works and articles quoted in the notes to the text have been set down only when they seemed to offer sufficiently general interest. Unless contrary indication is given, the place of publication is Paris; the date is that of the edition used (generally the most recent).

I For general background to the subject:
Histoire Générale des Civilisations, issued under the direction of M. Crouzet, volume V: *Le XVIIIe siècle, Révolution intellectuelle, technique et politique (1785-1815)*, by R. Mousnier and E. Labrousse, with the collaboration of M. Bouloiseau, 1953; volume VI: *Le XIXe siècle, L'Apogée de l'expansion européenne (1815-1914)*, by R. Schnerb, 1955
Destins du Monde, series issued under the direction of L. Febvre and F. Braudel, volume IX: *Les Bourgeois conquérants (XIXe siècle)*, by Ch. Morazé, 1957
F. Sternberg, *Le Conflit du siècle. Capitalisme et socialisme é l'épreuve de l'histoire*, 1958 (French translation by J. Rovan)
H. Heaton, *Histoire économique de l'Europe* (French translation by R. Grandbois), volume II: *De 1750 à nos jours* (with bibliography by P. Leuilliot)
H. Sée, *Histoire économique de la France*, volume II: *les temps modernes (1789-1914)*, 1951 (with bibliography by R. Schnerb)
E. Labrousse, *Aspects de l'évolution économique et sociale de la France et du Royaume-Uni de 1815 à 1900* (cours de Sorbonne, roneotyped, 1949)
M. Lévy, *Histoire économique et sociale de la France depuis 1848* (cours de l'Institut d'Etudes Politiques, roneotyped, 1951-52)
Ch. Morazé, *La France bourgeoise, XVIIe-XXe siècles*, 1947
Histoire du peuple francais, issued under the direction of L. H. Parias, volume IV: *De 1848 à nos jours*, by G. Duveau, 1953
F. Perroux, *Le Capitalisme*, 1948

II   On the development of French capitalism before the Revolution:

E. Labrousse, *Origines et aspects économiques et sociaux de la Révolution Française (1774-1791)* (cours de Sorbonne, roneotyped, 1952-53)

A. Soboul, *La France à la veille de la Revolution, I: Aspects économiques et sociaux* (cours de Sorbonne, roneotyped, 1959)

P. Léon, 'Tradition et machinisme dans la France du XVIIIe siècle', *L'Information Historique*, 1955, 5-15
'Recherches sur la bourgeoisie française de province au XVIIIe siècle', ibid, 1958, 101-5

Among the monographs devoted to the principal places of development of commercial capitalism:

P. Dardel, on Rouen, works examined by P. Leuilliot, *Annales*, 1947, 494-5, and 1955, 293-5; P. Richard, on Le Havre, cf P. Leuilliot, ibid, 1956, 508; J. Meyer, 'Le Commerce négrier nantais (1774-1792)' ibid, 1960, 120-9; G. Hubrecht, on Bordeaux, cf P. Leuilliot, ibid, 1956, 509; G. Rambert and others, *Histoire du commerce de Marseille*, in course of publication

G. Richard, 'Les corporations et la noblesse commerçante en France au XVIIIe siècle', *L'Information Historique*, 1957, 185-9; 'La noblesse commerçante à Bordeaux et à Nantes au XVIIIe siècle', ibid, 1958, 185-90 and 201; 'A propos de la noblesse commerçante à Lyon au XVIIIe siècle, ibid, 1959, 156-61

M. Reinhard, 'Elite et noblesse dans la seconde moitié du XVIIIe siècle', *Revue d'Histoire Moderne et Contemporaine*, 1956, 5-37

L. Dermigny, 'Circuits de l'argent et milieux d'affaires au XVIIIe siècle', *Revue Historique*, October 1954; 'La France à la fin de l'Ancien Régime: une carte monétaire', *Annales*, 1955, 480-93

B. Gille, *Les origines de la grande industrie métallurgique en France*, 1948
Les forges françaises en 1772, 1960

H. Lévy-Brühl, *Histoire de la lettre de change en France aux XVIIe et XVIIIe siècles*, 1933
Histoire juridique des sociétés de commerce aux XVIIe et XVIIIe siècles, 1938

R. de Roover, *L'évolution de la lettre de change (XIVe-XVIIIe siècles)* 1953

J. Bouchary, *Le marché des changes de Paris à la fin du XVIIIe siècle*, 1937
Les manieurs d'argent de Paris à la fin du XVIIIe siècle, 3 volumes, 1939-43
Les compagnies financières de Paris à la fin du XVIIIe siècle, 3 volumes, 1940-42

R. Bigo, *Les Bases historiques de la finance moderne*, 1948
La Caisse d'Escompte et les origines de la Banque de France (1776-1793), 1927

H. Lüthy, *La Banque protestante en France de la Révocation de l'Edit de Nantes à la Revolution*, volume I, 1960; volume II, in preparation

III   On the relationships between the economic situation and the development of capitalism the fundamental works are those of E. Labrousse already quoted; and, in their interest for methodology:
Esquisse du mouvement des prix et des revenus en France au XVIIIe siècle, 2 volumes, 1932
Las crise de l'economie française à la fin de l'Ancien Régime et au début de la Révolution, volume I, 1944

For the nineteenth century following the same methods:

A. Chabert, *Essai sur le mouvement des prix et des revenus en France de 1798 à 1820*, 2 volumes, 1945-49

Aspects de la crise et de la dépression de l'économie française au milieu du XIXᵉ siècle (volume XIX of the *Bibliothèque de la Révolution de 1848*, issued under the direction of E. Labrousse, 1956)

Works by economists on the study of economic fluctuations (among the most important may be quoted: J. Akerman, *Structures et cycles économiques*, French translation by Mme B. Marchal and Mlle G. Angot, 3 volumes, 1955-57) neglect almost completely their historical analysis.

One exception is:

J. Lescure, *Des crises générales et périodiques de surproduction*, 2 volumes, 1938

IV Monetary, banking and Stock Exchange aspects.

General works:

A. Pose, *La Monnaie et ses institutions. Histoire, théorie et techniques*, 2 volumes, 1942

R. Bigo, *Les Banques françaises au cours du XIXᵉ siècle*, 1947

G. Ramon, *Histoire de la Banque de France d'après les sources originales*, 1929 (Very 'official', but there exists no other serious work. That of A. Dauphin-Meunier, *La Banque de France*, 1937, is mediocre enough, as is *l'Histoire de la Banque*, 1951 by the same author)

P. Dupont-Ferrier, *Le marché financier de Paris sous le Second Empire*, 1925

The really systematic study of the subject has been begun by:

B. Gille, *La Banque et le Crédit en France de 1815 à 1848*, 1959 (the same author has devoted several works to the regional study of banking and credit: for Le Havre, *Annales de Normandie*, 1960; for Lyon, *Cahiers d'Histoire*, 1960; for Marseille, *Actes du 83ᵉ Congrès National des Sociétés Savantes*, Aix, 1958; for Dijon, *Annales de Bourgogne*, 1959 ...)

L. Girard, 'L'affaire Mirès', *Bulletin de la Société d'Histoire Moderne*, January 1951

J. Bouvier, *Le Credit Lyonnais de 1863 à 1882. Les années de formation d'une banque de dépôts* (in preparation; cf meanwhile, *L'information Historique*, 1959, 205-7)

Le Krach de l'Union Générale, 1960

Les Rothschild, 1960

'Aux origines de la IIIᵉ République: social reactions of business circles', *Revue Historique*, 1953, CCX, 271-301

'Des banquiers devant l'actualité politique en 1870-1871', *Revue d'Histoire Moderne et Contemporaine*, 1958, 137-151

'Les Péreire et l'affaire de la Banque de Savoie', *Cahiers d'Histoire*, 1960

Cl. Fohlen, 'Industrie et crédit dans la région lilloise (1815-1870)', *Mélanges L. Jacob, Revue du Nord*, XXXVI, 1954

D. S. Landes, 'Vieille banque et banque nouvelle: la révolution financière du XIXᵉ siècle', *Revue d'Histoire Moderne et Contemporaine*, 1956, 204-222

J. Labasse, *Les capitaux et la région. Le commerce et la circulation des capitaux dans la région lyonnaise*, 1955

Le commerce des soies à Lyon sous Napoléon et la crise de 1811 (concerning the Guérin bank)

G. Thuillier, 'Pour une histoire bancaire régionale: en Nivernais de 1800 à 1880', *Annales*, 1955, 444-512

'Pour une histoire monétaire de la France au XIXᵉ siècle. Le rôle des monnaies de cuivre et de billon', ibid, 1959, 65-90

On saving and investment, certain publications show an interest in the past:
J. Lescure, *L'épargne en France (1914-1934)*, 1936
'The financing of investment' (lectures at the International Banking Summer School, by E. Monick and others), 1951

V   On the major undertakings and, especially, on railway construction, the essential works are those of:
P. Dauzet, *Le siècle des chemins de fer en France, 1821-1938*, 1948
L. Girard, *La politique des travaux publics du Second Empire*, 1952
'L'affaire du chemin de fer Cette-Marseille (1861-1863)', *Revue d'Histoire Moderne et Contemporaine*, 1955, 107-26
L. M. Jouffroy, *L'ère du rail*, 1953

VI   Industrial aspects:
Besides the report of P. Léon on the industrial growth of France in the nineteenth and twentieth centuries (*Contributions-Communications* at the First International Conference of Economic History, Stockholm, 1960, 163-204), the numerous and important statements of P. Leuilliot in *Annales*, and the theses on regional geography (among the most recent and the most valuable may be quoted those of Cl. Prêcheur on iron and steelmaking in Lorraine and of M. Laferrère on industry in Lyon) the principal references are:
P. Léon, *La naissance de la grande industrie en Dauphiné (fin du XVIIᵉ siècle–1869)*, 2 volumes, 1954
P. Leuilliot, *L'Alsace au début du XIXᵉ siècle. Essais d'histoire politique, économique et religieuse (1815-1813)*, volume II: *les transformations économiques*, 1959
A. L. Dunham, *La Révolution Industrielle en France (1815-1848)*, 1953 (cf the review of B. Gille, *Revue d'Histoire Moderne et Contemporaine*, 1954, 156-60)
F. Dornic, *L'Industrie textile dans le Maine et ses débouchés internationaux (1650-1815)*, Le Mans, 1955
B. Gille, 'La concentration industrielle en France au début du Second Empire', *Bulletin de la Société d'Histoire Moderne*, November, 1952
G. Duveau, *La vie ouvrière en France sous le Second Empire*, 1946—contains an overall picture of industrial activity
Cl. Fohlen, *L'Industrie textile au temps du Second Empire*, 1956
'La Concentration dans l'industrie textile française au milieu du XIXᵉ siècle' *Revue d'Histoire Moderne et Contemporaine*, 1958, 46-58
'Esquisse d'une évolution industrielle: Roubaix au XIXᵉ siècle', *Revue du Nord*, 1951
P. de Rousiers, *Les syndicats industriels et producteurs en France et à l'étranger*, 1912
La concentration des entreprises industrielles et commerciales, by A. Fontaine and others, 1913

VII   The history of entrepreneurship remains too neglected a topic in France. Several recent works still yield to a 'hagiographic' treatment; useful books, but too obviously officially inspired or uncritical and not leading to a serious economic treatment are such works as:
C. J. Gignoux, *Histoire d'une entreprise française*, 1955 (Péchiney)
R. Sédillot, *Deux cent cinquante ans d'industrie en Lorraine. La maison de Wendel de 1704 à nos jours*, 1958

In the series under the same general editorship, *Histoire des grandes Entreprises:*
1 J. Choffel, *Saint-Gobain. Du miroir à l'atome*, 1960
2 R. Sédillot, *Peugeot. De la crinoline à la 404*, 1960
   Uneven, but valuable, is the symposium of:
J. Boudet and others, *Le Monde des affaires en France de 1830 à nos jours*, 1952
   The strictly systematic study of enterprise and of entrepreneurs was inaugurated in large measure by the *Bulletin du Centre de Recherches sur l'Histoire des Entreprises* (roneotyped, 1953) becoming in 1958 the journal *Histoire des Entreprises*. A first summing up may be found in:
L. Girard, *Histoire des entreprises au XIXe siècle* (Rapports du XIe Congrès International des Sciences Historiques, Stockholm, 1960, V, 97-106)
   and examples in:
J. Bouvier, 'Une dynastie d'affaires lyonnaise au XIXe siècle: les Bonnardel', *Revue d'Histoire Moderne et Contemporaine*, 1955, 185-205
Cl. Fohlen, *Une affaire de famille au XIXe siècle: Méquillet-Noblot*, 1955
B. Gille, *Recherches sur la formation de la grande entreprise capitaliste (1815-1848)*, 1959
G. Thuillier, *Georges Dufaud et les débuts du grand capitalisme dans la métallurgie en Nivernais au XIXe siècle*, 1959
   On the 'entrepreneur' and 'the spirit of enterprise' in France as seen from abroad:
D. S. Landes, 'French entrepreneurship and industrial growth in the XIXth century', *Journal of Economic History*, 1949; 'French Business and the Businessman', (in the symposium *Modern France*, issued under the editorship of E. M. Earle, Princeton, 1951)
S. B. Clough, 'Retardative factors in French economic development in the XIXth and XXth century', *Journal of Modern History*, 1946

VIII   On the social aspects of the subject, the broad features of a programme of research have been outlined by:
E. Labrousse, *Voies nouvelles vers une histoire de la bourgeoisie occidentale aux XVIIIe et XIXe siècles* (1700-1850) *Xe Congrès International des Sciences Historiques*, Rome, 1955, IV, 365-96; communications complémentaires, ibid, VII, 319-35; discussion, *Atti*, ibid, 514-35
   An obviously premature synthesis had been attempted by:
J. P. Palewski, *Histoire des chefs d'entreprise*, 1928
   A work to be used with profit, but with care, is the stimulating and systematic book of:
E. Beau de Loménie, *Les Responsabilités des dynasties bourgeoisies*, I (de Bonapartè à Macmahon), 1943; II (de Macmahon à Poincaré), 1947
   More objective is the recent 'Essai sur l'histoire sociale de France of:
J. Lhomme, *La grande bourgeoisie au pouvoir*, 1960
   A good monograph is:
J. Lambert-Dansette, *Essai sur les origines et l'évolution d'une bourgeoisie. Quelques familles du patronat textile de Lille Armentières (1789-1914)*, Lille, 1954
   A valuable source of documentation is:
A. Delavenne, *Recueil généalogique de la bourgeoisie ancienne* (first volume appearing in 1954)

IX External horizons

Particularly significant works remain as follows—on commercial policy, the monograph of:

A. L. Dunham, *The Anglo-French treaty of commerce of 1860 and the progress of the industrial revolution in France*, Michigan, 1930

and on the 'horizon of a port':

L. Dermigny, *Naissance et croissance d'un port—Sète de 1666 à 1880*, Montpellier, 1955

And, while waiting for the great *Histoire du Commerce de Marseille*, edited by G. Lambert, to reach the nineteenth century, there are the works of:

P. Guiral, 'Le monde vu de Marseille autour de 1820', *Provence Historique*, December 1956

    Marseille et Algérie (1830-1840), Gap, 1956

    'Marseille et l'Algérie de 1848 à 1870', *Revue Africaine*, 1956

On a great French overseas enterprise:

Le Canal Maritime de Suez, 1937 (publication of la Compagnie Universelle du Canal Maritime de Suez)

G. Edgar Bonnet, *Ferdinand de Lesseps*, 2 volumes, 1951-59

On external investments:

H. Feis, *Europe, the world's banker*, Yale University Press, 1933

H. D. White, *The French international accounts, 1880-1913*, Cambridge (Massachusetts), 1933

B. Gille, 'Investissements extérieurs et politique internationale (1815-1848)', *Bulletin de la Société d'Histoire Moderne*, 1960, XII, no 13

J. Bouvier, 'La "grande crise" des compagnies ferroviaires suisses', *Annales*, 1956, 458-60

    'L'installation des groupes financiers au Moyen-Orient', *Bulletin de la Société d'Histoire Moderne*, 1959, XII, no 10

    'Les intérêts financiers et la question d'Egypte (1875-1876)', *Revue Historique*, July, 1960, 75-104

R. E. Cameron, 'L'exportation des capitaux français, 1850-1880', *Revue d'Histoire Economique et Sociale*, 1955, 347-53

    'Le développement économique de l'Europe au XIXe siècle. Le rôle de la France', *Annales*, 1957, 243-7

For the relations of capitalist development and of colonialist expansion, one can go to:

H. Brunschwig, *Mythes et réalités de l'impéralisme colonial français, 1871-1914*, 1960, and its bibliography.

Index

In the original French edition the index consisted of names of historical personalities (in capitals) and of industrial and commercial families (in italics). This usage has been retained in the English edition but an attempt has been also been made to add names of authors of important works about capitalism and to indicate the main subjects dealt with.